THE MACHINE KNITTING BOOK

THE MACHINE KNITTING BOOK

JOHN · ALLEN
ASSISTED · BY · CLARE · ROWLAND

DK
DORLING KINDERSLEY · LONDON

CONTENTS

Editor Melanie Miller
Editorial Assistant Pie Dorling
Art Director Kieran Stevens
Designer Sandra Schneider
Machine Knitting Consultant Anne Smith
Managing Editor Amy Carroll

INTRODUCTION 6

KNITWEAR·DESIGN 10

STRIPES 26

JACQUARD 32

First published in Great Britain in 1985 by
Dorling Kindersley Publishers Limited,
9 Henrietta Street, London WC2E 8PS

Second impression 1985

British Library Cataloguing in Publication Data
Allen, John
The machine knitting book
1. Knitting, Machine 2. Knitting Patterns
I. Title II. Rowland, Clare
746.43'2041 TT687

ISBN 0-86318-034-5

Printed and bound in Italy

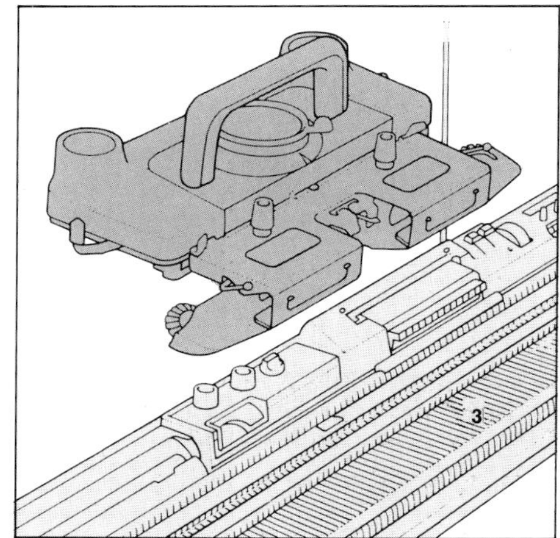
3

INTRODUCTION

In recent years a revolution has taken place in hand knitting. Gone is the old image of elderly hand knitters, in its place is a new market of sophisticated creators of stylish garments. Exciting yarns and designer patterns are now readily available and used by everyone. The confidence of hand knitters has developed to the point that now the most complicated stitches and patterns are undertaken.

Somehow machine knitting has not kept pace with this stimulating movement. While there are numerous publications available for hand knitters, containing interesting and unusual patterns, the garment patterns provided for machine knitters are often ordinary, unadventurous, even dull. I hope through this book to help redress that balance and start to fill the gap in the market for creative knitwear designs for machine knitters.

However, my aim in writing this book has not been merely to provide patterns for machine knitters. The knitting machine is an amazingly versatile instrument, capable of producing infinite fabric designs and pattern variations, given the right input from the machine knitter. I hope, after following some of the patterns and stitch techniques, readers will gain enough confidence not only to make any of the garments, but also to create their own variations from them. Readers should no longer be tied to printed instructions, but will be able to experiment with their machines and so devise their own, unique garment designs. There is no end to the different textures and fabrics a knitting machine can produce, if the machine is approached without preconceived ideas of its limitations. Through this book I hope to enable the reader to use the machine in a freer, more stimulating way than when he or she started.

Previous machine knitting publications stressed the speed and cheapness of producing garments on a knitting machine: while it is true that a machine dramatically reduces the time needed to knit a sweater, speed and cheapness should not be an end in themselves. Many of the techniques demonstrated in this book do take a little longer than plain stocking stitch, but you will be rewarded with ingenious fabrics and unusual surface interest.

Another way of creating more individual fabrics is to use fancy yarns, such as gimps or knops, snarls or loops. Even the simplest design may be given extraordinary surface interest by using these textured yarns, particularly if different types of yarns are combined in one garment, thus providing contrasts of textures. Try mixing crunchy cottons with fluffy mohair, shiny rayons with baby soft angora, to create interesting fabrics. Unusual yarns may take a little getting used to, but the results will be appreciated.

I am not a technical expert, but what I bring to knitting is a driving passion and love for design. As a teacher and also a practising designer my experience spans most fields of knitting. I hope, through this book, to share my enthusiasm, and to encourage readers to design their own garments.

John Allen

ABOUT THIS BOOK

The first section of the book, pages 8-25, provides general and specific information about designing knitwear: yarns, colours and styles.

The main part of the book, pages 26-113, contains twenty-five sweaters for men and women, all photographed in colour, with full making up instructions. The sweaters are divided into different sections according to the different techniques used, and as each new technique is introduced information

about it, and possible variations, is given. Each sweater is knitted in a suggested colourway, and in addition to this, on the double spread preceding each sweater approximately six different colour combinations or pattern variations are also shown. These demonstrate the radically different effects that may be produced either by manipulating the pattern, or by using alternative yarns, colours or tensions. The alternative samples can be used for guidance and inspiration, or, with the help of a shaping aid, they may be substituted for the colours and yarns used on the sweater. Full making-up instructions, including punchcards and shape guides, are given for all the sweaters.

The last part of the book, pages 114-125, consists of practical information about the basics of machine knitting; newcomers to machine knitting will find this section particularly useful. A brief introduction to the different types of knitting machine available is provided. Casting on, casting off, increasing and decreasing, making hems, ribs and tension swatches are just some of the techniques included. A very important, and often neglected area of making machine knitted garments is also covered – finishing off. Blocking, pressing and sewing together are dealt with in detail.

Finally, at the very back of the book is a list of useful addresses, including yarn suppliers and machine manufacturers.

NOTE FOR BEGINNERS

This book is *not* intended as a replacement for your machine manual. There are many different models of machines on the market, from different manufacturers, and controls vary from model to model, so familiarize yourself with your machine, using your manual, before embarking on any of the sweater patterns. The Basic Techniques section at the back of the book will also help you master your machine.

When you do make a garment from the book, be sure to start with an easy one – if the first pattern you attempt takes forever to finish, simply because you chose the most complicated one, using fancy yarns, you will be too discouraged to continue machine knitting. Information about how easy each sweater is to make is to be found on the chart overleaf. The "ease of making" for each sweater has been assessed in terms of the yarn used, the shaping needed, the stitch construction and the finishing. We could have given the patterns an overall rating of "easy", "medium", or "difficult", but this would not have made any allowances for the fact that some people find shaping relatively quick and easy to do, while others have difficulties. Also some of the sweaters as shown may be difficult to make, but if a straight yarn is substituted for a fancy one, a time-consuming pattern may become quicker and easier. When you get more adventurous, and want to try some of the more complicated stitch constructions and fancy yarns, spend a little time mastering the techniques on spare samples of knitting before embarking on a garment.

Don't be frightened of your machine. Every now and again something might go wrong, but don't panic, just calmly try to find out what has happened and rectify the mistake. Check that all the following are as they should be:

- Is the machine threaded up properly?
- If weights are needed are they in position?
- Is the stitch control set correctly?
- Are any of the needles damaged?

If none of these appear to be causing the problem, refer to your manual.

TECHNICAL INFORMATION

Machines
We have tried to make sure that the majority of the garments can be knitted on most of the popular domestic knitting machines. The patterns have been written for standard gauge, single bed punchcard machines. However, the punchcard may easily be drawn out on a graph for use with electronic machines, and many of the sweaters can be made on machines that use a manual method of needle selection. Since many knitters do have a ribbing attachment, some of the patterns include instructions for double bed ribs as well as hand knitted ribs.

Since the instructions have been written to be used by a wide range of knitting machines, it is important that you use the pattern instructions in conjunction with your machine manual, since some operations vary slightly from machine to machine. Some of the main things to look out for are listed below.

Pre-selection of needles Some punchcard machines (mainly Brother, Toyota and Singer) pre-select pattern needles, i.e. the pattern needles are selected before the carriage is taken across the knitting to knit the row. This means that you have to knit one row with the punchcard locked. For example:

Insert punchcard and lock on first row. *Set carriage for Fair Isle knitting.* Set RC at 000. Using yarn A, knit 1 row. Release card and continue in Fair Isle pattern with yarn A in feeder 1/A and yarn B in feeder 2/B . . .

If you have a machine which *does not* pre-select needles (mainly Knitmaster machines) you must ignore the first instruction "set carriage for Fair Isle knitting", and set your carriage for Fair Isle knitting when the instructions say "continue in Fair Isle pattern". If you do not do this then you may find that you drop stitches.

Lace knitting To produce transfer lace some lace carriages transfer stitches and knit them, others just transfer stitches. This means that different punchcards have to be used depending on the lace carriage. Further information is given about this in the lace knitting section.

Toyota punchcards For most machines the yarn in feeder 2/B knits the punched out pattern, and the yarn in feeder 1/A knits the background. For Toyota 747, 787 and 858 the reverse is true, so if you have one of these machines punch out your card in reverse.

Singer gauge Some Singer machines are made with a slightly different gauge from other standard gauge machines. However since the difference is not very great, providing you check the tension, and make any necessary adjustments to the tension dial, these Singer machines may be used with the patterns.

Yarns
Specific information as to the brand names of yarns has not been included since many yarns have a shelf life of only one season. Instead we have given a description of the yarn used, including information about thickness, composition and type (see pages 12-18). We have also included an actual size photograph of the yarns used in each sweater so you can see exactly what the yarn looks like. If you wish, you may substitute any yarn of a similar thickness for the yarn used. However, if you do this, remember that you may need more, or less than the weight of yarn stated in the pattern.

The yarn amounts stated are based on average requirements, and are therefore approximate. Remember that different fibres vary in weight – wool is much heavier than acrylic, for example, so it takes a greater weight of wool to knit a garment, than to knit the same garment in acrylic yarn. This is the main difference to be aware of when substituting yarns, but there are always variations from yarn type to yarn type.

It's always safer to buy more yarn than you think you may need, rather than less, since you can always use up left over yarn when sampling.

Shape guides
Garment outlines, with measurements, have been given, so that the patterns may be transferred to shaping aids (knit radar, knit leader, knit tracer), and any combination of yarns or stitch patterns used. Please note that the measurements given are those of the finished pieces, and should not be used to measure work on the machine.

Tension
If you are *not* using a shaping aid it is very important that you work to the tension stated in the pattern. Make a 10cm (4in) tension square. If the square has more stitches to 10cm than stated in the pattern, use a looser tension dial setting. If it has fewer stitches to 10cm, use a higher tension dial setting. Further instructions about making a tension square are to be found in the back of the book.

Measurements
Measurements on the garment outlines are given in centimetres. However, since most people think of their body measurements in terms of inches, we have given both inches and centimetres in the garment sizings. Figures in brackets refer to larger sizes; where there is only one set of figures, it refers to all sizes.

Right and wrong side
As the fabric is produced on a single bed knitting machine, the side facing

STANDARD GAUGE PUNCHCARD AND ELECTRONIC MACHINES SUITABLE FOR USE WITH THE PATTERNS

Please note that this list is not definitive, the machine manufacturers are constantly bringing out new models, so any machines introduced *after* the publication date of this book will not be included in the list, yet may be used with the patterns. Also the book may be used as a *design* book in conjunction with any type of knitting machine.

Jones+Brother	Knitmaster	Singer	Toyota
KH 830	SK 500	Singer Memo-matic	901
KH 840	SK 560	KE 2400*	787*
KH 860	600	KE 2500*	747.*†
KH 881	700	KE 2600*	858†
KH 910	260K or KL	Memo II	
KH 820*	360K or KL	Models 400 & 600	
	321*	Memo-matic model 2310	
	323*	KE 1200*†	
	325*	SB 100	
	326*		
	328*		
	329*		

* Discontinued models.
† The punchcards for these machines have a twelve stitch pattern repeat, however many of the punchcard patterns given may be adapted for use with these machines.

the knitter is the purl side, the side facing away from the knitter is the knit side. Throughout the book we refer to the knit side of the fabric as the right side, and the purl side as the wrong side.

Pattern sequence
Any repeated pattern or yarn sequence that is used throughout the sweater is given at the beginning of the pattern instructions.

Blocking and pressing
The instructions concerning blocking and pressing given in the pattern instructions apply only to the yarns and stitch constructions actually used in the sweaters shown. If you have substituted different types of yarn, or a different stitch, then refer to the ball or cone band, and page 124 for blocking and pressing instructions.

Abbreviations
Standard abbreviations have been used in the pattern instructions. A full list, with explanations, is given below.

Samples
The samples are used to show the different effects you can achieve. They may show colour and yarn variations of the pattern used, or they may show possible developments of the technique. Usually, as long as you can produce a tension square with the same number of stitches and rows to 10cm as stated in the pattern (it does not matter what the actual tension dial setting is), then you can substitute any yarns you like for the ones used in the sweater. However, if your tension square does not measure 10cm then you must use a shaping aid to create the garment using alternative yarns.

ABBREVIATIONS

cm centimetre(s)
g gram(s)
HP holding position
in inch(es)
k knit
mm millimetre(s)
MT main tension
MT − 2 set tension dial two full sizes lower than main tension
MT + 2 set tension dial two full sizes higher than main tension
NWP non-working position
p purl
RC row counter
st(s) stitch(es)
st st stocking stitch
UWP upper working position
WP working position
( ) round brackets at the end of a sentence denote a total number of stitches, rows or needles

EASE OF MAKING

KEY

EASY 1 **MEDIUM 2** **DIFFICULT 3**

	YARNS	SHAPING	STITCH CONSTRUCTION	FINISHING
STRIPES				
Cheerleader *(p. 27)*	1	1	1	1
Popsicle *(p. 29)*	1	1	2	1
JACQUARD				
Black Magic Jumper *(p. 34)*	1	1	1	1
Black Magic Cardigan *(p. 36)*	1	3	1	2
Bib and Tucker *(p. 40)*	2	3	1	2
Chequerboard *(p. 44)*	1	3	1	2
Zigzag *(p. 46)*	3	1	1	1
Man's Fair Isle *(p. 49)*	1	1	1	1
Woman's Fair Isle *(p. 52)*	2	2	1	2
TUCK STITCH				
Neon *(p. 56)*	3	2	3	3
Classic Cardigan *(p. 59)*	1	2	2	3
Arabian Nights *(p. 63)*	2	2	2	1
WEAVING				
Heather Mist *(p. 68)*	2	2	2	1
Cocoon *(p. 72)*	2	1	2	3
Turkish Delight *(p. 76)*	2	1	2	1
Peaches and Cream *(p. 78)*	2	1	3	1
Batwing *(p. 82)*	2	2	3	1
INTARSIA				
Patches *(p. 85)*	1	1	2	1
LACE KNITTING				
Northern Lights *(p. 90)*	2	2	2	1
Pinstripe *(p. 93)*	2	2	2	2
Guinivere *(p. 98)*	2	2	2	1
HAND SELECTED NEEDLE KNITTING				
Anchors Away *(p. 101)*	2	2	3	2
Candy Floss *(p. 105)*	3	3	3	2
Confetti *(p. 109)*	2	2	3	1
Stardust *(p. 112)*	3	1	3	1

KNITWEAR·DESIGN

The aim of this book is to introduce you to just some of the enormous wealth of design ideas and fabric constructions that are possible if you are willing to experiment and invent. To start, it is important to be familiar with the four basic elements that make up any knitted garment. These are:

1 Colour
2 Yarn
3 Stitch construction
4 Style/shape

In this section, I hope to show you how and where to find inspiration for choosing and using these, so you can design your own sweaters, or individualize patterns to suit yourself. To create unusual, interesting fabrics you need a little time, patience, and a working knowledge of your machine.

Although any one of the four basic elements may be used individually as a starting point for designing a garment (you may want a big, baggy sweater, for example, so you decide on the shape first, then colour, yarn and finally stitch construction), a more creative, open approach, combining colour, yarn and stitch construction usually brings more interesting results. The technique which combines these three elements (colour, yarn and stitch construction) is known as sampling.

Sampling means sitting down at your machine, with a whole host of different colours and yarns, and one stitch construction or pattern. Experiment by knitting the stitch construction or pattern in lots of different yarns and colours until you find one you particularly like. Then design the shape of the garment around the fabric you have created. A soft, draping fabric lends itself to tops, skirts or dresses, while a stiffer sample might be used for jackets and coats. Very elaborate textures or multi-coloured fabrics are best used on simple garments, while plain, subdued or classic patterns are well suited to more complicated garment designs. Alternatively, instead of designing your own garment shape, you can, with the help of a shaping aid, use the fabric you have designed with one of the sweater shapes I have provided.

SAMPLING

To get the most out of sampling you need to have a variety of different colours, textures and thicknesses of yarns at hand, but experiment with only one stitch construction or pattern at a time. When sampling remember these two guidelines:

- There is no such word as can't, always be open-minded and adaptable.
- Try all sorts of yarns and mixtures of yarns – some of the most interesting effects are achieved by mixing yarns, i.e. plain with fancy, matt with shiny, thick with thin.

This stage of working out ideas is one that most home knitters neglect; they spend far too little time on it, often sampling becomes simply the knitting of colourways. The opposite is the case with professional designers. I spend much more time sampling, sorting and trying out ideas, than actually knitting finished garments. If done creatively it can be the most interesting and exciting form of knitting, since the knitter is totally free to try anything within a given stitch construction.

How to sample

1 Using the cast-on method you find quickest and easiest to do, cast on about fifty stitches.
2 Whatever stitch construction you are sampling, whether it is tuck stitch, jacquard, weaving, or anything else, work a few rows in a plain straight yarn to check that the stitch is forming correctly, then start experimenting in different ways.
3 There are a number of different things you can do:

- Change the tension several numbers higher
- Change the tension several numbers lower
- Use different colours of yarns
- Use different textures of yarns
- Change the yarn colour every so often, to produce colour striping

Since you may find it rather confusing if you experiment with all these different elements at once, it's probably a good idea to concentrate on one variation at a time, i.e. experiment with extremes of tension to start with, then experiment with different yarns.
4 Only knit about 5-8cm (2-3in) of an idea unless you really like it, in which case knit a sample 20-25cm (8-10in) long. Make a note of the yarns and tension used, either in a book, or by pinning a label to the knitting.
5 When you have exhausted all the possibilities that interest you, remove your knitting from the machine (it will probably look like a long, multi-coloured scarf), steam press or block it (see page 124), then lay it out to view the samples.
6 You may find that some of the samples look particularly good next to one another, or you may find you prefer the reverse, "purl" side of the fabric to the right, "knit" side. Cut out and file any yarn, colour and stitch combinations that you particularly like, and put them in a scrapbook with a note of the tension, and the yarns used. If you do this regularly your scrapbook will become an invaluable reference source.

Using two or more different thicknesses of yarns

When knitting with two or more different types of yarns, you should always try to set a tension for them which is a compromise between the ideal for each, but which will allow you to knit the mixture without having to fiddle around with the tension while actually working. In some cases this does not work, i.e. one of the yarns you have chosen will knit, while one will not. To get around this problem you can sometimes change the tension while working, according to which yarn is being knitted. This technique is a little time-consuming, but it is worth the extra effort as it solves the problem and allows you to mix very contrasting yarns to produce interesting surfaces and textures. The only drawback is, if the extremes of tensions for the different yarns are too great, the sides of your knitting will distort.

Using alternative yarns and colourways

Some of the samples that I have made while designing the sweaters are shown with the sweaters. In most cases the garment pattern given can easily be worked in one of these samples, if preferred. I hope by the time you, the reader, have produced one or two sweaters, you will be sampling and using some of your own fabrics in the patterns.

The samples opposite show the same stitch pattern repeated with different colours, textures and tensions.

KNITTING YARNS

NATURAL

ANIMAL

WOOL
from sheep

HAIR
fleece from any other animal, often sold blended with sheep's wool

SILK
from silkworm

WILD
coarse, irregular

CULTIVATED
resilient, lustrous, soft

FILAMENT
silk sold as it is made in one long filament thread

SPUN
waste filament spun together, poorer quality, less shine than filament

MOHAIR
from Angora goat

ANGORA
from Angora rabbit

CASHMERE
from Kashmir goat, very soft

WOOLLEN
short fibres, lightweight so less wool is used

WORSTED
longer fibres, smoother, stronger, more lustrous than woollen

PURE NEW WOOL
all new fibres

ALL WOOL
mixed new and reprocessed fibres

SHODDY
all reprocessed fibres

TWEED
(Donegal, Harris)
most tweed yarns are slightly coarse, hardwearing

ARAN
thick, soft yarn, usually found in natural colours

SHETLAND
also hardwearing, but softer than tweed yarns

BOTANY
fine quality, made from the best wool, with long, staple fibre

VEGETABLE

LINEN
very strong yarn, lacking in elasticity, often blended with other fibres

MAN-MADE

SYNTHETIC
coal and/or oil based

METALLIC THREAD
aluminium coated in plastic, used for decoration in knitting, e.g. lurex

REGENERATED
wool/cellulose based

NYLON
strong, long-lasting, non-absorbent thus quick drying, can be uncomfortable, best blended with wool

ACRYLIC
feels more like wool than other synthetics although less durable, tendency to stretch

VISCOSE RAYON
cheap to buy, often comes with a decorative finish, not hardwearing, melts under hot iron, tendency to crease, stretch and shrink

ACETATE RAYON
slightly tougher and more resilient than viscose, still liable to melt and shrink

COTTON

UNTREATED
lacking in elasticity so tricky to knit, strong, long-lasting, does not shrink

MERCERISED
cotton treated with caustic soda which swells the individual fibres giving a lasting lustre, easy to knit with

EGYPTIAN & SEA ISLAND
most expensive, best quality

AMERICAN
good quality

INDIAN
poor quality

YARN

A bewildering array of different yarns is available to the machine knitter. Yarns may be differentiated in three ways: by their composition (wool, acrylic, cotton etc), construction (straight, loop, gimp etc), and by their thickness, or "weight" (fine-weight, double knitting, chunky etc). These three different factors affect the way a yarn knits, and the fabric that results.

COMPOSITION

Basically yarns can be made from natural fibres, such as wool, cotton, or silk, or they can be manufactured, such as acrylic or nylon. Some yarns are a blend of natural and man-made fibres. The table above provides a brief breakdown of most of the different compositions of yarns available, suitable for use on knitting machines.

CONSTRUCTION

As already mentioned, the raw material that yarns are made from may be natural or manufactured fibres. The fibres come in two different forms, staple and filament. Staple fibre is made up of lots of separate pieces, their lengths depending on what the fibre is made from. Staple fibres are turned into yarn by twisting or spinning them together. Filament yarn is made of one continuous long length. Generally *most* natural fibres are staples (the exception being silk), while manufactured fibres are produced in filament form. The latter may be chopped up into staple, and then spun.

Worsted and woollen yarns

Yarn fibres have to be twisted together to form long lengths. In the case of wool, there are two different ways of doing this, producing either worsted, or woollen yarns. Other yarns are then said to be produced on the worsted or woollen systems.

Worsted yarn is produced when the longer staple fibres are separated from the shorter staple fibres and laid as nearly parallel to one another as possible, before being twisted together. The resulting yarn is smooth, strong and hardwearing, for example Botany.

Woollen yarn is produced when the shorter fibres are first laid parallel, and then deliberately and evenly tangled before spinning. This produces a fuzzy yarn which is not as strong as worsted yarn. However it has greater warmth for less weight. Shetland wool is produced by this method.

Twisting

Yarn may be twisted in a clockwise, or an anti-clockwise direction, thus producing an "s" or "z" twist, depending on the direction of the twist. Apart from the direction of the twist, the amount of twist may also vary. Very loosely twisted yarn such as Icelandic lopi cannot be knitted on a standard gauge knitting machine, but may be used for laying in by hand. The yarns most commonly used on standard gauge knitting machines are medium twist yarns such as three- and four-ply yarns in any fibres.

Doubling

The spinning process produces a single strand, or ply, which may be used as it is, or may be twisted with one or more strands of the same, or different yarns. This process is known as doubling. The way strands are doubled produces different effects, such as loops, slubs, tweeds etc. Most of the different constructions of yarns are shown on the yarn charts, below.

Straight yarns

For standard, straight knitting yarn two, three or four single strands are twisted together uniformly, to produce standard two-, three- or four-ply yarn. Although the term four-ply is commonly used to denote yarn of a certain thickness, in actual fact it refers to the number of strands twisted together, which can, of course, be of any thickness. Straight yarns may be made from any fibres.

Cotton

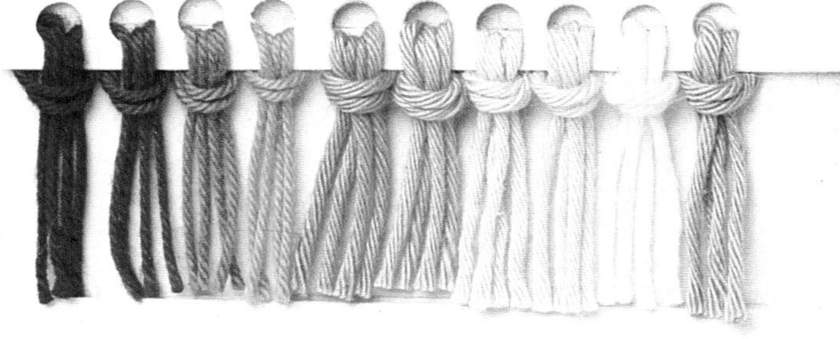

Wool

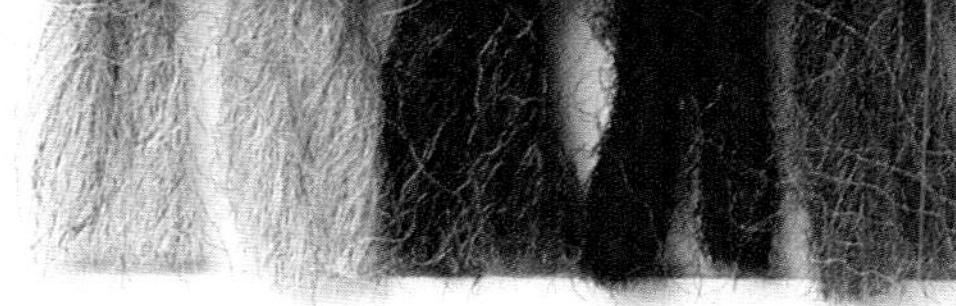

Wool

Silk

Acrylic/Wool mixtures

Crêpe yarns
Crêpe yarns are produced when yarn is twisted as much as possible, without doubling back on itself. When woven or knitted crêpe yarns produce a gravelly surface.

Fluffy yarns
Angora and mohair are the most commonly used fluffy yarns. Mohair is very expensive, so manufacturers produce mohair mixture yarns, and even some acrylic yarns which simulate the same hairy effect. Angora is very soft and fluffy, and even more expensive than mohair. However, it does not work so well in mixtures. To produce the best effect, fluffy yarns should be knitted on a fairly loose tension. After knitting, the fabric may be brushed with a teazle brush to make it even fluffier.

Slub yarns
Slub yarns are irregular in appearance, being quite thick in some places, and fine in others. This is caused by deliberate uneven spinning, so that sections of tightly twisted yarn alternate with sections of soft fibres that are hardly twisted. They are often doubled with a straight yarn.

Gimp yarns
Gimp yarns are produced by feeding two yarns into the doubling machine at slightly different speeds, so that one of them creates small bumps around the other. They may be made from any fibre.

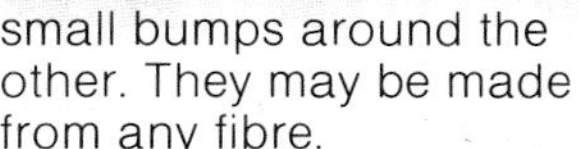

Snarl yarns
Snarl yarns are formed in the same way as gimp yarns, but the difference in speed between the two yarns is even greater, so that little twists, rather than bumps of the second yarn are formed.

Loop yarns
Loop yarns are produced by twisting two strands of yarn tightly around each other, while introducing a third strand at an increased speed. This causes an excess of yarn in the third strand, which shows up as loops, usually evenly-spaced along the length of the yarn. Any fibres may be used to form loop yarn, but the most commonly found compositions are wool, mohair and rayon. Bouclé and poodle yarns are types of loop yarn.

Chenille yarns
Chenille yarn is actually made from fabric, cut into strips. The cloth is specially woven with a very fine, strong thread going in one direction, and a much thicker, bulkier thread in the other. It is then cut into strips, following the direction of the fine threads. These strips are only one or two threads thick. As the fabric is cut the bulkier yarn forms a "fringe". Chenille may be made from natural or synthetic fibres, but is generally considered best when made from pure cotton, as the characteristic silky, luxurious feel is not produced with other fibres.

Knop yarns
These are formed when two or three yarns are fed through a feeder, and the doubling machine is stopped periodically. This causes the doubling yarns to pile up on themselves, producing lumps, or "knots" of thread along the yarn.

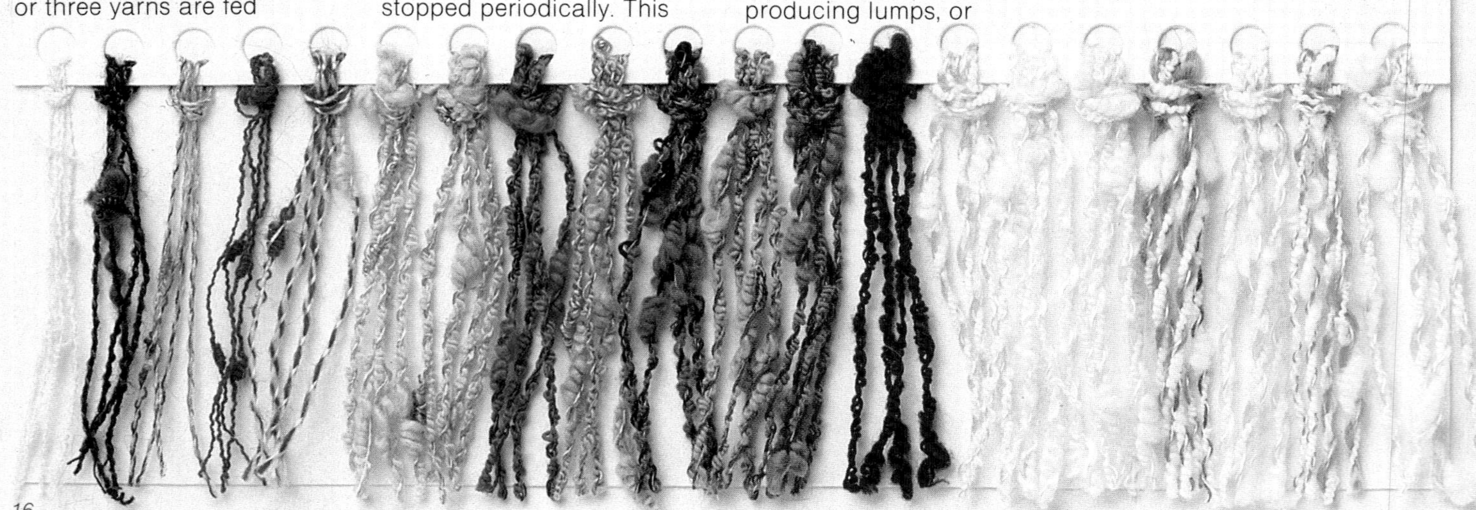

Tape yarns
Tape yarns have recently become popular. They are made from narrow knitted or woven strips of fabric. They are usually quite bulky, and should be treated as chunky yarns.

Mixture yarns
Yarns are also produced that are a hybrid of the different types of yarns already described. For example:

Fluffy gimp

Fluffy slub

Fancy gimp

Fancy knop

Slub gimp

Knop gimp

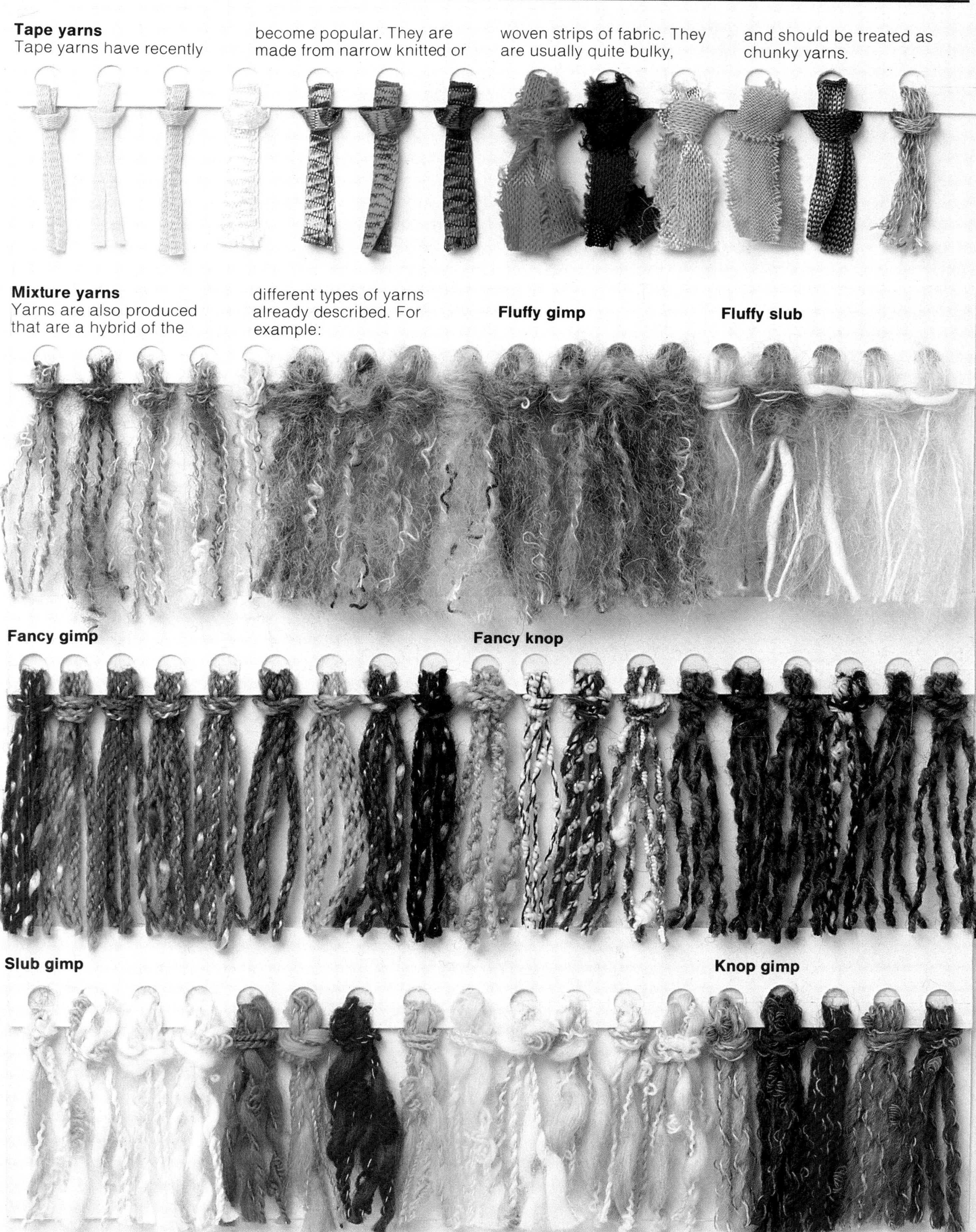

THICKNESS

Most of the different types of yarns shown on the previous pages are available in different thicknesses, or weights. It's difficult to standardize the different thicknesses of yarns – a rather complicated "count" system is used in industry, but it isn't universal – so for the purposes of this book, we have "standardized" the yarns used on the sweaters so you can purchase similar yarns. The photographs below are all to actual size, as are the photographs of the yarns shown with each sweater pattern.

When using a standard gauge knitting machine, the thickest yarn that can easily be knitted is a medium-weight yarn. However, by knitting on only every other needle, thicker yarns may be used as long as they fit easily in the needle hook. Another way of using thicker yarns is to lay them in by hand. There is no limit to how fine a yarn may be knitted, and interesting fabrics may be formed when using fine yarns with tuck stitch. Two or three fine yarns may be knitted together, or a fine yarn may be used with a thicker one to produce interesting effects.

KNITABILITY

Very interesting textures and unusual fabrics may be created by using fancy yarns. The only way to know if these will knit is to try them; try them on different tensions, try them with more weights than usually used, and have patience. Sometimes a yarn which is difficult to knit at the start becomes easier as you and the machine become more familiar to working with it. Remember to take the carriage across the knitting slowly to begin with, give yourself time, and be prepared to use extremes of tension.

When knitting it is very important that the yarn is fed into the machine smoothly and evenly. In order to do this, your yarn may need winding or waxing. See the Basic Techniques section for more information about these two processes.

	STRAIGHT YARNS	FANCY YARNS
Very fine Anything thinner than fine		
Fine Equivalent to standard 2-ply		
Medium The same as, or slightly thicker or thinner than standard 4-ply		
Thick Equivalent to standard double knitting		
Chunky Anything thicker than the above		

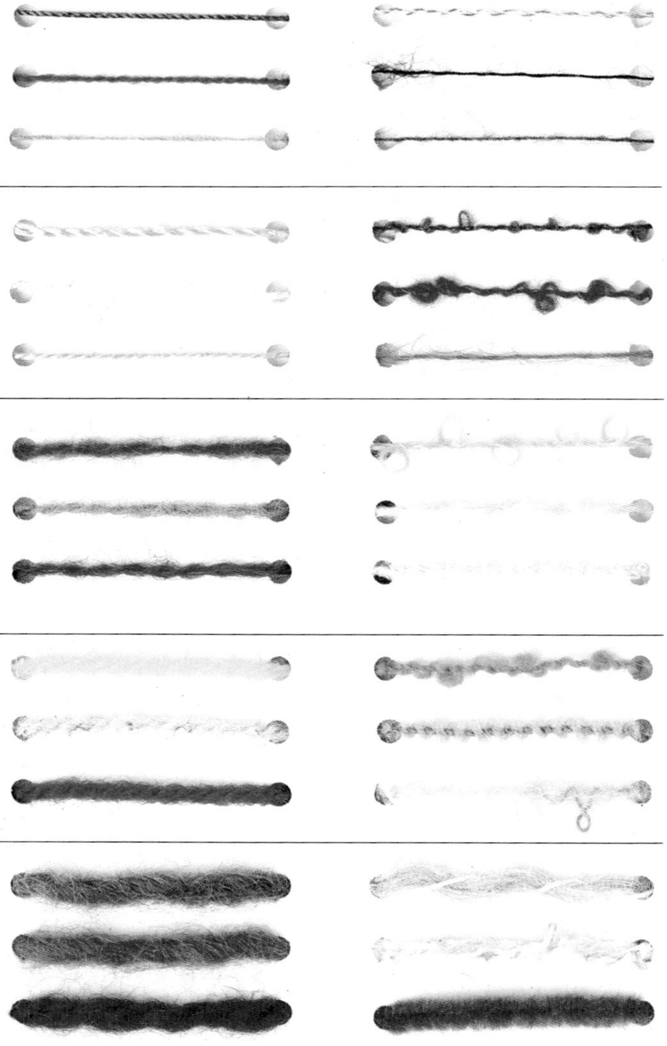

STITCH STRUCTURE

Different stitches add yet another dimension to machine knitting. Plain stocking stitch combined with fancy yarns can produce interesting garments, but many more fabric variations are possible if different stitch constructions are explored.

Stitch constructions add a decorative element to knitting, but, depending on the yarn used, they can also contribute to the physical quality of the fabric. For example, all-over tuck stitch produces a bulky, non-curling fabric. Using the jacquard technique results in a warm fabric – since two colours are used, a double layer of fabric is formed. Weaving produces fabric with little lateral stretch, while lace knitting creates soft, draping fabric. These are just some of the variations possible. These stitch constructions, plus variations of them, are introduced and explored throughout the book, illustrated in samples and in sweaters. You may already be familiar with some of them, but I hope to show you some of the endless variations you may not have encountered.

There are no right and wrong rules concerning the stitch construction you choose to use. As with the choice of colours and yarns, be adventurous, be prepared to try anything once. Sample extensively with different yarns and stitch structures. Having said that, there are a few things that probably should be avoided, simply because they cause practical problems. For example, jacquard designs with widely spaced shapes will produce long floats on the reverse side of the fabric,

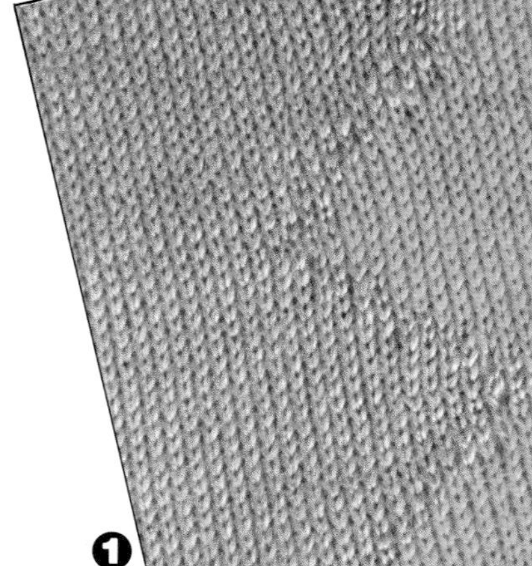

which may get in the way. As you sample you will discover exactly what is and what isn't feasible.

Remember, too, that there is no accurately defined "right" and "wrong" side to the fabric you produce. If the so-called wrong, or purl side looks more attractive to you, then use it for the right side of your garment.

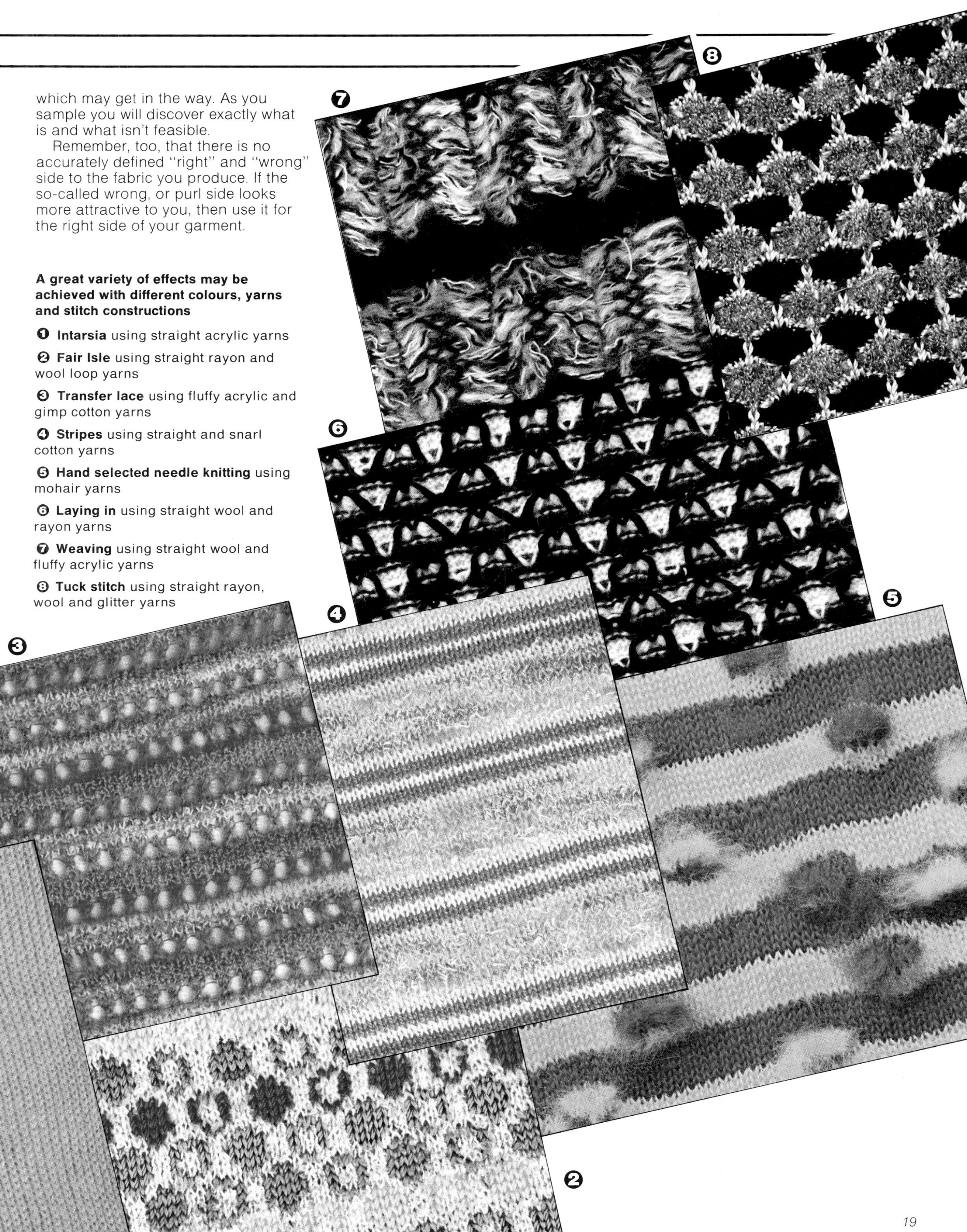

A great variety of effects may be achieved with different colours, yarns and stitch constructions

❶ **Intarsia** using straight acrylic yarns

❷ **Fair Isle** using straight rayon and wool loop yarns

❸ **Transfer lace** using fluffy acrylic and gimp cotton yarns

❹ **Stripes** using straight and snarl cotton yarns

❺ **Hand selected needle knitting** using mohair yarns

❻ **Laying in** using straight wool and rayon yarns

❼ **Weaving** using straight wool and fluffy acrylic yarns

❽ **Tuck stitch** using straight rayon, wool and glitter yarns

STYLING

This is where the professional designer is an expert. Simply by altering an ordinary crew neck in an inventive way a somewhat dull pattern can become interesting. It is no good pretending you can become an innovating stylist just by reading this book, but you will increase your awareness of styling details. I hope, even in some small way, to help you to understand about styling, and by so doing encourage you to try your hand at making your own pattern styles, in a more original way than you would have done previously.

Styling sources

The first thing to do is to look at as many fashion magazines as possible. Don't look only at knitting magazines; inspiration for knitwear designs can also be found in garments made from fabric. Look at the way interesting tops and jackets are put together; the way they are seamed, how fastenings are used. It is often the detailing of necks and openings which distinguish designer sweater styles from those of the amateur. By looking at high fashion clothes in glossy magazines, you will find stimulating ideas for your own pattern designs and adaptations.

I am not advocating copying a style, but simply suggesting that you observe the details of garments you like – at some later date you might be able to use this information for your own garment patterns. For example, you might see a woven dress with the seams placed in the centre front and back, rather than at the sides. By noting this, you might try putting the seams of a sweater in an unconventional place. You could develop this further by joining seams so that the naturally curly edge of a piece of knitting shows on the outside of a seam. This would create a raised effect down the join, and give your sweater a distinctive look. This may be an obvious example, but it illustrates how looking at high fashion ideas can help you. To emphasize this point, I have made some line drawings showing just a few of my ideas for styling necks, sleeves, sweater openings and insets. I hope these will help you to take a closer look at the obvious, and give you ideas of how to make a more stylish sweater. Of course you need not design a complete new garment; by adding interesting styling details to existing patterns you can create different-looking sweaters.

An interesting exercise that you can do is to look at a simple crew neck sweater, draw it out on paper, and then see how many different ideas can be invented around one basic shape, by just changing styling details.

COLLARS

ROUND NECKS

SQUARE NECKS AND BOAT NECKS
V NECKS
STRAPS
NECK INSETS

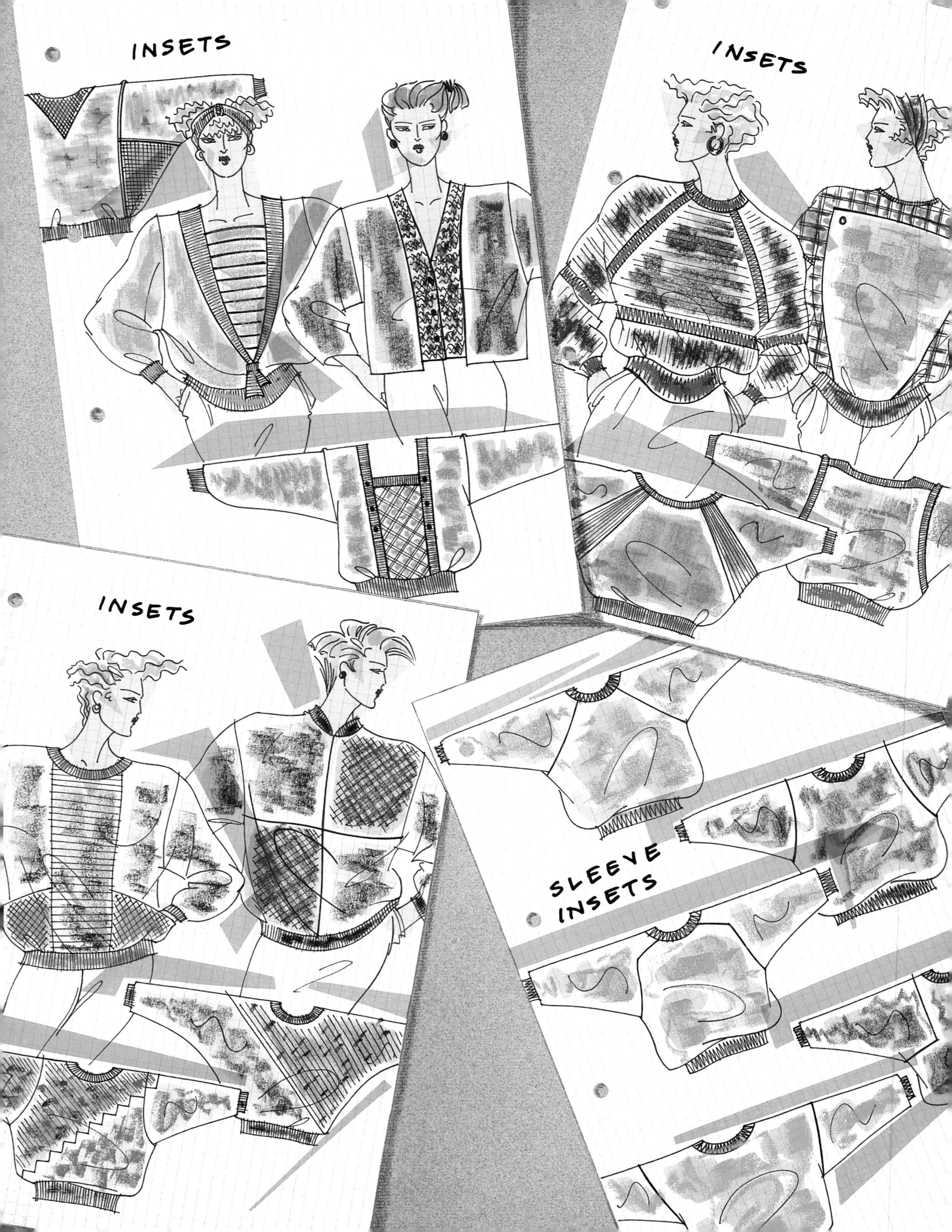
INSETS
INSETS
INSETS
SLEEVE
INSETS

COLOUR

Colour is the single most important element in any design; no matter how good a sweater shape, if its colours have been used crudely or poorly it will lose its attraction. A person's attention is always attracted first by colour. Watch shoppers reacting in a store. They approach a rail of garments, drawn by its colours, then they feel the garments, and only then, if both these elements satisfy them, do they pull out the garments to look at their styling.

There are many books already written about colour, and it is not my intention here to go into a detailed analysis of it, but simply to make some salient points. A colour sense, unlike, say, perfect pitch in music, is not a gift, but something that can be developed and improved. It is worth knowing a little about the characteristics of different colours. Reds, oranges and browns are warm colours, and evoke a similar feeling. Greens, blues and greys are cool colours; they can be made even cooler looking by being mixed with white. In the same way, colours can be made to take on different tones simply by placing them next to other colours. For example, if red is placed near blue, the red appears yellower. Place the same red next to yellow, and it appears bluer. If a dark colour is placed near a lighter colour it appears darker, while the lighter colour appears lighter. Combination of tones and shades can be used to great effect when combining colours in knitting. For example bright green used with the complimentary bright red in a small jacquard design, will seem to shimmer as the two colours clash. The same bright green used with bright yellow in the same pattern will be much calmer. More information about colour basics is illustrated overleaf.

Obviously not everyone responds to colours in exactly the same way, but general responses to colours are well documented. The following list shows how most people would describe the mood evoked by certain colours:

	Red – exciting, stimulating, vibrant
	Yellow – sunny, cheerful
	Blue – soothing, calm, cool
	Purple – regal
	Black – sophisticated, mysterious
	White – innocent, pure
	Green – tranquil
	Grey – safe, cool, calm
	Brown – earthy
	Pink – sweet, gentle
	Orange – friendly, cheerful

Colour combinations

The primaries – red, yellow and blue are the pure colours from which all other colours are derived.

Neutrals – white, off-white, beiges, greys – can look sophisticated and elegant. Often look good enlivened by the addition of a bright contrast colour.

Pastels – soft looking, ice cream colours to which white has been added.

Warm colours – red, oranges, browns – give out a warm feeling.

Cool colours – greens, blues, greys – can be made even cooler by mixing them with white.

Monochromatic colour schemes – use several shades of one colour.

Colour contrasts

Combining different colours can produce unexpected results. Contrasts may be intensified by contrasting textures, note the effect achieved by placing smooth, glossy yarns next to soft fluffy yarns. Colour contrasts can be dramatic, such as navy and ginger, turquoise and brown, pink and green.

Colour contrasts can be subtle, such as grey and yellow, brown and apricot, pink and beige.

Colour sources

By being aware of how colour is used, your own use of it will improve, and you will become more adventurous and confident. Start your own reference book, making careful notes of the colours that attract you in your everyday surroundings. This information may come from something obvious, such as the autumn colours of the trees in your garden. See how nature uses reds, yellows, rusts, browns and greens of every shade together.

Or you might observe something more personal, like the reflection of light on your carpet or a range of kitchen utensils displayed against some brilliantly coloured wall. Make notes, keep references, cut out all types of photographs from magazines which show colours that interest you.

Save small amounts of every yarn you use and keep them in jars or bottles, not only do they look attractive, they are also extremely useful in helping you to see colours differently and creatively. I use large, transparent cake boxes, one for each colour, and along with the coloured scraps of yarn, I also add bits of fabric and paper of the same colour. If you do the same, you will be astonished at just how many tones and shades of one colour there really are. Only by immersing yourself in colour will you improve your use of it. All the information you collect can eventually be used in actual knitting, but instead of sitting at the machine mindlessly knitting colours together, you will consciously start to use colour and exploit all its great potential.

Shade cards

Try to get colour and shade cards from yarn companies. Most places now charge for these, but they are well worth the money. Seasonal colour forecasting cards may be purchased from the International Wool Secretariat, their address is given on p. 126. It's always extremely useful to know the fashion season's forecast, and these cards often indicate interesting colour combinations, which provide good reference points.

Learning to use colour

How can we learn to use colour more adventurously? Just as with stitch constructions, sampling is the key to gaining confidence in the use of colour. Try unusual combinations with different coloured yarns in different textures, such as shiny colours with contrasting matt shades. Mix subtle combinations of similarly toned colours and add just a single row of a contrast colour. Simply playing with colour in sampling will help you gain confidence and enable you to become more aware of how colours react with or against each other.

Alternatively, try one of the methods given on the right. You may be encouraged to combine colours you would not normally have considered putting together, and you are not under the same pressure as when sitting in front of the machine, being very conscious of the amount of yarn you're using.

- Buy lots of coloured paper, or colour some of your own. Cut these sheets into strips of different widths and lay them next to each other. When you get a combination you like, cut out a 15cm square of these and stick them on to backing paper. Use these as reference sources the next time you use your knitting machine. Try altering the proportions of the colours used, as one combination may work in one way, but not in another. This will help you to learn about colour in relation to proportion.

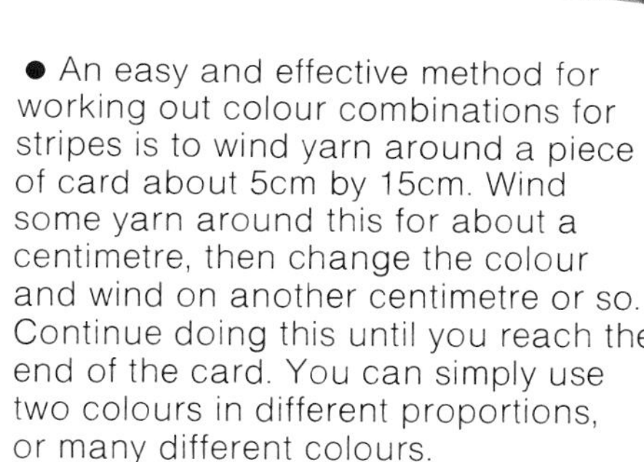

- An easy and effective method for working out colour combinations for stripes is to wind yarn around a piece of card about 5cm by 15cm. Wind some yarn around this for about a centimetre, then change the colour and wind on another centimetre or so. Continue doing this until you reach the end of the card. You can simply use two colours in different proportions, or many different colours.

STRIPES

Stripes are one of the most useful, and easy-to-use design ideas that may be incorporated in knitted garments. They can be made in plain knitting, or with a textured stitch construction. If you are knitting regular horizontal stripes in two colours, remember that it is more practical to work an even number of rows in each colour. If only one row, or an odd number of rows are worked, you will have to break the yarn at the end of each row and take it across to the opposite side of the machine. As well as being time-consuming at the knitting stage, it will also be tedious to darn in all the ends when sewing the garment pieces together. When knitting stripes in more than two colours, work out the pattern so that the yarn is dropped on the side where it will later be picked up.

Stripe width
Depending on the number of rows worked in each yarn or colour, stripes can be broad or narrow. Narrow stripes tend to produce busy, eye-catching designs, while broad stripes give a calmer effect, especially if a few similarly toned shades of yarn are used. Thick and thin stripes may be combined to good effect in one garment, or the widths of stripes may be graded from the bottom to the top of a sweater.

Illusion of shape
The careful use of stripes can appear to change the shape of your body. Narrow stripes tend to make people look thinner, especially when they run vertically, while broad stripes, running horizontally, have the opposite effect. In the striped sweater shown opposite, I have balanced the wide horizontal stripes by introducing a broad central panel in a contrasting colour. Apart from being more interesting to look at, this combination gives a flattering effect when worn.

Experimenting with colours and yarns
Dark colours and similar tones of colours tend to create flat looking surfaces. However, additional interest can be introduced by making stripes in different stitch constructions, or by the use of textured or fancy yarns. Shiny, reflective yarns such as rayon or lurex, for example, can be used to exaggerate these effects.

Making up
Always be on the lookout for new and inventive ways of putting your garments together. Knitted pieces need not be sewn up with the stripes all running in the same direction. Experiment with small swatches and rough drawings until you get a pleasing result.

Using stripes on a raglan-sleeved garment provides an interesting design possiblity. Use horizontal stripes for the body and sleeves, then carefully match the stripes at the raglan when sewing together. This will create a very flattering yoke.

Cheerleader **pattern variations**
Samples show the effects of using different colours and yarns, and working different numbers of rows of each yarn.

CHEERLEADER

This cosy, roll-neck sweater has a plain central panel front and back, and striped side panels. Shaped armbands to match the central panel are sewn on afterwards. Here it's made up in brightly coloured mohair, but it would look just as effective in subtler shades of a tweedy slub yarn.

For speed and accuracy in sewing together, mark the plain panel on the rows where the striped panel is to be attached at colour change points.

PATTERN INSTRUCTIONS FOR
CHEERLEADER

MATERIALS

Yarn
Yarn A 175 (200)g medium-weight mohair (dark green)
Yarn B 200 (225)g medium-weight mohair (blue)
Yarn C 150 (175)g medium-weight mohair (yellow)
Yarn D 50 (75)g medium-weight mohair (pink)

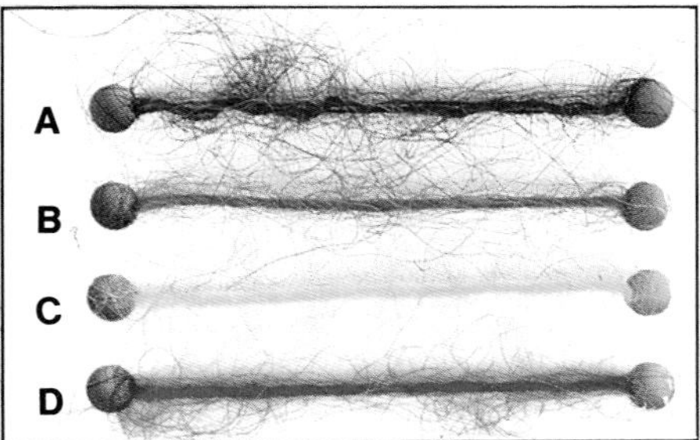

Needles
If you don't have a ribber, you need 1 pair size 2¾mm knitting needles.

MEASUREMENTS

To fit chest 86-91 (97-102)cm (34-36, 38-40in)
Actual chest size 112 (120)cm (44, 47in)
Length to shoulder 61 (65)cm (24, 25½in)
Sleeve seam 43 (46.5)cm (17, 18¼in)

MAIN TENSION (MT)

24 sts and 30 rows measure 10cm over stocking stitch (tension dial set at approximately 10).

STRIPE PATTERN

K 14 (15) rows yarn B, 14 (15) rows yarn D, 14 (15) rows yarn B, 14 (15) rows yarn C, 14 (15) rows yarn D and 14 (15) rows yarn C. These 84 (90) rows form the pattern.

BACK

Machines with ribber
With ribber in position and carriage at right, set machine for 1 × 1 rib. Using yarn C, cast on 136 (146) sts in 1 × 1 rib. Work 5 tubular/circular rows. Carriage is at right. Set carriage for 1 × 1 rib knitting. Set RC at 000. Using MT – 4, work 20 rows. Transfer sts for st st.
Machines without ribber
Using 2¾mm needles and yarn C, cast on 136 (146) sts. Work in k1, p1 rib until work measures 5cm. Push 136 (146) needles to WP. Transfer sts to machine needles.
All machines
Push 90 (96) needles at left to HP. Using waste yarn, knit a few rows over 46 (50) sts at right and release from machine. Push 44 (46) needles at centre from HP to UWP. Using waste yarn, knit a few rows and release from machine. With carriage at left, push remaining 46 (50) needles from HP to UWP. Continue on these sts for first side panel.
First side panel
Set RC at 000. Using MT, continue in stripe pattern and knit 112 (120) rows.
Shape armhole: Cast off 4 sts at the beginning of the next and following alternate row. Decrease 1 st at armhole edge on every row until 30 sts remain. Knit 45 rows. RC shows 168 (180). Cast off.
Second side panel
Push 46 (50) needles to WP. With carriage at right and purl side facing, replace 46 (50) sts below waste yarn at right on to needles. Unravel waste yarn. Finish to correspond with first side panel.
Centre panel
Push 44 (46) needles to WP. With carriage at right and purl side facing, replace 44 (46) sts below waste yarn at centre on to needles. Unravel waste yarn. Set RC at 000 *. Using MT and yarn A, knit 168 (180) rows, placing marker at each end of every 14th (15th) row. Cast off.

FRONT

Work as given for the back as far as *. Using MT and yarn A, knit 152 (164) rows, placing marker at each end of every 14th (15th) row.
Shape neck: Using a length of yarn A, cast off centre 18 (20) sts. Push 13 needles at left to HP and continue on remaining sts for first side. Decrease 1 st at neck edge on every row until 1 st remains. Fasten off. With carriage at left, push needles from HP to WP and finish to correspond with first side.

SLEEVES

Machines with ribber
With ribber in position and carriage at right, set machine for 1 × 1 rib. Using yarn C, cast on 60 sts in 1 × 1 rib. Work 5 tubular/circular rows. Carriage is at right. Set carriage for 1 × 1 rib knitting. Set RC at 000. Using MT – 4, work 20 rows. Transfer sts for st st.
Machines without ribber
Using 2¾mm needles and yarn C, cast on 60 sts. Work in k1, p1 rib until work measures 5cm. Push 60 needles to WP. Transfer sts to machine needles.
All machines
Set RC at 000. Using MT and yarn B, shape sides by increasing 1 st at each end of every 5th row until there are 104 (108) sts. Knit 5 rows. RC shows 115 (125).
Shape top: Cast off 4 sts at the beginning of the next 4 rows. Decrease 1 st at each end of every row until 72 sts remain, then on every following alternate row until 32 sts remain. Cast off.

ARMBANDS

Push 16 needles to WP. Using MT and waste yarn, cast on and knit a few rows ending with carriage at right. Set RC at 000. Using yarn A, shape sides by increasing 1 st at each end of every 8th row until there are 26 sts. Knit 70 (86) rows. Decrease 1 st at each end of next and every following 8th row until 16 sts remain. Knit 7 rows. RC shows 150 (166). Using waste yarn, knit a few rows and release from machine.

COLLAR

The collar is made in two pieces.
Machines with ribber
With ribber in position and carriage at right, set machine for 1 × 1 rib. Using yarn C, cast on 115 sts in 1 × 1 rib. Work 5 tubular/circular rows. Carriage is at right. Set carriage for 1 × 1 rib knitting. Set RC at 000. Using MT – 4, work 54 rows. Cast off loosely. Make another collar piece to match.
Machines without ribber
Using 2¾mm needles and yarn C, cast on 115 sts. Work in k1, p1 rib until work measures 17cm. Cast off loosely. Make another collar piece to match.

FINISHING

With purl side of work facing, block each piece by pinning out to correct measurements. Depending on yarn used, press carefully following instructions on ball or cone band, or dampen with cold, clean water and leave to dry naturally. Join centre panel to side panels. Join shoulder, side and sleeve seams. Set in sleeves gathering tops slightly. Join collar seams and sew in position. Graft ends of armbands, fold in half and join long seams. Sew in position 1cm in front of armhole seam, taking them down in a straight line to the side seams.

SHAPE GUIDE
All measurements are given in centimetres. Figures in brackets refer to the larger size. Where there is only one figure it applies to both sizes.

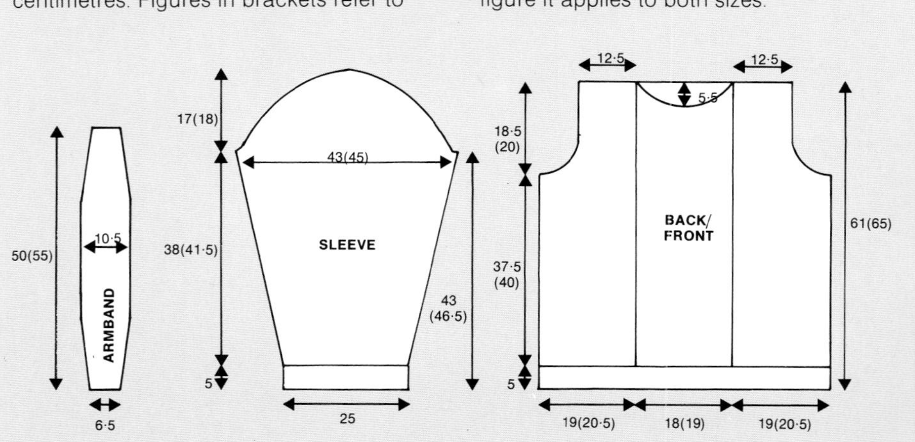

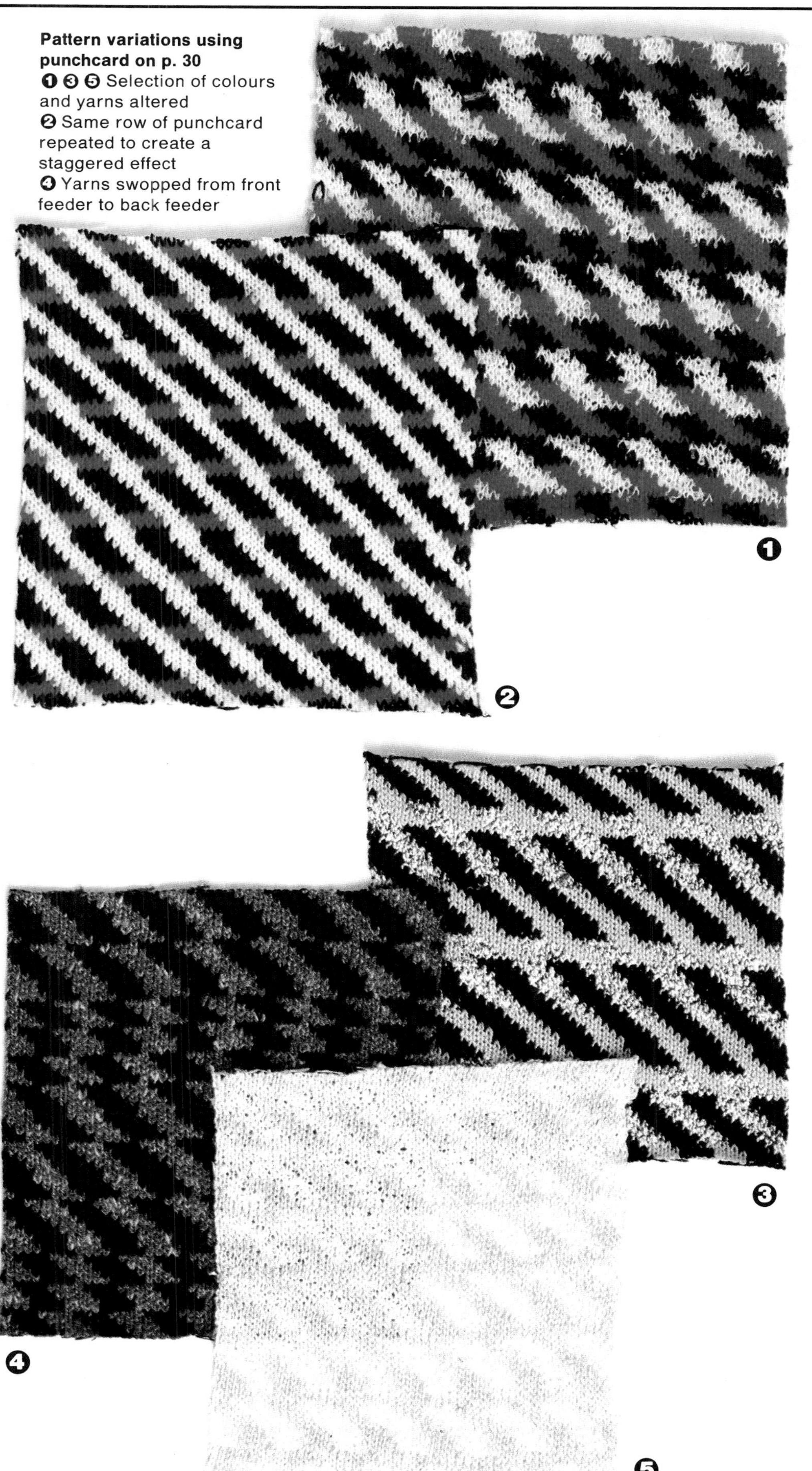

Pattern variations using punchcard on p. 30
❶ ❸ ❺ Selection of colours and yarns altered
❷ Same row of punchcard repeated to create a staggered effect
❹ Yarns swopped from front feeder to back feeder

VERTICAL & DIAGONAL STRIPES

In addition to forming horizontal stripes by changing the yarn colour every few rows, as discussed on the previous pages, you can also make vertical or diagonal stripes by using a punchcard or electronic graph with the secondary yarn feeder. This is how I have achieved the striped effect on the sweater *Popsicle,* overleaf.

Experimenting with colours and yarns
The samples show how different effects can be achieved when using the same basic design. One method is to use different coloured or textured yarns, another is to change the number of rows worked in each yarn. Swopping the yarns used from the front feeder to the back feeder provides yet more scope for modifying this design (sample 4). Another way of changing the appearance of the stripe is to use the same row of the punchcard more than once, thus creating a stepped effect (sample 2).

I had intended to use only one type of yarn throughout this sweater (the plain mercerised cotton), but found that the resulting fabric was flat and dead. Consequently, during sampling, I changed the white cotton yarn for a textured, natural-coloured one, and immediately the whole fabric improved in handling and appearance.

Do not be afraid to mix yarns. A very ordinary, conventionally knitted sweater can be made distinctive by the clever use of textured and straight yarn combinations.

Transferring alternate stitches
After experimenting with colours and yarns I found a combination that I particularly liked, but I felt that the sweater might be a little bland without the addition of another, different effect. So working from right to left, I transferred every alternate stitch on to the next needle along, and put the empty needles out of action. This created a lighter, more open fabric.

This technique of transferring alternate stitches, which results in an effect known as continental rib, does not have to be carried out across the entire piece of knitting, as it has been in this particular sweater, the transferring could be worked in blocks, or diagonal stripes. This might take longer to do, but the finished sweater would have greater design interest.

PATTERN INSTRUCTIONS FOR

POPSICLE

This loose-fitting, one-size summer top is based on a very simple square shape. Extra interest is added at the shoulders with a row of pretty, pastel-coloured buttons. The continental rib at the top of the sweater draws the work in tighter, helping to hold the shoulder line in place. The armbands and shoulder bands are knitted with a tighter tension on the inside to enable them to lay flat.

MATERIALS

Yarn

Yarn A 75g fine-weight mercerised cotton (lilac)
Yarn B 75g fine-weight mercerised cotton (pale green)
Yarn C 75g fine-weight mercerised cotton (blue)
Yarn D 100g medium-weight gimp cotton (natural)

Notions

16 buttons 1cm in diameter

MEASUREMENTS

To fit chest 81-101cm (32-40in)
Actual chest size 104cm (41in)
Length to back neck 54.5cm (21½in)

MAIN TENSION (MT)

32 sts and 37 rows measure 10cm over Fair Isle Pattern using yarns A, B and C (tension dial set at approximately 5)
32 sts and 42 rows measure 10cm over Fair Isle Pattern using yarns A, B, C and D (tension dial set at approximately 5)
32 sts and 40 rows measure 10cm over continental rib using yarns A, B, C and D (tension dial set at approximately 5)

SPECIAL NOTE

Needles in non-working position are counted as stitches throughout.
When working in Fair Isle pattern, read two colour rows as follows: thread first colour stated in feeder 1/A to knit the background, and second colour stated in feeder 2/B to knit the contrast pattern.

BACK

Push 84 needles at left and 83 needles at right of centre 0 to WP (167 needles). Push every alternate needle back to NWP. Using MT and waste yarn, cast on and knit a few rows ending with carriage at right. Set row counter at 000. Using MT – 3, continue in stripes as follows:

* Knit 2 rows yarn A, 2 rows yarn B, 2 rows yarn A and 2 rows yarn C. Repeat from * twice more. Knit 4 rows yarn A. ** Knit 2 rows yarn C, 2 rows yarn A, 2 rows yarn B and 2 rows yarn A. Repeat from ** twice more. Row counter shows 52. Push needles from NWP to WP and make a hem by placing loops of first row worked in yarn A evenly along the row. Unravel waste yarn when work is completed. Insert punchcard and set to first row. (Do not lock card.) Set carriage for Fair Isle patterning. Set row counter at 000. Using MT, continue in Fair Isle pattern. *** Knit 2 rows yarn A only (st st), 4 rows yarns B/A and 4 rows yarns C/A. Repeat from *** 3 times more. Knit 2 rows yarn A only (st st) and 8 rows yarns D/A. Row counter shows 50. **** Knit 2 rows yarn D only (st st), 4 rows yarns D/A, 4 rows yarns D/C and 4 rows yarns D/B. Repeat from **** twice more. Row counter shows 92. Place marker at each end for armholes. Continue in Fair Isle pattern. Repeat from **** 4 times more. Remove punchcard and continue in stocking stitch. Knit 2 rows yarn D. Row counter shows 150.

Continental rib: Transfer every alternate st on to adjacent needles and push empty needles to NWP. Continue in stripes as follows: ***** Knit 2 rows yarn D, 2 rows yarn A, 2 rows yarn D, 2 rows yarn C, 2 rows yarn D and 2 rows yarn B. Repeat from ***** twice more. Knit 2 rows yarn D. Row counter shows 188. Push needles from NWP to WP and place loop from row below adjacent st on to empty needles ******. Using MT and yarn B, knit 9 rows. Using MT – 1, knit 9 rows. Make a hem by placing loops of first row worked in yarn B on to corresponding needles. Knit 1 row. Cast off.

FRONT

Work as given for the back as far as ******. Using MT and yarn B, knit 4 rows. Counting from each end, make buttonholes by transferring the 7th and every following 8th st on to its adjacent needle 7 times in all (7 buttonholes each side). With empty needles in WP, knit 5 rows. Using MT – 1, knit 5 rows. Make buttonholes over same sts as before. Knit 4 rows. Make a hem by placing loops of first row worked in yarn B on to corresponding needles. Knit 1 row. Cast off.

FRONT ARMBANDS

Push 80 needles to WP. With purl side facing, pick up 80 sts from top of shoulder band to marker on front and place on to needles. * Set row counter at 000. Using MT and yarn B, knit 1 row. Counting from shoulder edge, make a buttonhole by transferring the 4th st on to adjacent needle. With empty needle in WP, knit 8 rows. Using MT – 1, knit 8 rows. Make a buttonhole over same st as before. Knit 1 row. Make a hem by placing loops of first row worked in yarn B on to corresponding needles. Knit 1 row. Cast off.

BACK ARMBANDS

Push 80 needles to WP. With purl side facing, pick up 80 sts from top of shoulder band to marker on back and place on to needles. Work as given for the front armbands from *, omitting buttonholes.

FINISHING

With purl side of work facing, block each piece by pinning out to correct measurements. Depending on yarn used, press carefully following instructions on ball or cone band, omitting welts and continental rib, or dampen with cold, clean water and leave to dry naturally. Join side seams. Neaten open ends of armbands. Sew on buttons.

PUNCHCARD
Punch this card before starting to knit.

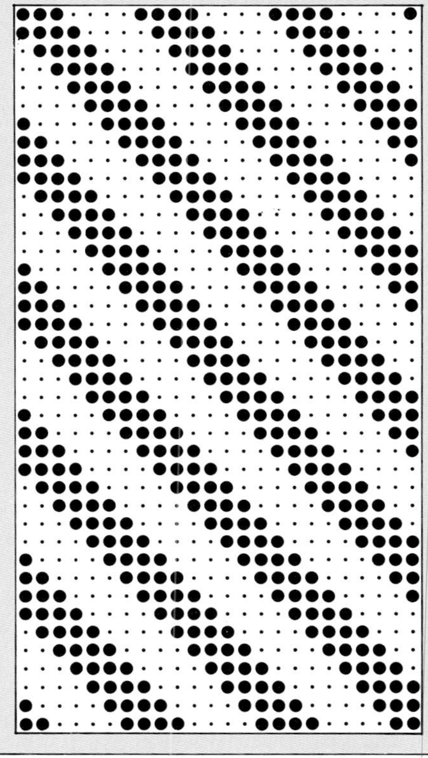

SHAPE GUIDE
All measurements are given in centimetres.

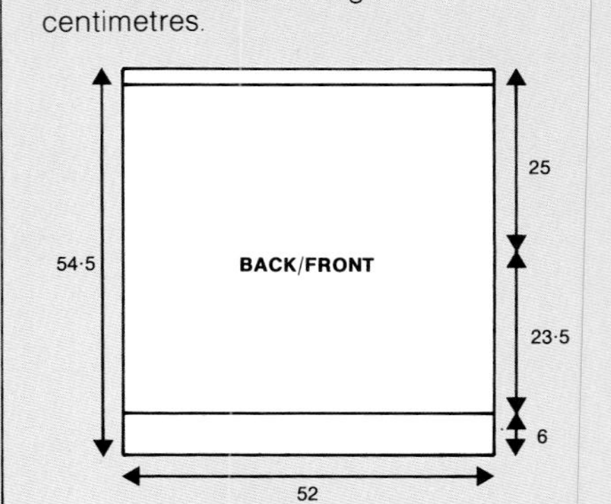

Choose buttons in pretty pastel shades to tone with the sweater.

JACQUARD

Jacquard and Fair Isle are two different terms used in machine knitting to describe the same technique, namely the use of two different coloured yarns in one row. I usually use the term Fair Isle to refer to the multi-coloured patterns based on traditional motifs from the islands north of Scotland, and the term jacquard to refer to multi-coloured design patterns generally, hence the heading for this section. However, it should be noted that some machine manufacturers use the term Fair-Isle to refer to knitting with two colours of yarn in a row, and to create the jacquard patterns in this section you will have to set your machine for "Fair Isle patterning" if you use one of these machines.

The technique

By using two different yarns in the two yarn feeders, jacquard knitting may be produced as quickly as plain stocking stitch on punchcard and electronic machines. The jacquard design is punched on to the punchcard or drawn on the graph. The needles corresponding to the filled-in squares knit one colour of yarn, and the needles corresponding to the holes knit the second colour. (On most machines the yarn in feeder 2/B knits the punched-out pattern, and the yarn in feeder 1/A knits the "background".) Since there are only two yarn feeders, only two colours may be used in any one row, but the yarn may be changed in either or both of the feeders at the start of each new row, so you can use as many colours as you wish on one garment. The more changes of colour that are made, the longer the sweater takes to knit, but with certain designs the results are well worth the extra effort.

The fabric

When constructing jacquard patterns, the yarn not being knitted produces a strand of yarn, or *float* across the back of the knitting. Because of this, the fabric produced is much thicker than a plain, stocking stitch fabric. While you can use this to advantage – a warm garment may be produced from relatively fine yarn – it may be a hindrance if the fabric is too bulky for your required purpose. This is an important factor to consider if, as in the twin set shown on pages 34-37, two garments are to be worn together in layers. One way around this problem is to limit the use of the jacquard pattern to small, selected areas on the underneath garment. This possibility is explored further in the section *Jacquard Insets*, page 38.

Working out jacquard designs

The easiest way of working out jacquard designs is to draw them on squared graph paper. Beginners should try small motifs to begin with, such as those used on the *Chequerboard* and *Bib and Tucker* sweaters. Get used to manipulating these into interesting repeats, and then start working out more complex designs. Do remember that your designs, when knitted, may not come out looking exactly as they do on the graph paper; since stitches are often longer than they are wide, the knitted design may be more elongated than the graph paper design. It is possible to buy special stitch proportioned graph paper which makes working out designs easier. Single stitches, also, do not always come out exactly as expected. However, if this happens, do not let it discourage you, the abstract motif you end up with might look more attractive than the original concept.

Pattern repeats

A design motif can be repeated several times to form an all-over repeat. This is known as putting a design into repeat. There are many different ways a motif can be structured into a repeat, some of the most common are illustrated on the right.

Not every design or motif can be repeated in the same way; the punchcard machine knitter is slightly

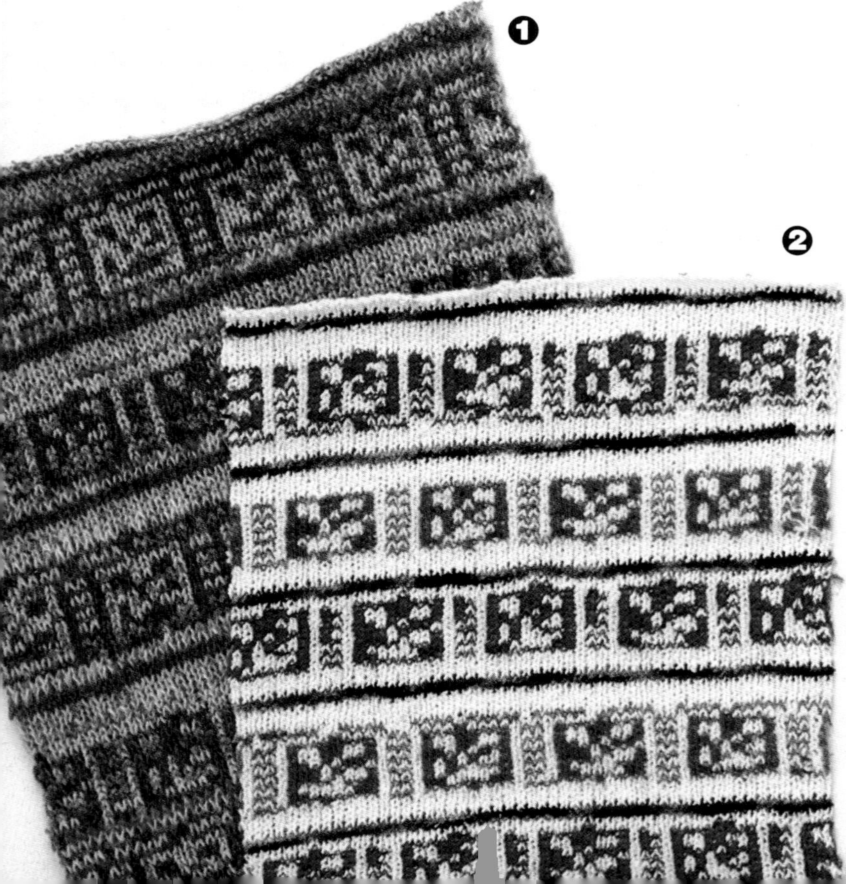

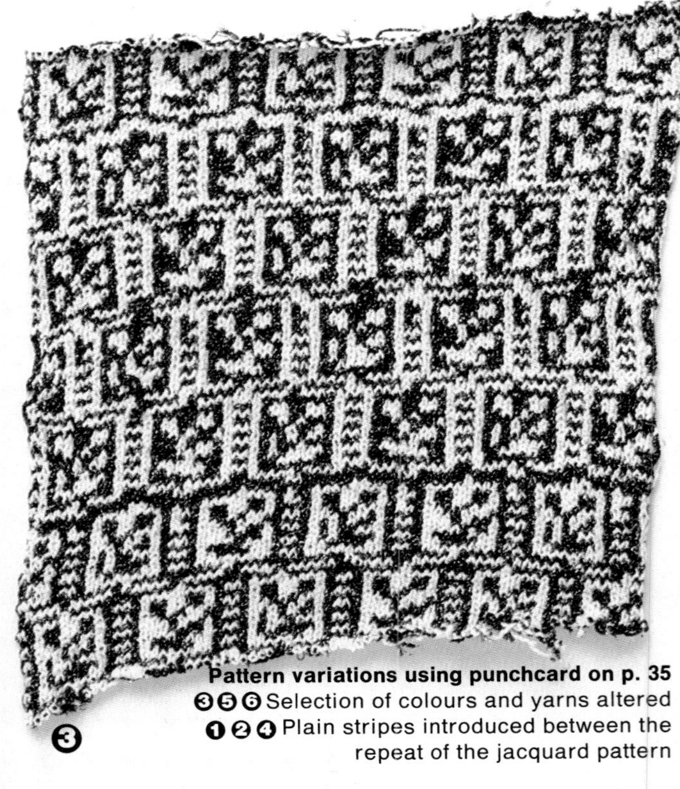

Pattern variations using punchcard on p. 35
❸❺❻ Selection of colours and yarns altered
❶❷❹ Plain stripes introduced between the repeat of the jacquard pattern

limited by the size of the punchcard, and this must be borne in mind when working out a repeating pattern. Since punchcards are 24 stitches wide, the width of the pattern repeat has to be a number of stitches that will divide into 24 exactly. That means patterns 2, 3, 4, 6, 8, or 12 stitches wide may be used. The length of the pattern repeat may be more varied – it can be anything up to 60 rows long, or 120 rows if the elongating facility found on many machines is utilised. For even longer patterns, blank punchcard bought on a roll may be used, or two punchcards may be joined together. These limitations do not apply to electronic machines, these can produce even larger designs.

PATTERN REPEATS The coloured area indicates the pattern repeat

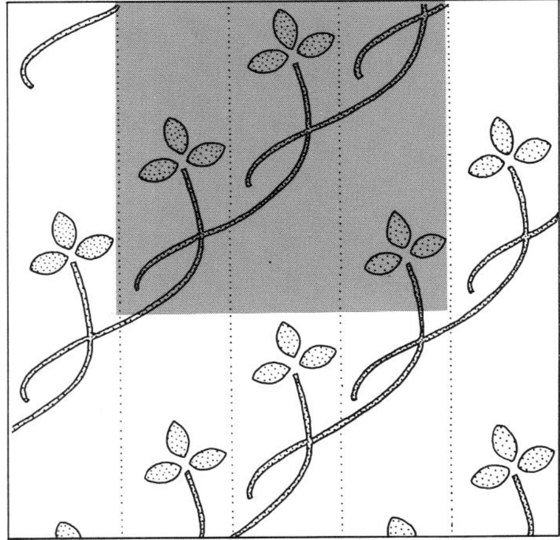

Drop repeat

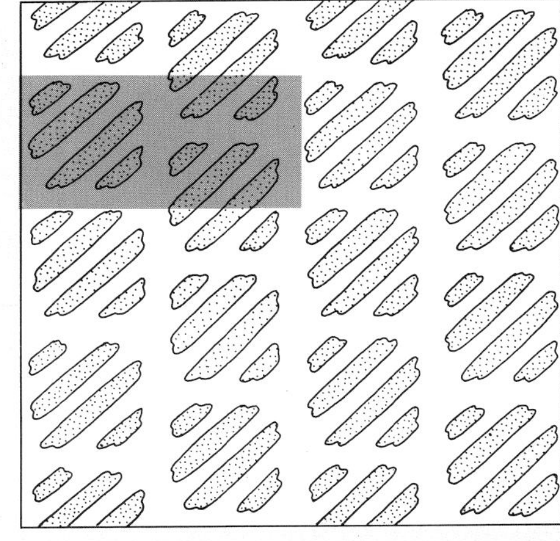

Half drop repeat

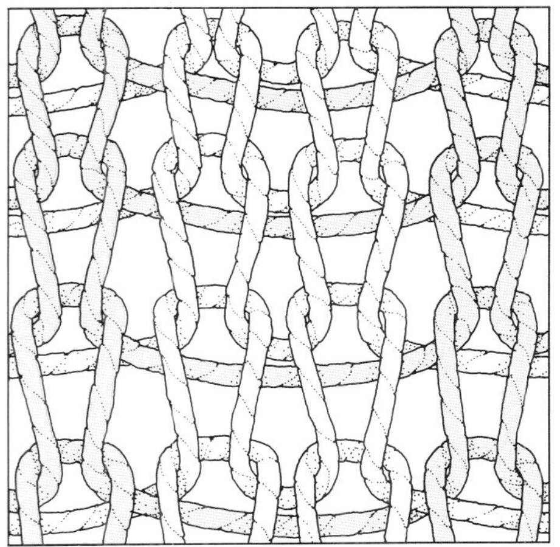

Stitch construction The yarn not being knitted produces a float along the back of the knitting.

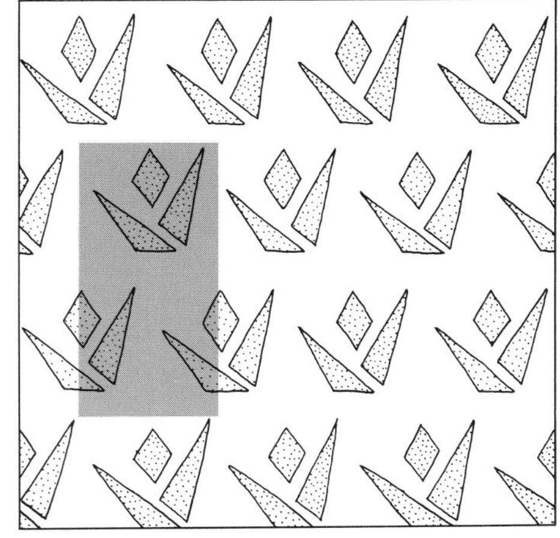

Brick repeat

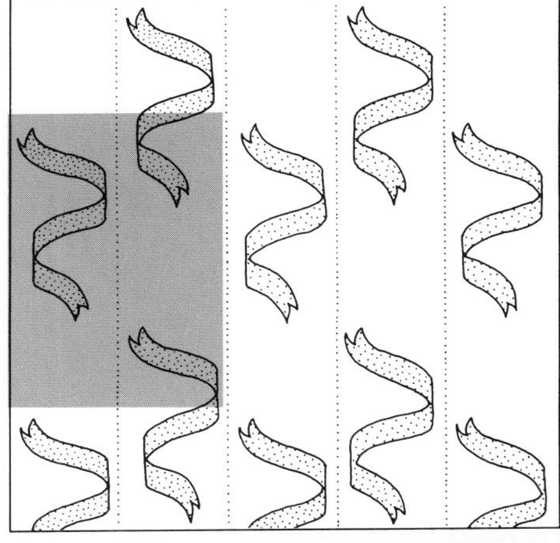

Step repeat

❹

❺

❻

PATTERN INSTRUCTIONS FOR
BLACK MAGIC SWEATER

The combination of a black mohair-type yarn and a pale grey fancy yarn make a classic winter twinset. Bands of an abstracted flower motif are featured on the sweater, the same design is used as an all-over pattern on the cardigan, p. 36. For summer wear use soft, pastel sahdes of mercerised cotton.

MATERIALS

Yarn

Yarn A 225 (250)g fine-weight fluffy acrylic yarn, used double (black)
Yarn B 50 (50)g medium-weight acrylic gimp (pale grey)

A

B

Needles
If you don't have a ribber, you need 1 pair size 2¼mm knitting needles.

MEASUREMENTS

To fit chest 81 (86)cm (32, 34in)
Actual chest size 87 (92)cm (34, 36in)
Length to shoulder 57.5cm (22¾in)
Sleeve seam 12.5cm (5in)

MAIN TENSION (MT)

30 sts and 43 rows measure 10cm over Fair Isle pattern (tension dial set at approximately 7)
28 sts and 40 rows measure 10cm over stocking stitch (tension dial set at approximately 7)

BACK

Machines with ribber
With ribber in position and carriage at right, set machine for 1 × 1 rib. Using yarn A, cast on 122 (130) sts in 1 × 1 rib. Work 5 tubular/circular rows. Set carriage for 1 × 1 rib knitting. Set RC at 000. Using MT—3, work 26 rows. Transfer sts for st st.
Machines without ribber
Using yarn A and 2¼mm needles, cast on 122 (130) sts. Work 5cm in k1, p1 rib. Push 122 (130) needles to WP. With carriage at right, transfer sts to machine needles.
All machines
Set RC at 000. Using MT, knit 7 rows. Insert punchcard and lock on first row. Set carriage for pattern. Knit 1 row. Release card and continue in Fair Isle with yarn A in feeder 1/A and yarn B in feeder 2/B. Knit 16 rows. Remove card. Continue in st st and yarn A. Knit 98 rows. RC shows 122.
Shape armholes: Cast off 8 sts at the beginning of the next 2 rows. Decrease 1 st at each end of every following alternate row until 98 (104) sts remain *. Knit 60 (58) rows. RC shows 192.
Shape neck: Using a length of yarn, cast off centre 30 sts. Push 34 (37) needles at left to HP and continue on remaining sts for first side. Decrease 1 st at neck edge on every row until 24 (27) sts remain, then on every following alternate row until 21 (24) sts remain. Knit 4 rows. Cast off. With carriage at left, push remaining needles from HP to WP and finish to correspond with first side reversing shapings.

FRONT

Work as for back to *. Knit 50 (48) rows. RC shows 182.
Shape neck: Using a length of yarn, cast off centre 30 sts. Push 34 (37) needles at left to HP and continue on remaining sts for first side. Decrease 1 st at neck edge on every row until 24 (27) sts remain, then on every following alternate row until 21 (24) sts remain. Knit 14 rows. Cast off. With carriage at left, push remaining needles from HP to WP and finish to correspond with first side reversing shapings.

SLEEVES

Machines with ribber
With ribber in position and carriage at right, set machine for 1 × 1 rib. Using yarn A, cast on 78 (84) sts in 1 × 1 rib. Work 5 tubular/circular rows. Set carriage for 1 × 1 rib knitting. Set RC at 000. Using MT—3, work 13 rows. Transfer sts for st st.
Machines without ribber
Using yarn A and 2¼mm needles, cast on 78 (84) sts. Work 2.5cm in k1, p1 rib. Push 78 (84) needles to WP. With carriage at left, transfer sts to machine needles.
All machines
Set RC at 000. Using MT, knit 3 rows. Shape sides by increasing 1 st at each end of next row, knit 3 rows. Insert punchcard and lock on first row. Set carriage for pattern. Increase 1 st at each end of next row. Release card and continue in Fair Isle with yarn A in feeder 1/A and yarn B in feeder 2/B. Increase 1 st at each end of every 4th row until there are 90 (96) sts. Remove card. Continue in st st and yarn A. Increase 1 st at each end of every 4th row until there are 96 (102) sts. Knit 5 rows. RC shows 41.
Shape top: Cast off 8 sts at the beginning of the next 2 rows. Decrease 1 st at each end of every following alternate row until 70 (76) sts remain, then on every following 6th row until 50 (58) sts remain, then on every following alternate row until 24 (26) sts remain, then on every row until 16 (18) sts remain. Cast off 5 sts at the beginning of the next 2 rows. Cast off remaining 6 (8) sts.

BACK NECKBAND

Machines with ribber
With ribber in position and carriage at right, set machine for 1 × 1 rib. Using yarn A, cast on 118 sts in 1 × 1 rib. * Work 5 tubular/circular rows. Set carriage for 1 × 1 rib knitting. Set RC at 000. Using MT—3, work 10 rows. Transfer sts to main bed. With purl side of back facing, pick up sts around neck edge and place on to needles. Cast off *.
Machines without ribber
With right side of back facing, join yarn A to neck at right shoulder and using 2¼mm needles, pick up and knit 118 sts around neck edge. Work 2cm in k1, p1 rib. Cast off in rib.

FRONT NECKBAND

Machines with ribber
With ribber in position and carriage at right, set machine for 1 × 1 rib. Using yarn A, cast on 132 sts in 1 × 1 rib. Work as for back neckband from * to * reading front for back.
Machines without ribber
With right side of front facing, join yarn A to neck at left shoulder and using 2¼mm needles, pick up and knit 132 sts around neck edge. Work 2cm in k1, p1 rib. Cast off in rib.

FINISHING

With purl side of work facing, block each piece by pinning out to correct measurements. Depending on yarn used, press carefully following instructions on ball or cone band, or dampen with cold, clean water and leave to dry naturally. Join shoulder, neckband, side and sleeve seams. Set in sleeves gathering tops.

SHAPE GUIDE
All measurements are given in centimetres. Figures in brackets refer to the larger size. Where only one figure is given, it applies to both sizes.

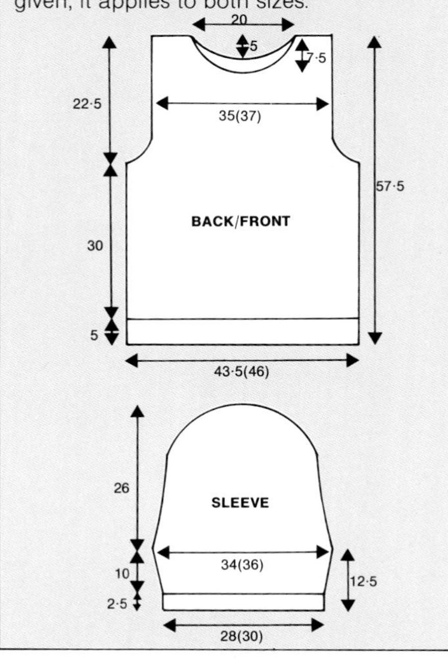

PUNCH CARD
Punch this card before starting to knit.

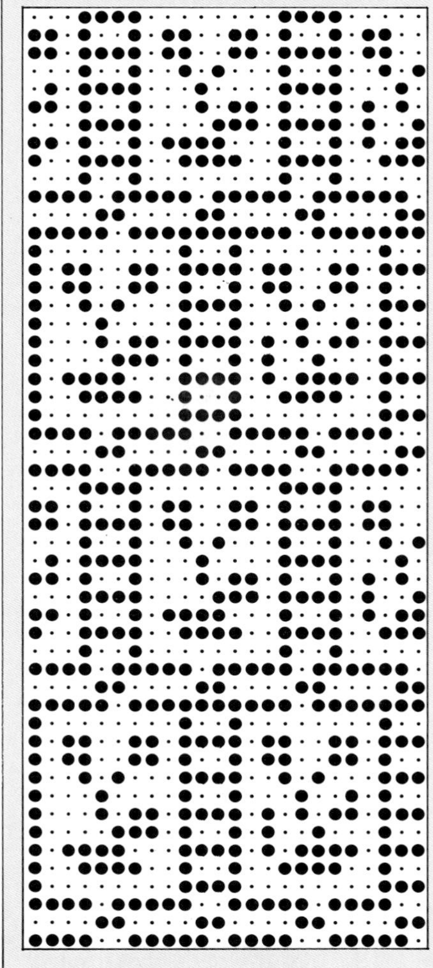

PATTERN INSTRUCTIONS FOR

BLACK MAGIC CARDIGAN

This round-necked cardigan buttons right up to the neck for warmth. Handy pockets are incorporated into the design.

MATERIALS

Yarn
Yarn A 250 (300)g fine-weight fluffy acrylic yarn, used double (black)
Yarn B 300 (325)g medium-weight acrylic gimp (pale grey)

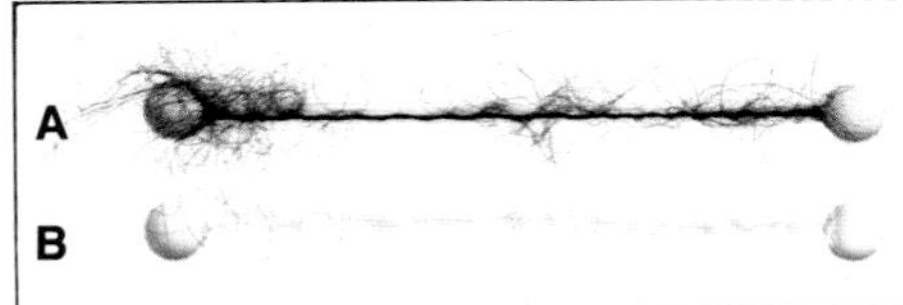

Notions
11 buttons, 1cm in diameter
2 stitch holders

Needles
If you don't have a ribber, you need 1 pair size 2¼mm knitting needles

MEASUREMENTS

To fit chest 81 (86)cm (32, 34in)
Actual chest size 93 (98)cm (36½, 38½in)
Length to shoulder 59 (65)cm (23¼, 25½in)
Sleeve seam 44cm (17¼in)

MAIN TENSION (MT)

The same as the twinset sweater p. 35.

SPECIAL NOTE

Use the same punchcard as the twinset sweater p. 35.

BACK

Machines with ribber
With ribber in position and carriage at right, set machine for 1 × 1 rib. Using yarn A, cast on 140 (148) sts in 1 × 1 rib. Work 5 tubular/circular rows. Set carriage for 1 × 1 rib knitting. Set RC at 000. Using MT—3, work 26 rows. Transfer sts for st st.

Machines without ribber
Using yarn A and 2¼mm needles, cast on 140 (148) sts. Work 5cm in k1, p1 rib. Push 140 (148) needles to WP. With carriage at right, transfer sts to machine needles.

All machines
Insert punchcard and lock on first row. Set carriage for pattern. Set RC at 000. Using MT, knit 1 row. Release card and continue in Fair Isle with yarn A in feeder 1/A and yarn B in feeder 2/B. Knit 129 (155) rows. RC shows 130 (156).

Shape armholes: Cast off 8 sts at the beginning of the next 2 rows. Decrease 1 st at each end of every alternate row until 112 (118) sts remain. Knit 91 (89) rows. RC shows 235 (261). Cast off.

RIGHT FRONT

Machines with ribber
With ribber in position and carriage at right, set machine for 1 × 1 rib. Using yarn A, cast on 80 (84) sts in 1 × 1 rib. Work 5 tubular/circular rows. Set carriage for 1 × 1 rib knitting. Set RC at 000. Using MT—3, work 4 rows. Counting from left edge, make a buttonhole over 7th, 8th and 9th sts. Work 22 rows. Transfer sts for st st.

Machines without ribber
Using yarn A and 2¼mm needles, cast on 80 (84) sts. Work 4 rows in k1, p1 rib.

1st buttonhole row: Rib 6, cast off next 3 sts, rib to end.

2nd buttonhole row: Rib to end, casting on 3 sts over those cast off in previous row. Continue in rib to 5cm. Push 80 (84) needles to WP. With carriage at right and buttonhole at left, transfer sts to machine needles.

All machines
** Slip 14 sts at left on to a stitch holder for front band. Insert punchcard and lock on first row. Set carriage for pattern. Set RC at 000. Using MT, knit 1 row. Release card and continue in Fair Isle with yarn A in feeder 1/A and yarn B in feeder 2/B. Knit 26 rows. Knit 1 row extra for left front.
Pocket opening: Using nylon cord, knit 21 (25) sts at right by hand taking needles down to NWP. Note number on row counter and pattern row on card. Continue on remaining sts for first side. Knit 65 rows. Using nylon cord, knit sts by hand taking needles down to NWP. With carriage at right, unravel nylon cord over 21 (25) needles at right bringing needles back to WP. Lock card on number previously noted. Set carriage for pattern and take to left without knitting. Set RC on number previously noted. Release card and continue in Fair Isle. Knit 65 rows. Unravel nylon cord over 45 needles at left bringing needles back to WP. Continue in Fair Isle pattern, knit 38 (64) rows. RC shows 130 (156), 131 (157) when working left front.
Shape armhole: Cast off 8 sts at the beginning of the next row, knit 1 row. Decrease 1 st at armhole edge on every following alternate row until 52 (55) sts remain. Knit 65 (63) rows. (26 rows less have been worked to shoulder than on back.)
Shape neck: Cast off 10 sts at the beginning of the next row. Decrease 1 st at neck edge on every row until 36 (39) sts remain, then on every following alternate row until 30 (33) sts remain. Knit 7 rows. Cast off **.

LEFT FRONT

Work as for right front to * omitting buttonhole, then from ** to ** reversing shaping, noting alteration in number of rows worked and reading left for right and right for left.

SLEEVES

Machines with ribber
With ribber in position and carriage at right, set machine for 1 × 1 rib. Using yarn A, cast on 56 (60) sts in 1 × 1 rib. Work 5 tubular/circular rows. Set carriage for 1 × 1 rib knitting. Set RC at 000. Using MT−3, work 26 rows. Using waste yarn, work a few rows and release from machine.
Machines without ribber
Using yarn A and $2\frac{1}{4}$mm needles, cast on 56 (60) sts. Work 5cm in k1, p1 rib.
All machines
Push 64 (68) needles to WP. With carriage at right, place sts on to needles as follows: 1 st on to each of first 3 (5) needles, leave 1 needle empty, * 1 st on to each of next 7 needles, leave 1 needle empty; repeat from * across the row ending with 1 st on to each of last 4 (6) needles. Pick up a loop from row below adjacent st and place on to empty needle. Insert punchcard and lock on first row. Set carriage for pattern. Set RC at 000. Using MT, knit 1 row. Release card and continue in Fair Isle with yarn A in feeder 1/A and yarn B in feeder 2/B. Shape sides by increasing 1 st at each end of every 6th row until there are 112 (116) sts. Knit 24 rows. RC shows 169.
Shape top: Cast off 8 sts at the beginning of the next 2 rows. Decrease 1 st at each end of every row until 76 (80) sts remain, then on every following 3rd row until 38 (44) sts remain. Knit 1 row. Decrease 1 st at each end of every row until 14 sts remain. Cast off.

BUTTON BAND

Machines with ribber
With ribber in position, set machine for 1 × 1 rib. Arrange 14 needles for 1 × 1 rib. With purl side of left front facing, replace band sts on to needles. Set RC at 000. Using MT−3, and yarn A, work 200 (220) rows. Cast off.
Machines without ribber
With knit side of left front facing, join in yarn A and using $2\frac{1}{4}$mm needles, pick up 14 sts from stitch holder and work in k1, p1 rib until band, when slightly stretched, fits up left front edge. Cast off in rib. Mark positions for 10 buttons on this band, the top one two rows below top edge and the others evenly spaced.

BUTTONHOLE BAND

Machines with ribber
With ribber in position, set machine for 1 × 1 rib. Arrange 14 needles for 1 × 1 rib. With purl side of right front facing, replace band sts on to needles. Set RC at 000. Using MT−3 and yarn A, work 0 (2) rows. * Counting from left edge, make a buttonhole over 7th, 8th and 9th sts. Work 22 (24) rows. Repeat from * 8 times more. Make another buttonhole over the same needles as before. Work 2 rows. Cast off.
Machines without ribber
With knit side of right front facing, join in yarn A and using $2\frac{1}{4}$mm needles, pick up 14 sts from stitch holder and work in k1, p1 rib as given for button band, making buttonholes as markers are reached as follows:
1st buttonhole row (right side): Rib 6, cast off next 3 sts, rib to end.
2nd buttonhole row: Rib to end casting on 3 sts over those cast off in previous row.

NECKBAND

Machines with ribber
With ribber in position and carriage at right, set machine for 1 × 1 rib. Using yarn A, cast on 140 sts in 1 × 1 rib. Work 5 tubular/circular rows. Set carriage for 1 × 1 rib knitting. Set RC at 000. Using MT−3, decrease 1 st at each end of the next 10 rows. Cast off.
Machines without ribber
Using yarn A and $2\frac{1}{4}$mm needles, cast on 140 sts. Work 1 row in k1, p1 rib. Working in rib, decrease 1 st at each end of the next 10 rows. Cast off in rib.

POCKET BANDS

Machines with ribber
With ribber in position and carriage at right, set machine for 1 × 1 rib. Using yarn A, cast on 14 sts in 1 × 1 rib. Work 5 tubular/circular rows. Set carriage for 1 × 1 rib knitting. Set RC at 000. Using MT−3, work 60 rows. Cast off.
Machines without ribber
Using yarn A and $2\frac{1}{4}$mm needles, cast on 14 sts. Work in k1, p1 rib until band, when slightly stretched, fits along pocket opening. Cast off in rib.

POCKET LININGS

Using yarn A, cast on 23 sts by hand. Set RC at 000. Using MT, knit 1 row. Increase 1 st at left edge on every row until there are 33 sts, then on every following alternate row until there are 40 sts. Knit 32 rows. Decrease 1 st at right edge on every row until 12 sts remain. Cast off.
Knit second lining by reversing shapings and reading left for right and right for left.

FINISHING

With purl side of work facing, block each piece by pinning out to correct measurements. Depending on yarn used, press carefully following instructions on ball or cone band, or dampen with cold, clean water and leave to dry naturally. Join shoulder, side and sleeve seams. Set in sleeves. Sew front bands in position. Sew on cast off edge and shaped ends of neckband. Sew on pocket bands to front edge of pocket openings. Sew pocket linings to back edge of pocket opening then sew remaining edges in position. Finish buttonholes and sew on buttons to correspond.

SHAPE GUIDE
All measurements are given in centimetres. Figures in brackets refer to the larger size. Where only one figure is given, it applies to both sizes.

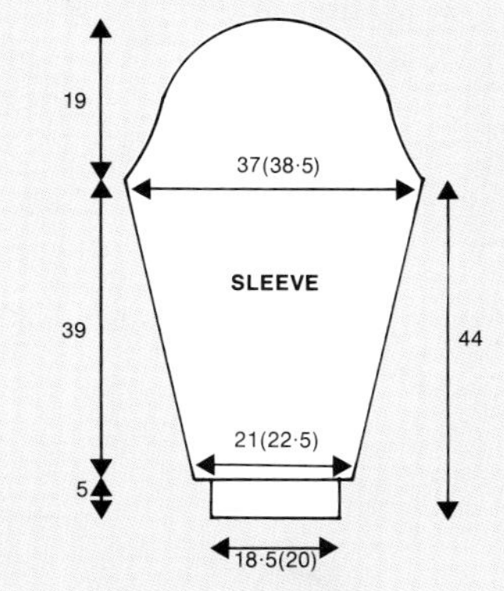

JACQUARD INSETS

The simplest way of using the jacquard technique is as an all-over pattern, as shown on the *Man's Fair Isle*, the *Woman's Fair Isle*, and the cardigan of the *Black Magic Twin Set*. However, it can also be very effective when used as an inset. There are three reasons for using jacquard patterns as insets:

1. Economy – in order to achieve maximum effect from the limited use of an expensive yarn.
2. Weight – in order to use jacquard patterning on a garment and yet not produce a thick and bulky fabric.
3. Design – by exploring this process interesting design concepts can be achieved.

Economy

I wanted to show the use of angora, a soft and luxurious, but expensive yarn. After producing a pleasing, simple jacquard pattern, I worked out a sweater design that was styled to include an inset in which only a limited amount of angora was used, while the rest of the sweater was knitted in a cheaper yarn. In this design the angora was used only in a bib-shaped inset, on the front of the sweater, and in a narrow band around the welt, cuffs and collar. Other ideas for insets may be found on pages 20-22.

Weight

This problem has already been mentioned when discussing the design of the *Black Magic Twin Set*, where I wanted to create two garments that could be worn layered without creating too much bulk. I limited the use of the jacquard pattern to small bands around the body and sleeves of the short sleeved top. You can get ideas for a variety of sweater styles by sketching your garment shape and filling in small areas of pattern in as many different ways as possible. Several alternatives that could have been used on the *Black Magic* sweater are shown on the right.

Design

Jacquard patterning is ideally suited to breaking up a sweater surface into different areas of colour and texture. Again, drawing your sweater shape and then filling in various areas with jacquard patterning is a good way of working out the possibilities. This idea of using jacquard patterns as insets, or on only parts of a garment, can open up a whole new area of sweater design. With experience, making such garments becomes quite simple.

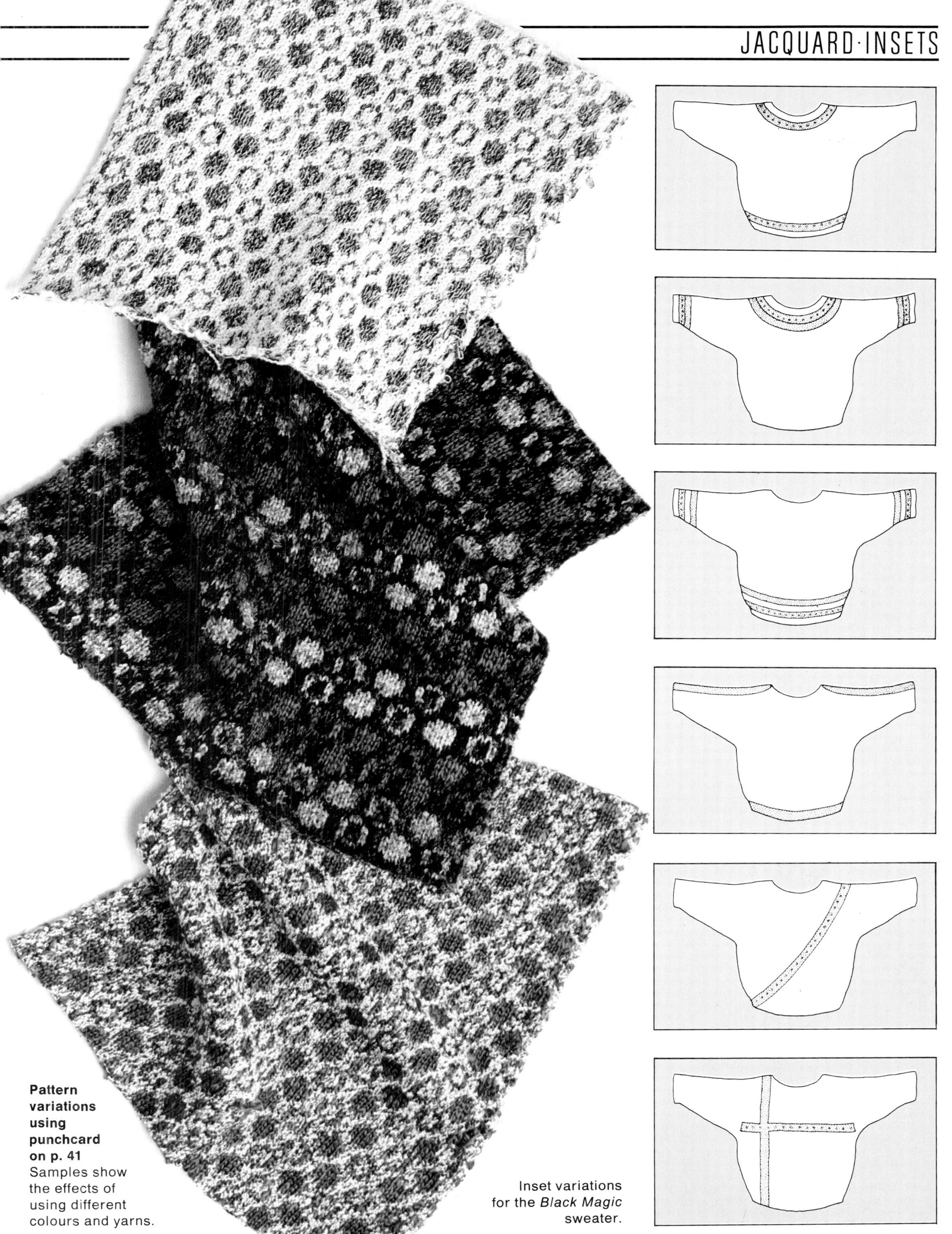

Pattern variations using punchcard on p. 41
Samples show the effects of using different colours and yarns.

Inset variations for the *Black Magic* sweater.

PATTERN INSTRUCTIONS FOR

BIB AND TUCKER

This sweater has been made in three different colourways to show the effect colour can have on design. To keep the cost of the yarn reasonable, confine the use of angora to the bib inset, and narrow stripes around the sleeves and welt. Carefully brush the angora from the right side to bring the hairs through from the back of the fabric.

MATERIALS

Yarn
Yarn A 250 (300, 350)g medium-weight acrylic yarn (blue)
Yarn B 40 (40, 40)g medium-weight angora (mustard)

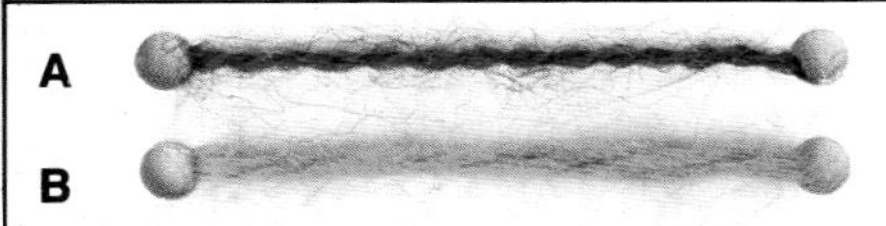

Notions
1 button
2 hooks and eyes
Needles
1 pair size $2\frac{3}{4}$mm

MEASUREMENTS

To fit chest 81 (86, 91)cm (32, 34, 36in)
Actual chest size 91 (96, 100)cm ($35\frac{3}{4}$, $37\frac{3}{4}$, $39\frac{1}{2}$in)
Length to shoulder 60 (60.5, 61)cm ($23\frac{1}{2}$, $23\frac{3}{4}$, 24in)
Sleeve seam 45cm ($17\frac{3}{4}$in)

MAIN TENSION (MT)

25 sts and 34 rows measure 10cm over stocking stitch (tension dial set at approximately 10).

SPECIAL NOTE

These instructions are written for punchcard machines whose pattern needles come out to upper working position, and for single motif punchcard machines with point cams. Instructions differ slightly for these two different types of machines.

BACK

Using $2\frac{3}{4}$mm needles and yarn A, cast on 114 (120, 126) sts. Work 6cm in k1, p1 rib. Push 114 (120, 126) needles to WP. With carriage at right, transfer sts to machine needles. Set RC at 000. Using MT and yarn B, knit 2 rows *. Change to yarn A and knit 110 rows. RC shows 112.
Shape armholes: Cast off 4 sts at the beginning of the next 2 rows. Decrease 1 st at each end of the next and every following alternate row until 96 (100, 104) sts remain. Knit 61 rows. RC shows 184 (186, 188). Cast off.

FRONT

Work as for Back to *. Change to yarn A and knit 87 rows (88 rows for single motif machines).

BIB

Single motif machines
Set machine for single motif Fair Isle. Set point cams to pattern over centre 4 sts. Working in Fair Isle * knit 1 row. Move point cam opposite end to carriage 4 sts out. Knit 1 row. Move point cam opposite end to carriage 4 sts out *. Repeat from * to * 3 more times. Then repeat from * to * 5 times but move point cams out by 3 sts. Repeat from * to * 2 more times but move point cams out by 2 sts. RC shows 112.
Shape armholes: Repeat from * to * of Bib moving point cams 1 needle out, until all needles are knitting Fair Isle. At the same time, cast off 4 sts at the beginning of the next 2 rows. Decrease 1 st at each end of the next and every following alternate row until 98 (104, 110) sts remain. Knit 1 row. RC shows 122.

Other machines
Insert punchcard and lock on first row. Set carriage for pattern. Knit 1 row. Push all needles except centre 4 back to WP. Release card and continue in Fair Isle pattern with yarn A in feeder A and yarn B in feeder B. Knit 1 row. Push all needles except centre 12 back to WP. Knit 1 row. Knit 3 rows, working 3 more sts each side of centre panel into pattern on every row. Knit 8 rows, working 2 more sts each side of centre panel into pattern on every row. Knit 5 rows, working 1 more st each side of centre panel into pattern on every row. Knit 4 rows, working 1 more st at each side of centre panel into pattern on next and every following alternate row. RC shows 112.
Shape armholes: Work 1 more st each side of centre panel into pattern on next and every following alternate row, and at the same time, cast off 4 sts at the beginning of the next 2 rows. Decrease 1 st at each end of the next and every following alternate row until 98 (104, 110) sts remain. Knit 1 row. RC shows 122.

All machines
Divide for front opening: Using nylon cord knit 49 (52, 55) sts at left by hand taking needles down to NWP. Note pattern row on card and position of pattern. Continue on remaining sts for first side. Continue to decrease at armhole edge on every alternate row from previous decrease until 48 (50, 52) sts remain, and at the same time, knit 13 (19, 25) rows, working 1 more st at side of centre panel into pattern on the next and every following alternate 3rd row. RC shows 135 (141, 147). Knit 28 (24, 20) rows. RC shows 163 (165, 167).
Shape neck: Cast off 6 sts at the beginning of the next row. Decrease 1 st at the neck edge on every row until 34 (36, 38) sts remain, then every following alternate row until 30 (32, 34) sts remain. Knit 8 rows. RC shows 188 (190, 192). Cast off. With carriage at right, unravel nylon cord over remaining 49 (52, 55) needles bringing back needles to WP. Lock card on number previously noted. Set carriage for pattern and take to left without knitting. Rest RC to 122. Release card and continue in Fair Isle pattern. Keeping pattern correct finish to correspond with first side, reversing shapings.

SLEEVES

Using $2\frac{3}{4}$mm needles and yarn A, cast on 64 (66, 68) sts. Work 6cm in k1, p1 rib. Push 64 (66, 68) needles to WP. With carriage at right transfer sts to machine needles. Set RC at 000. Using MT and yarn B, knit 2 rows. Change to yarn A and shape sides by increasing 1 st at each end of the next and every following alternate row until there are 88 (90, 92) sts. Knit 109 rows. RC shows 134.
Shape top: Cast off 4 sts at the beginning of the next 2 rows. Decrease 1 st at each end of the next and every following alternate row until 24 sts remain. Knit 1 row. Cast off.

COLLAR

With carriage at right and using yarn B, cast on 98 sts by hand. Set RC at 000. Using MT, knit 2 rows. Change to yarn A and knit 12 rows. Using MT-2, knit 6 rows; MT-4, knit 6 rows; MT-6, knit 10 rows. Cast off.

SHAPE GUIDE
All measurements are given in centimetres. Figures in brackets refer to larger sizes. Where only one figure is given, it applies to all sizes.

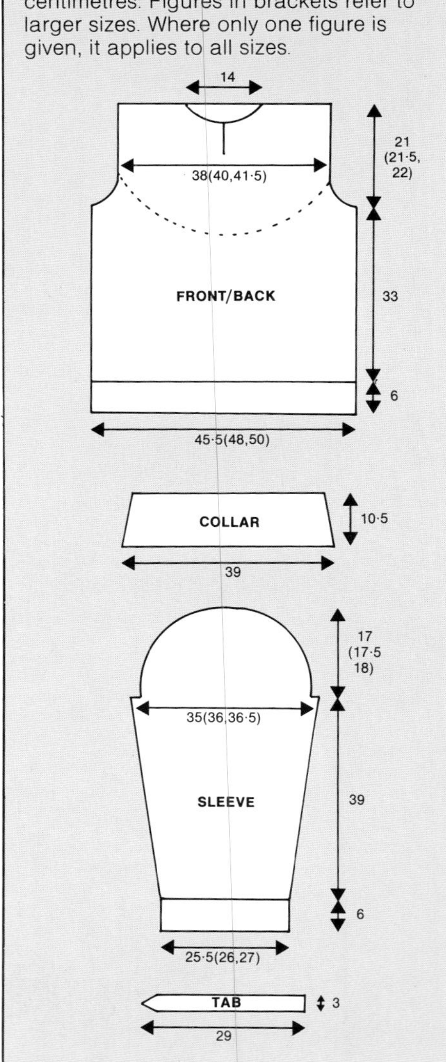

TAB

With carriage at right and using yarn B, cast on 2 sts by hand. Set RC at 000. Using MT, increase 1 st at each end of every alternate row until there are 8 sts. Knit 93 rows. RC shows 99. Cast off.

FINISHING

With purl side of work facing, block each piece by pinning out to correct measurements. Depending on yarn used, press carefully following instructions on ball or cone band, or dampen with cold, clean water and leave to dry. Join shoulder seams. Set in sleeves. Join side and sleeve seams. Lay sweater flat. With cast off edge of tab to neck, centre tab on top of slit. Stitch edge of tab to right side of slit, about 1.5cm from edge of slit. Stitch across tab in horizontal line below slit. Hold down end tab with a button. Sew cast off edge of collar to neck, beginning and ending at centre front. Sew one hook and eye to neck edge, and one half way down opening.

PUNCHCARD
Punch this card before starting to knit.

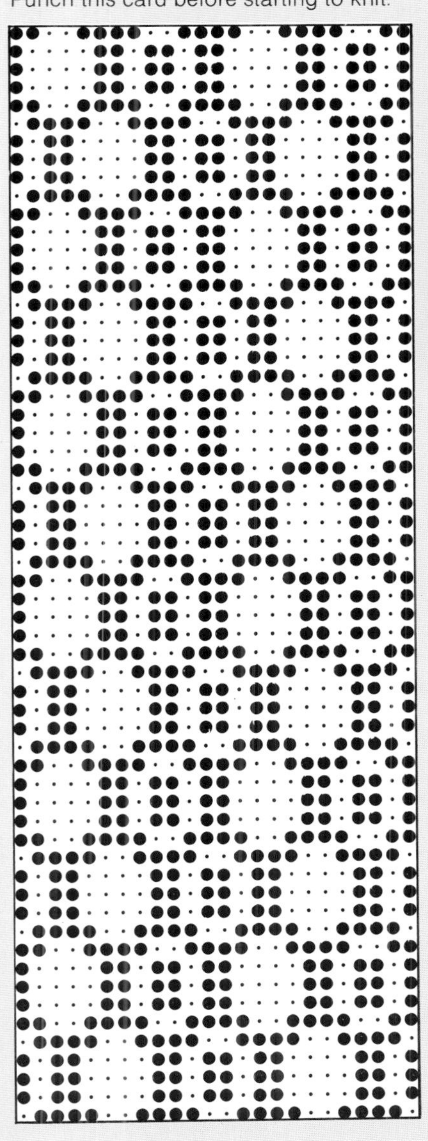

Black and white yarns produce a sophisticated sweater suitable for evening wear.

COMBINING·JACQUARD·PATTERNS

We have already discussed the use of all-over jacquard, and jacquard insets; yet another development of the technique is to combine two or more jacquard patterns, as shown on the *Subtle Squares* sweater. Here, I have used two related jacquard designs both based on the fleur-de-lis motif. Combining small designs in this way produces the effect of a larger design when the sweater is made up, but a successful result depends on good use of one's imagination in manipulating the garment pattern pieces.

Working out the design

Draw out the two jacquard designs you wish to use on graph paper. Cut out a paper pattern of your proposed sweater shape. Imagine breaking up the paper shape with lines, creating proportions that are pleasing to the eye. Then try to imagine the separate areas filled in with your jacquard designs. When you find a combination you like, use crayons or felt tip pens to fill in the various areas.

To start, treat this simply as an experiment. Only when you have gained confidence, and drawn out a few different designs, should you think of how your design ideas may be realised. If you start thinking practically too soon, you will stifle your creative instincts.

When you do begin to think seriously about knitting one of your designs, don't panic if it seems impossible to make. Think about how sweaters are usually put together, and try to find some new, alternative ways

Pattern variations using punchcards on pp. 44-45
Samples show the effects of using different colours and yarns.

of making yours. For instance, the actual knitting may run across a sweater, from side to side, instead of from top to bottom. Seams can run in any direction, and not just down the sides. For inspiration, look at dress-making patterns to see the different ways of putting garment pieces together. If you are prepared to spend a little more time than usual at the finishing stage, what appeared impossible at first may in fact be achieved, and you will be able to create original, unusual sweater designs.

Knitting two different yarns together for the background produces an attractive mottled effect.

PATTERN INSTRUCTIONS FOR
CHEQUERBOARD

In order to create a large, chequerboard effect, this sweater has been made in an unconventional way. The seams run down the centre front and back, instead of down the sides, and a separate panel is sewn to the sleeves.

MATERIALS

Yarn
Yarn A 250 (275, 300)g medium-weight Shetland wool (grey)
Yarn B 275 (300, 325)g medium-weight Shetland wool (brown)
Yarn C 75 (100, 125)g fine-weight acrylic loop (blue)

Needles
If you don't have a ribber, you need 1 pair size 2¾mm knitting needles.

MEASUREMENTS

To fit chest 91-97 (97-102, 102-107)cm (36-38, 38-40, 40-42in)
Actual chest size 105 (110, 115)cm (41¼, 43¼, 45¼in)
Length to shoulder 61 (63, 65)cm (24, 24¾, 25½in)
Sleeve seam 56cm (22in)

MAIN TENSION (MT)

32 sts and 40 rows measure 10cm over Fair Isle pattern (tension dial set at approximately 6)

LEFT FRONT AND BACK

With carriage at right and using yarns B and C together, cast on 168 (176, 184) sts by hand. Insert punchcard 1 and lock on first row. Set carriage for Fair Isle pattern. Set RC at 000. Using MT, knit 1 row. Release card and continue in Fair Isle with yarns B and C together in Feeder 1/A and yarn A in Feeder 2/B. Knit 105 (111, 117) rows. Remove card. Insert punchcard 2 and lock on first row. Knit 1 row. Release card. RC shows 107 (113, 119).
Shape armhole: Using a length of yarn, cast off centre 24 sts. Using nylon cord, knit 72 (76, 80) sts at right by hand taking needles down to NWP. Note pattern row on card. Continue on remaining sts for Back. Knit 99 (101, 103) rows. Remove card. Insert punchcard 1, lock on first row. Knit 1 row. Release card. RC shows 207 (215, 223).
Shape neck: Cast off 28 sts at the beginning of next row (44, 48, 52 sts). Knit 19 rows. Cast off. Remove card. With carriage at left, unravel nylon cord over remaining needles bringing needles back to WP. Insert punchcard 2 and lock on row previously noted. Take carriage to right without knitting. Release card and continue in Fair Isle. Knit 80 (82, 84) rows.
Shape neck: Cast off 12 sts at the beginning of the next row. Decrease 1 st at the neck edge on every row until 47 (51, 55) sts remain, then on every following alternate row until 44 (48, 52) sts remain. Cast off.

RIGHT FRONT AND BACK

Work as for left front and back reversing shapings, and reading left for right and right for left, and using Punchcard 1 in place of Punchcard 2 and Punchcard 2 in place of Punchcard 1.

LEFT SLEEVE

Using yarns B and C together, cast on 64 (66, 68) sts by hand. Insert punchcard 1 and lock on first row. Set carriage for Fair Isle pattern. Set RC at 000. Using MT, knit 1 row. Release card and continue in Fair Isle with yarns B and C together in Feeder 1/A and yarn A in Feeder 2/B. Shape sides by increasing 1 st at each end of every 4th row until there are 144 (152, 154) sts, then on every following 6th row until there are 154 (158, 160) sts. Knit 5 rows. RC shows 196.
Shape underarm: Using nylon cord, knit 77 (79, 80) sts at left by hand taking needles down to NWP. Note pattern row on card. Continue on remaining sts for first side. Continue to increase at side edge on every 6th row from previous increase until there are 80 (82, 83) sts. Knit 3 rows. Cast off. With carriage at right, unravel nylon cord over remaining needles bringing needles back to WP. Lock card on row previously noted. Take carriage to left without knitting. Release card and continue in Fair Isle. Finish to correspond with first side reversing shapings.

SHAPE GUIDE

All measurements are given in centimetres. Figures in brackets refer to the larger sizes. Where only one figure is given, it applies to all sizes.

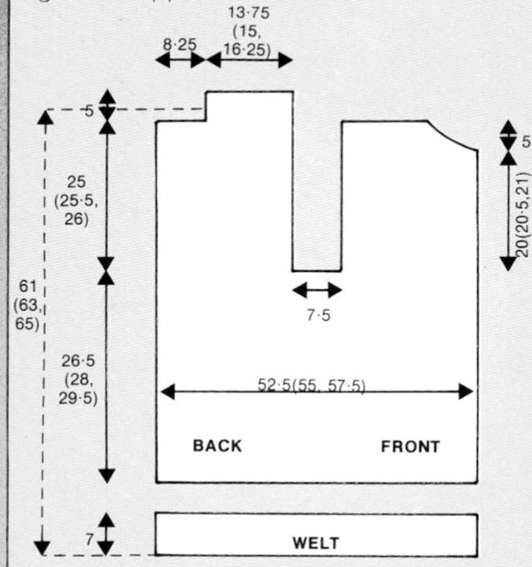

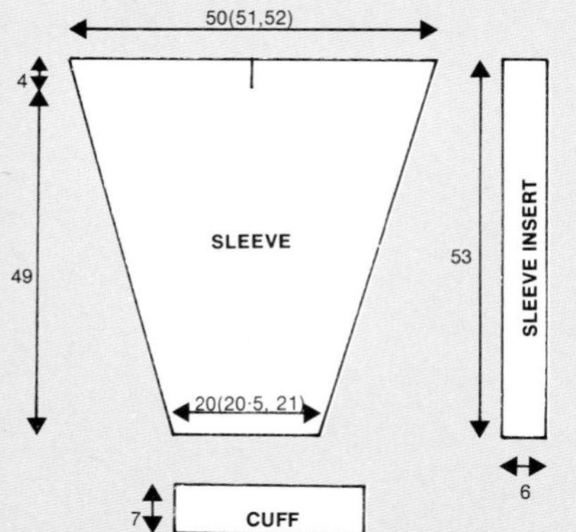

RIGHT SLEEVE

Work as for left sleeve using Punchcard 2 in place of Punchcard 1.

LEFT SLEEVE INSERT

Using yarns B and C together, cast on 20 sts by hand. Insert punchcard 2 and lock on first row. Set carriage for pattern. Set RC at 000. Using MT, knit 1 row. Release card and continue in Fair Isle with yarns B and C together in Feeder 1/A and yarn A in Feeder 2/B. Knit 211 rows. Cast off.

PUNCHCARDS

Punch these cards before starting to knit.

Punchcard 1

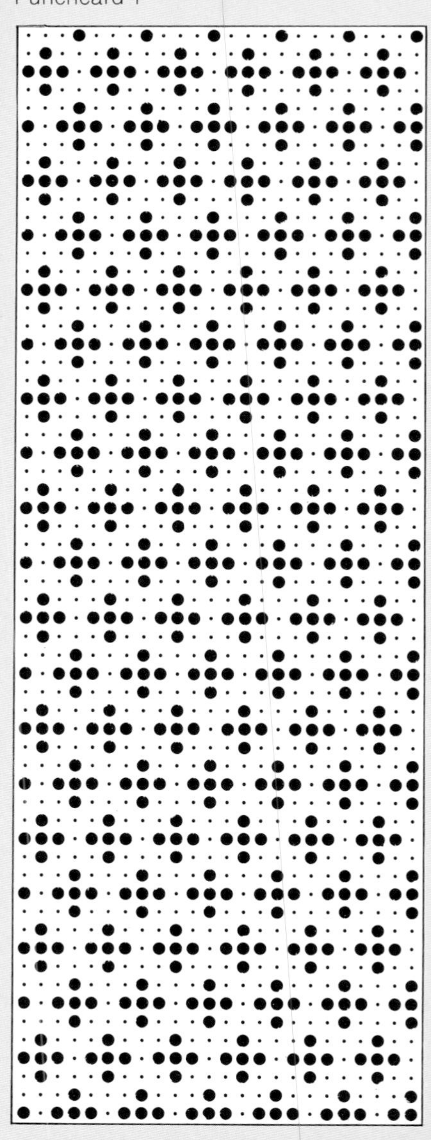

RIGHT SLEEVE INSERT

Work as for left sleeve insert using Punchcard 1 in place of Punchcard 2.

WELTS

Machines with ribber
With ribber in position, set machine for 1 × 1 rib. Using yarns B and C together, cast on 168 (176, 184) sts in 1 × 1 rib. * Work 5 tubular/circular rows. Set carriage for 1 × 1 rib knitting. Set RC at 000. Using MT – 1/MT – 1, work 32 rows. Cast off.
Machines without ribber
Using 2¾mm needles and yarns B and C together, cast on 168 (176, 184) sts. Work 7cm in k1, p1 rib. Cast off.

CUFFS

Machines with ribber
With ribber in position, set machine for 1 × 1 rib. Using yarns B and C together, cast on 84 (86, 88) sts in 1 × 1 rib. Work as for welts from *.
Machines without ribber
Using 2¾mm needles and yarns B and C together, cast on 84 (86, 88) sts. Work 7cm in k1, p1 rib. Cast off.

Punchcard 2

NECKBAND

The neckband is made in two pieces.
Machines with ribber
With ribber in position, set machine for 1 × 1 rib. Using yarns B and C together, cast on 110 sts in 1 × 1 rib. Work 5 tubular/circular rows. Set carriage for 1 × 1 rib knitting. Set RC at 000. Using MT – 1/MT – 1, work 40 rows. Cast off. Make another neckband piece to match.
Machines without ribber
Using 2¾mm needles and yarns B and C together, cast on 110 sts. Work 9cm in k1, p1 rib. Cast off. Make another neckband piece to match.

FINISHING

With purl side of work facing, block each piece by pinning out to correct measurements. Depending on yarn used, press carefully following instructions on ball or cone band, or dampen with cold, clean water and leave leave to dry naturally. Join shoulder, centre front and centre back seams. Join sleeve inserts to sleeves. Set in sleeves. Sew welts, cuffs and neckband in position. Fold neckband in half and catch down on inside.

COPING·WITH FLOATS

Jacquard designs which produce long floats on the back of the work should, generally, be avoided. However, in particular circumstances methods of overcoming this problem may be devised. For example, you may be able to design a garment in which the jacquard fabric is used on its side. Since the floats then lay vertically, they don't "catch" so easily when the garment is put on or taken off. This does not eliminate the problem completely, but, for the *Zigzag* sweater shown opposite, it provides an acceptable, practical way of using a jacquard design with long floats.

Another way of coping with long floats involves modifying a design slightly. If your jacquard design features large areas of one colour which create long floats of a second colour, break up these large areas with scattered stitches of another colour. Alternatively lay long floats in the needle hooks so they are knitted in.

PATTERN INSTRUCTIONS FOR ZIGZAG

This comfortable, flattering, one-size design has been knitted up in thick rayon, creating a glossy, shiny sweater suitable for evening wear. Slippery rayon like this can be quite difficult to knit with – take care that you don't drop any stitches. Inexperienced knitters might prefer to knit the same design in mercerised cotton or botany wool.

MATERIALS

Yarn

Yarn A 250g medium-weight viscose rayon (blue)

Yarn B 225g medium-weight viscose rayon (pink)

Needles

If you don't have a ribber, you need 1 pair size $2\frac{3}{4}$mm knitting needles.

MEASUREMENTS

To fit chest 86-97cm (34-38in)
Actual chest size 106cm ($41\frac{3}{4}$in)
Length to shoulder 53cm (21in)

MAIN TENSION (MT)

30 sts and 36 rows measure 10cm over Fair Isle pattern (tension dial set at approximately 7)

BACK

Push 67 needles at left and 1 needle at right of centre 0 to WP * (68 needles). Using MT and waste yarn, cast on and knit a few rows ending with carriage at left. Insert punchcard 1 and lock on first row. Set carriage for Fair Isle knitting. Set RC at 000. Using yarn A, knit 1 row. Release card and continue in Fair Isle pattern with yarn A in feeder 1/A and yarn B in feeder 2/B. Knit 1 row. Increase 1 st at right edge on every row until there are 106 sts. Knit 1 row. Cast on 48 sts at the beginning of the next row (154 sts). Knit 15 rows. RC shows 57. Remove punchcard. (Push pattern needles back to WP on machines whose pattern needles come out to UWP.) Take carriage to right without knitting. Insert punchcard 2 and lock on first row. Set carriage for Fair Isle pattern. Take carriage to left without knitting. Reset RC at 57. Release card and continue in Fair Isle pattern. Knit 8 rows. Lock card. Continue in st st and yarn A. Knit 23 rows. Set carriage for Fair Isle pattern. Knit 1 row. (Note that this row is worked in st st but allows pre-selection machine needles to be set for pattern.) Release card and continue in Fair Isle pattern. Knit 4 rows. RC shows 93

Shape neck: Decrease 1 st at left edge on the next and the following alternate row. Remove punchard. Insert punchcard 1 and lock on 9th row. Continue in Fair Isle and knit 1 row. Release card and continue to decrease as before at left edge on every following alternate row until 139 sts remain. Knit 31 rows. Increase 1 st at left edge on next and every following alternate row until there are 154 sts. Knit 51 rows. Cast off 48 sts at the beginning of the next row. Knit 1 row. Decrease 1 st at right edge on every row until 68 sts remain. Continue in st st and yarn A. Knit 1 row. RC shows 274. Using waste yarn, knit a few rows and release from machine.

FRONT

Push 13 needles at left and 55 needles at right of centre 0 to WP. Work as for back from * to end, reversing shapings and reading left for right and right for left.

NECKBAND

Join left shoulder seam.

Machines with ribber

With ribber in position, set machine

Pattern variations

Samples show the effects achieved using the pattern on p. 47 with an electronic machine.

for 1 × 1 rib. Using yarn A, cast on 162 sts in 1 × 1 rib. Work 5 tubular/circular rows. Set carriage for 1 × 1 rib knitting.
Set RC at 000. Using MT — 5, work 10 rows. Transfer sts to main bed. With purl side facing, pick up 162 sts around neck edge and place on to needles. Cast off.

Machines without ribber
With knit side facing and using 2¾mm needles, join in yarn A to back neck at right shoulder and pick up and knit 162 sts around neck. Work 2cm in k1, p1 rib. Cast off in rib.

CUFFS

Join right shoulder and neckband seam.

Machines with ribber
With ribber in position, set machine for 1 × 1 rib. Using yarn A, cast on 136 sts in 1 × 1 rib. Work 5 tubular/circular tows. Set carriage for 1 × 1 rib knitting. Set RC at 000. Using MT — 5, work 10 rows. Transfer sts to main bed. With purl side facing, replace 136 sts from lower edge of sleeve on to needles. Cast off.

Machines without ribber
With knit side facing and using 2¾mm needles and yarn A, pick up 136 sts from lower edge of sleeve. Work 2cm in k1, p1 rib. Cast off in rib.

WELTS

Machines with ribber
With ribber in position, set machine for 1 × 1 rib. Using yarn A, cast on 160 sts in 1 × 1 rib. Work 5 tubular/circular rows. Set carriage for 1 × 1 rib knitting. Set RC at 000. Using MT — 5, work 10 rows. Transfer sts to main bed. With purl side facing, pick up 160 sts from lower edge and place on to needles. Cast off.

Machines without ribber
With knit side facing and using 2¾mm needles, and yarn A, pick up and knit 160 sts from lower edge. Work 2cm in k1, p1 rib. Cast off in rib.

FINISHING

With wrong side of work facing, block each piece by pinning out to correct measurements. Depending on yarn used, press carefully following instructions on cone or ball band, or dampen with cold, clean water and leave to dry naturally. Join side, sleeve, cuff and welt seams.

SHAPE GUIDE
All measurements are given in centimetres.

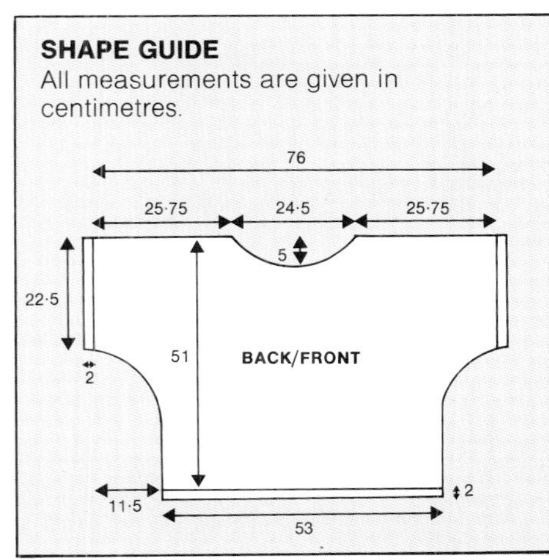

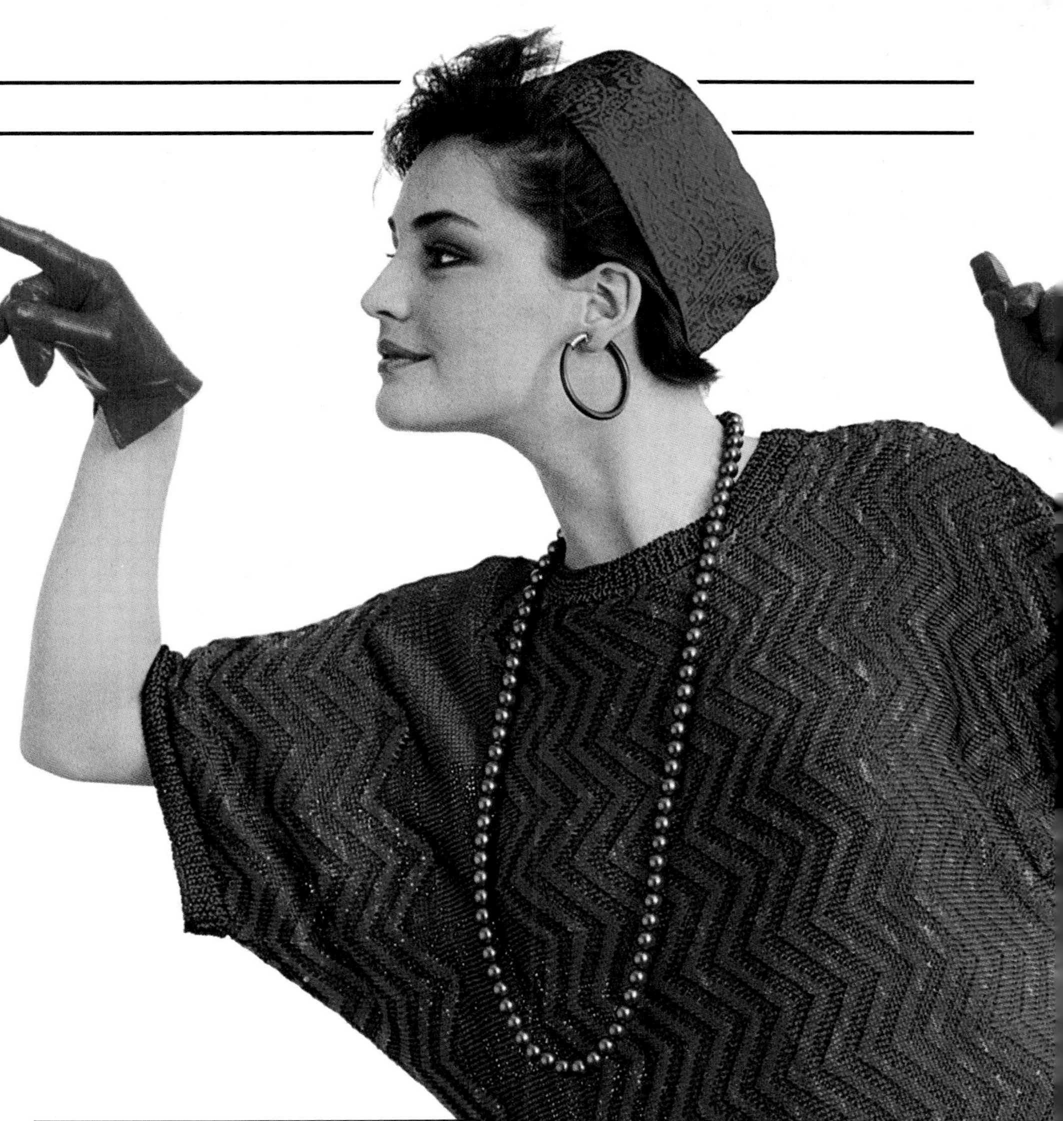

PUNCHCARDS
Punch these cards before starting to knit.
Punchcard 1

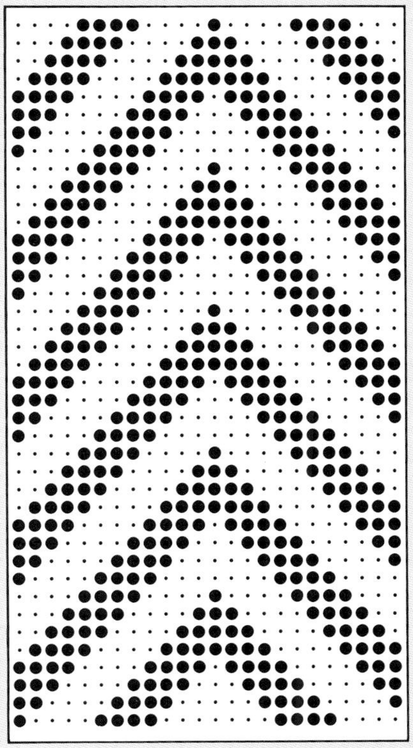

Punchcard 2

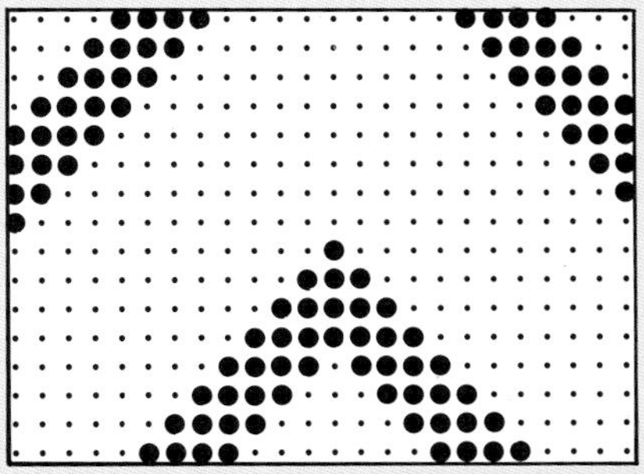

FAIR·ISLE

As already mentioned, I use the word Fair Isle to refer to two-colour knitting using traditional patterns, while the machine manufacturers tend to use it to refer to any two-colour knitting. Traditional patterns like these originated in Fair Isle, a tiny island to the north of Scotland, half way between Orkney and Shetland. Shetland knitwear was first marketed in London in the middle of the nineteenth century, but it was not until the twentieth century that the multi-coloured Fair Isle designs became popular. In the 1920s and 1930s sweaters with all-over Fair Isle patterns became fashionable after the Prince of Wales was seen wearing one.

It is interesting to note that Fair Isle knitting today is usually produced in 100% Shetland wool. In the 1920s and 1930s silk was often used, mixed with good quality wool, producing garments that were soft and luxurious to handle. Traditionally Fair Isle sweaters are hand knitted on circular needles and, amazingly, some of the knitters reach speeds of up to 200 stitches per minute.

Working out Fair Isle patterns

As with other jacquard patterns, plan your design by colouring in squared graph paper before punching a punchcard. Most Fair Isle patterns are composed from small, fairly simple geometric motifs, often containing diagonal rather than vertical lines. Inspiration for Fair Isle-type patterns may be found from numerous sources, such as tapestry samplers, Scandinavian folk art, and, of course, the original Fair Isle sweaters themselves. There are several books on Scottish Fair Isle knitting containing graphed motifs which may easily be transferred on to punchcards, but do try inventing your own, original pattern shapes.

Experimenting with colours and textures

Traditionally Fair Isle patterns are produced on a background of natural wool colours – white, grey, cream or brown, and the multi-coloured look is built up by continually changing the background and pattern colours. However, Fair Isle patterns can be just as attractive when knitted in only two or three colours, as shown in the samples. After working out a design, try sampling it in different shades of one colour using only straight yarns, then try different shades of one colour using textured yarns. Then sample with contrasting colours, using straight *and* fancy yarns. The permutations are endless, and by creative sampling a wide variety of fabric types can be produced. The different weights of fabrics will help you devise ideas for garment shapes – a light, soft fabric might suggest a wide, full sweater with gathered sleeves; a heavier, stiffer fabric could be used to make a more architectural, squared off garment.

Fair Isle patterns can also look very effective when worked in bands, as borders for garments, rather than as all-over patterns. See pages 38-39 for ways of developing this idea.

Remember, there are no rules to stick to. Fair Isle patterning really comes alive with the imaginative use of different colours and textures of yarns, as shown by the samples on these two pages.

Pattern variations using punchcard on p. 50
Samples show the effects of using different colours and yarns.

PATTERN INSTRUCTIONS FOR

MAN'S FAIR ISLE

Shetland wool, as used in traditional Fair Isle knitting, has been used for this bright sweater. The bold primary colours were chosen to give this ethnic sweater a modern look, but it would be equally effective made up in softer shades of Shetland yarn.

MATERIALS

Yarn

Yarn A 225 (250, 275)g medium-weight Shetland wool (red)
Yarn B 225 (250, 275)g medium-weight Shetland wool (blue)
Yarn C 100 (125, 150)g medium-weight Shetland wool (yellow)
Yarn D 75 (100, 125)g medium-weight Shetland wool (green)

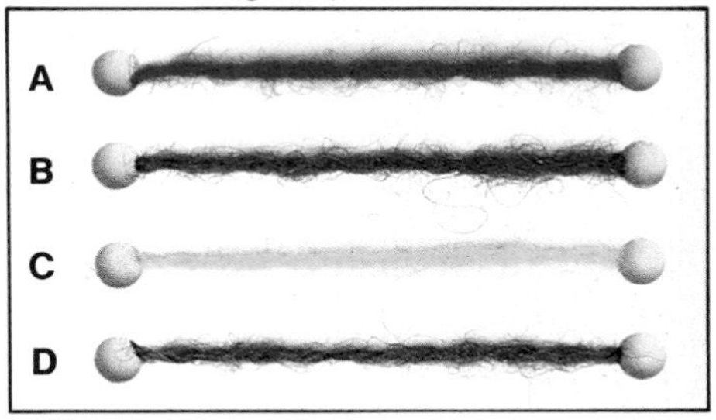

MEASUREMENTS

To fit chest 97 (102, 107)cm, (38, 40, 42in)
Actual chest size 110 (115, 120)cm ($43\frac{1}{4}$, $45\frac{1}{4}$, $47\frac{1}{4}$in)
Length to shoulder 64cm ($25\frac{1}{4}$in)
Sleeve seam 54cm ($21\frac{1}{4}$in)

MAIN TENSION (MT)

32 sts and 40 rows measure 10cm over Fair Isle pattern (tension dial set at approximately 6).

SPECIAL NOTE

The punchcard for this pattern is 64 rows long, so punch it on blank punchcard from a roll, or join two punchcards.
When working Fair Isle pattern, read two colour rows as follows: thread first colour stated in feeder 1/A to knit the background, and second colour stated in feeder 2/B to knit the contrast pattern.
To avoid long floats on the back of the work, pick up any long, loose strands and place them on to needles.

FAIR ISLE PATTERN

Knit 16 rows A/B, 4 rows C/B, 2 rows C/D, 6 rows A/D, 2 rows B/D, 4 rows B/C, 2 rows A/D, 4 rows A/C, 1 row A only, 3 rows A/B, 2 rows B/D, 6 rows C/B, 2 rows A/D, 2 rows C/D, 2 rows A/D, 1 row A only, 1 row A/D, 2 rows A/B and 2 rows C/B. These 64 rows form the pattern.

BACK AND FRONT (alike)

Push 176 (184, 192) needles to WP. * Push the 3rd and every following alternate needle back to NWP. Using MT and waste yarn, cast on and knit a few rows ending with carriage at left. Set RC at 000. Using MT — 3 and yarn B, knit 60 rows. Push needles from NWP to WP and make a hem by placing loops of first row worked in yarn B evenly along the row. Unravel the waste yarn when work is completed. Insert punchcard and lock on first row. Set carriage for pattern. Set RC at 000. Using MT, knit 1 row. Release card and continue in Fair Isle pattern *. Knit 208 rows. RC shows 209. Transfer the 3rd and every following alternate st on to adjacent needle and push empty needles to NWP. Set RC at 000. Using MT — 2 and yarn A, knit 60 rows. Make a hem by placing loops of first row worked in yarn A on to corresponding needles. Cast off loosely.

PUNCHCARD

Punch this card before starting to knit. For the *Man's Fair Isle* sweater use the punchcard as it appears. For the *Woman's Fair Isle* sweater insert the punchcard the other way up and start it at the row marked with a red line.

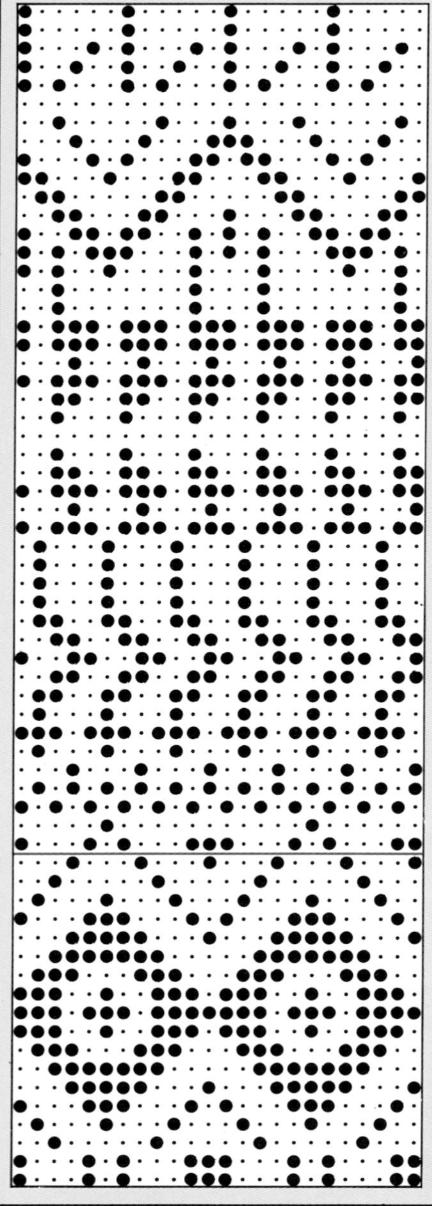

SLEEVES

Push 88 (92, 96) needles to WP. Work as for back and front from * to *. Shape sides by increasing 1 st at each end of every following 4th row until there are 176 (180, 184) sts. Knit 16 rows. RC shows 193. Cast off loosely.

FINISHING

With purl side of work facing, block each piece by pinning out to correct measurements. Depending on yarn used, press carefully following instructions on ball or cone band, or dampen with cold, clean water and leave to dry naturally. Join shoulder seams, leaving approximately 24cm open for neck. Join side and sleeve seams. Sew in sleeves with centre of sleeve to shoulder seam. Press seams.

SHAPE GUIDE

All measurements are given in centimetres. Figures in brackets refer to the larger size. Where only one figure is given, it applies to all sizes.

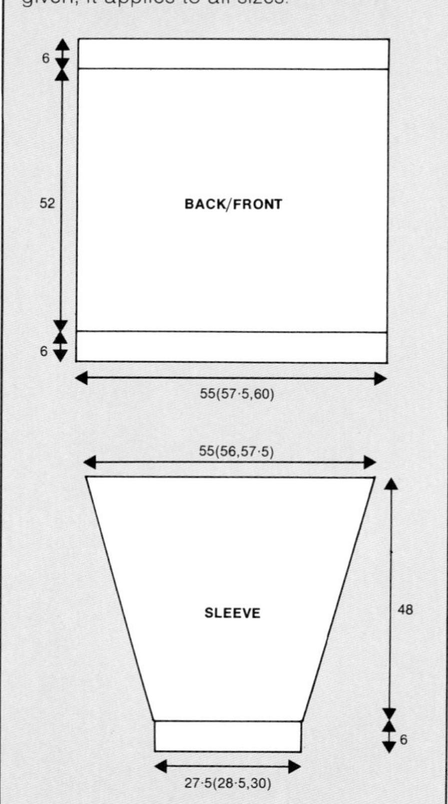

PATTERN INSTRUCTIONS FOR
WOMAN'S FAIR ISLE

This cardigan features the same jacquard pattern as used on the Man's Fair Isle sweater, but by using different yarns, a softer, drapable fabric is produced. The cardigan has been designed to show this off, with full sleeves and a large shawl collar. The use of a looped yarn gives the fabric a rich, textural surface, but when knitting with loop yarns remember to keep checking that the needles have picked up the yarn, and not just a loop.

MATERIALS

Yarn
Yarn A 100 (125)g fine Botany wool (pink)
Yarn B 75 (75)g fine fluffy acrylic loop (rust)
Yarn C 100 (125)g fine Botany wool (purple)
Yarn D 150 (175)g fine Botany wool (green)

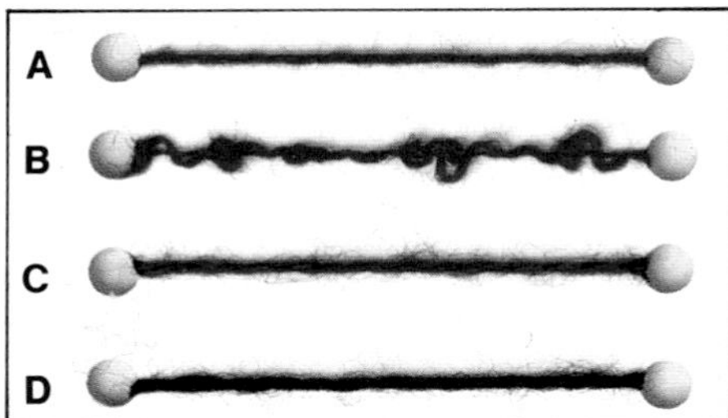

Notions
10 buttons, 1cm in diameter
Needles
1 pair size 2¾mm

MEASUREMENTS

To fit chest 81-86 (91-97)cm (32-34, 36-38in)
Actual chest size 100 (110)cm (39½, 43¼in)
Length to shoulder 57cm (22½in)
Sleeve seam 57 (22¼in)

MAIN TENSION (MT)

32 sts and 40 rows measure 10cm over Fair Isle pattern (tension dial set at approximately 6)

SPECIAL NOTE

The punchcard used for this pattern is the same one as used for the *Man's Fair Isle* sweater, page 50, inserted into the machine the other way up, and started on the row marked with a red line.

FAIR ISLE PATTERN

Knit 16 rows C/B, 2 rows C/A, 4 rows D/B, 1 row A/B, 1 row B only, 4 rows A/C, 2 rows B/D, 4 rows B/A, 4 rows B/C, 2 rows D/C, 1 row C/A, 1 row C only, 2 rows C/A, 2 rows C/D, 6 rows B/D, 2 rows A/D, 6 rows C/A and 4 rows C/D. These 64 rows form the pattern.

BACK

Push 80 (88) needles at left and 81 (89) needles at right of centre 0 to WP (161, 177 needles). With carriage at right and using yarn C, cast on by hand. Insert punchcard and lock on first row. Set carriage for pattern. Set RC at 000. Using MT, knit 1 row. Release card and continue in Fair Isle pattern. Knit 128 rows. RC shows 129.
Shape armholes: Cast off 20 sts at the beginning of the next 2 rows (121, 137 sts). Knit 78 rows. RC shows 209. Cast off loosely.

LEFT FRONT

Push 44 (52) needles at left and 36 (36) needles at right of centre 0 to WP (80, 88 needles). * With carriage at right and using yarn C, cast on by hand. Insert punchcard and lock on first row. Set carriage for pattern. Set RC at 000. Using MT, knit 1 row. Release card and continue in Fair Isle pattern. Knit 128 rows. RC shows 129.
Shape armhole: Cast off 20 sts at the beginning of the next row (60, 68 sts). Knit 64 rows. RC shows 194.
Shape neck: Cast off 10 sts at the beginning of the next row, then decrease 1 st at neck edge on every row until 45 (53) sts remain. Knit 9 rows. RC shows 209. Cast off.

RIGHT FRONT

Push 35 (35) needles at left and 45 (53) needles at right of centre 0 to WP (80, 88 needles). Work as for left front from * to end, reversing shapings and reading left for right.

RIGHT SLEEVE FRONT AND LEFT SLEEVE BACK

Push 97 (89) needles at left and 89 (97) needles at right of centre 0 to WP * (186 needles). With carriage at right and using yarn C, cast on by hand. Insert punchcard and lock on first row. Set carriage for pattern. Set RC at 000. Using MT, knit 1 row. Release card and continue in Fair Isle pattern. Knit 80 rows. Remove card. Using waste yarn, knit a few rows in st st and release from machine.

LEFT SLEEVE FRONT AND RIGHT SLEEVE BACK

Push 88 (96) needles at left and 98 (90) needles at right of centre 0 to WP. Work as for right sleeve front and left sleeve back from * to end.

COLLAR (make two)

Push 55 needles at left and 60 needles at right of centre 0 to WP (115 needles). Using MT and waste yarn, cast on and knit a few rows ending with carriage at right. Set RC at 000. Using MT and yarn D, knit 6 rows. Push the 2nd and every following 4th needle to HP. Knit 7 rows. Push all needles back to WP. Insert punchcard and lock on first row. Set carriage for pattern. Set RC at 000. Knit 1 row. Release card and continue in Fair Isle pattern. Knit 6 rows. Make a hem by placing loops of first row worked in yarn D on to corresponding needles. Continue in pattern and knit 58 rows. RC shows 65. Cast off, working 2 sts together across the row. Knit second piece reading left for right and right for left.

BACK WELT

Machines with ribber
Push 107 (114) needles to WP. With purl side facing, pick up 107 (119) sts evenly along cast on edge of back and place on to needles. * Using MT and yarn D, knit 1 row. With ribber in position, set machine for 1 × 1 rib knitting. Transfer every alternate st on to corresponding needle on ribber. Set RC at 000. Using MT—3/MT—3, knit 30 rows. Cast off.
Machines without ribber
With knit side facing and using 2¾mm needles and yarn D, pick up and knit 107 (119) sts evenly along cast on edge of back **.
1st rib row: P1, * k1, p1; repeat from * to end.
2nd rib row: K1, * p1, k1; repeat from * to end.
Repeat these 2 rows for 5cm, ending with a 1st rib row. Cast off in rib.

FRONT WELTS

Machines with ribber
Push 53 (59) needles to WP. With purl side facing, pick up 53 (59) sts evenly along cast on edge of front and place on to needles. Work as for back welt from * to end.
Machines without ribber
With knit side facing and using 2¾mm needles and yarn D, pick up and knit 53 (59) sts evenly along cast on edge of front. Work as for back welt from ** to end.

CUFFS

Remove waste yarn from sleeves and graft upper sleeve seams.
Machines with ribber
Push 57 needles to WP. With purl side facing, pick up 57 sts evenly along lower edge of sleeve and place on to needles. Work as for back welts from * to end.
Machines without ribber
With knit side facing and using 2¾mm needles and yarn D, pick up and knit 57 sts evenly along lower edge of sleeve. Work as for back welts from ** to end.

BUTTON BAND

Using 2¾mm needles and yarn D, cast on 12 sts. Work in k1, p1 rib until band, when slightly stretched, fits up front edge. Cast off in rib. Tack band in position, then mark position of buttons with pins, the first to come on the fifth row from the beginning, the last to come on the fifth row from the top edge and the remaining eight spaced evenly in between.

BUTTONHOLE BAND

Work to match button band, making buttonholes to correspond with markers as follows:
1st buttonhole row: (Knit side) Rib 5, cast off 2, rib to end.
2nd buttonhole row: Rib to end, casting on 2 sts over those cast off.

SHAPE GUIDE

All measurements are given in centimetres. Figures in brackets refer to the larger size. Where only one figure is given, it applies to both sizes.

FINISHING

With purl side of work facing, block each piece by pinning out to correct measurements. Depending on yarn used, press carefully following instructions on ball or cone band, or dampen with cold, clean water and leave to dry naturally. Join shoulder seams. Sew in sleeves. Join side and sleeve seams. Sew on front bands with buttonhole band on right front. Join collar seam. Sew cast off edge of collar to neck edge, starting and ending in centre of front bands. Press seams. Sew on buttons.

TUCK·STITCH

Tuck stitch is one of the basic stitch constructions available to the machine knitter. It is formed by holding the yarn on a selected needle without knitting it, so that there is a knitted stitch as well as new yarn over the selected needle. When the needle is returned to its starting position both the old stitch and the new yarn are retained. This retaining of the old stitch and the new yarn may be done several times in succession on the same needle, so that a drawn-up, tuck effect results.

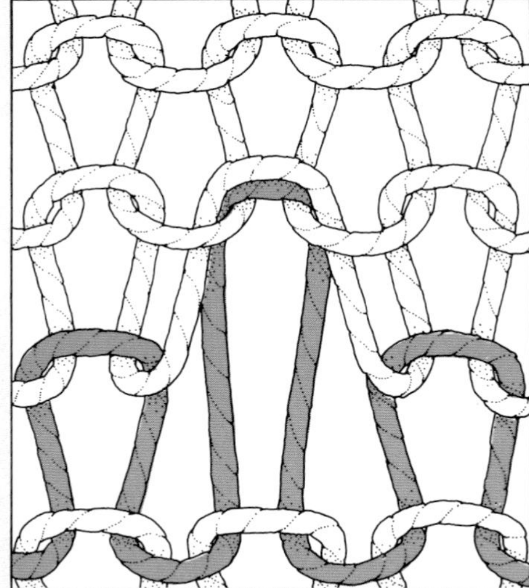

Stitch construction Tucking stitch held over two rows

The fabric

The fabric created by tuck stitch usually has a textural, three-dimensional quality. Depending on how the tucking needles have been spaced, very different-looking fabrics may be produced using the same technique. An all-over small scale brick repeat pattern produces a honeycomb effect, a more spaced-out use of tuck stitch will produce less raised pattern areas.

All-over tuck stitch produces a bulky, non-curling fabric with fewer stitches and many more rows to the centimetre than normal. The bulk makes it a warm fabric, and the lack of curl means it is easy to join pieces together.

A special quality of tuck stitch is that the back of the fabric can be as interesting as the front, as shown in the *Arabian Nights* sweater. This is due to the use of certain combinations of yarn and needle selection.

Needle selection

The needles chosen for tucking may be selected by hand, or automatically, with a punchcard or an electronic graph. Using automatic selection is much faster than using manual selection, however the shape, size and positioning of the tuck may be varied randomly if needles are selected by hand. Refer to your machine manual in order to set up your machine for tuck stitch.

Tuck stitch is usually selected on only one stitch at a time, since knitted stitches are needed on either side to hold the tucked yarn in place. The same needle cannot be selected to tuck continuously – every so often the tucking needle must be allowed to knit. If you allow the needles to tuck over too many rows, the stitches will pile up on the needles and eventually jump off, or jam the machine. Unfortunately there are no defined rules. Knitters must simply learn by trial and error. In my own experience, each case is determined by the type of yarn used and the tension of the knitting. Using finer yarns or extra weights will allow more rows to be tucked.

Punchcards may be obtained that give standard tuck stitch patterns. The examples illustrated on the right show tucking over two or four rows.

Choice of yarn

Although you *can* tuck with any yarn, some yarns are easier to use than others. It's difficult to use yarns which have no "give" in them, such as cotton or chenille, so if you are a beginner start your experiments with more elastic yarns, such as wool. While experimenting note how some yarns, particularly wool, produce more three-dimensional effects than other yarns of a similar thickness.

With the tuck stitch technique you can use different thicknesses of yarn on one garment without changing the punchcard or the tension. To demonstrate this, yarns ranging from fine rayon to medium-weight wool have been used on the *Neon* sweater, overleaf.

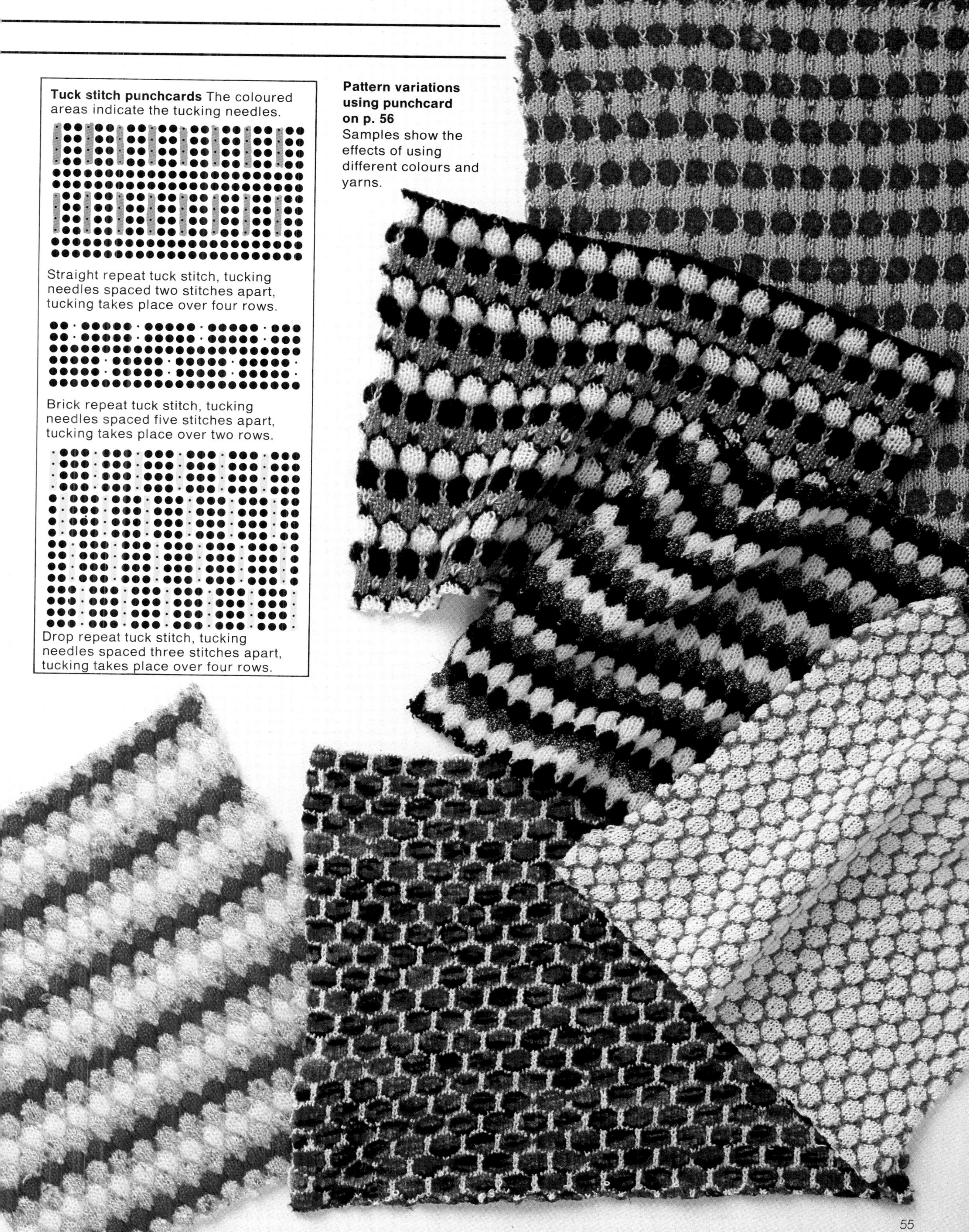

Tuck stitch punchcards The coloured areas indicate the tucking needles.

Straight repeat tuck stitch, tucking needles spaced two stitches apart, tucking takes place over four rows.

Brick repeat tuck stitch, tucking needles spaced five stitches apart, tucking takes place over two rows.

Drop repeat tuck stitch, tucking needles spaced three stitches apart, tucking takes place over four rows.

Pattern variations using punchcard on p. 56
Samples show the effects of using different colours and yarns.

PATTERN INSTRUCTIONS FOR

NEON

This sweater has been designed to show how many different yarns may be combined to good effect in one sweater – the yarns used range from very fine rayon, to medium-weight wool.

It appears as if the sleeves and body have been knitted in one – in fact the pieces have been knitted separately and then neatly grafted to each other so the join is almost invisible from the right side.

MATERIALS

Yarn

Yarn A 125g fine weight fluffy yarn (pink)
Yarn B 50g medium-weight wool (red)
Yarn C 50g fine-weight angora (turquoise)
Yarn D 75g fine-weight cotton (blue)
Yarn E 75g very fine-weight rayon (green)
Yarn F 75g very fine-weight rayon (brown)
Yarn G 75g very fine-weight rayon (gold)
Yarn H 75g fine-weight cotton (turquoise)
Yarn I 75g fine-weight cotton (orange)

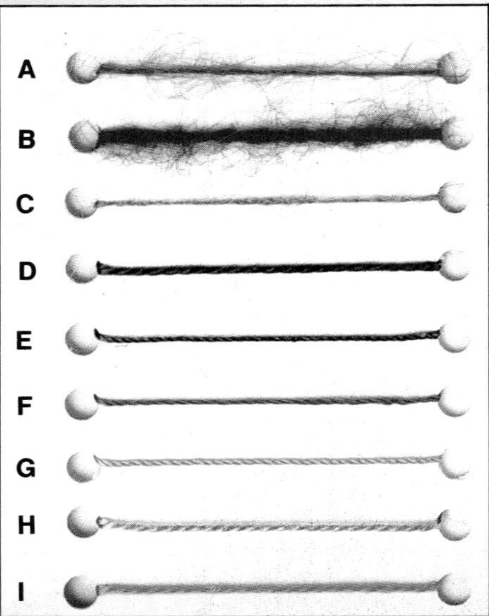

Needles

If you don't have a ribber, you need 1 pair size 2½mm knitting needles.

MEASUREMENTS

To fit chest 81-86cm (32-34in)
Actual chest size 93cm (36½in)
Length to shoulder 64cm (25¼in)
Sleeve seam 48cm (19in)

MAIN TENSION (MT)

32 sts and 63 rows measure 10cm over tuck stitch pattern (tension dial set at approximately 6)

SPECIAL NOTE

Since so many different yarns are used on this sweater, you will probably find it helpful if you label the different cones you are using A, B, C and so on before you start knitting.

BODY

Push 75 needles at left and right of centre 0 to WP (150 needles). Using MT and waste yarn, cast on and knit a few rows ending with carriage at left. Insert punchcard and lock on first row. Set carriage for pattern. Set RC at 000. Using yarn F, knit 1 row. Release card and continue in tuck stitch.

*K 7 rows F, 1 row I, 6 rows E, 1 row H, 7 rows B, 1 row I, 6 rows D, 1 row H, 7 rows E, 1 row I, 6 rows C, 1 row H, 7 rows G, 1 row I, 6 rows F, 1 row H, 7 rows A, 1 row I, 6 rows E, 1 row H, 7 rows G, 1 row I, 6 rows B, 1 row H **, 7 rows F, 1 row I, 6 rows D, 1 row H, 7 rows C, 1 row I, 6 rows G, 1 row H, 7 rows D, 1 row I, 6 rows A, 1 row H *. Repeat from * to * once more, then from * to ** once. RC shows 361.

Shape neck: Using a length of yarn H, cast off the centre 64 sts, then cast them on again.

*** K 7 rows B, 1 row I, 6 rows G, 1 row H, 7 rows E, 1 row I, 6 rows A, 1 row H, 7 rows F, 1 row I, 6 rows G, 1 row H, 7 rows C, 1 row I, 6 rows E, 1 row H, 7 rows D, 1 row I, 6 rows B, 1 row H, 7 rows E, 1 row I, 6 rows F ****, 1 row H, 7 rows A, 1 row I, 6 rows D, 1 row H, 7 rows G, 1 row I, 6 rows C, 1 row H, 7 rows D, 1 row I, 6 rows F and 1 row H ***. Repeat from *** to *** once more then from *** to **** once. Knit 1 row F. RC shows 721. Using waste yarn, knit a few rows in st st and release from machine.

PUNCHCARD

Punch this card before starting to knit.

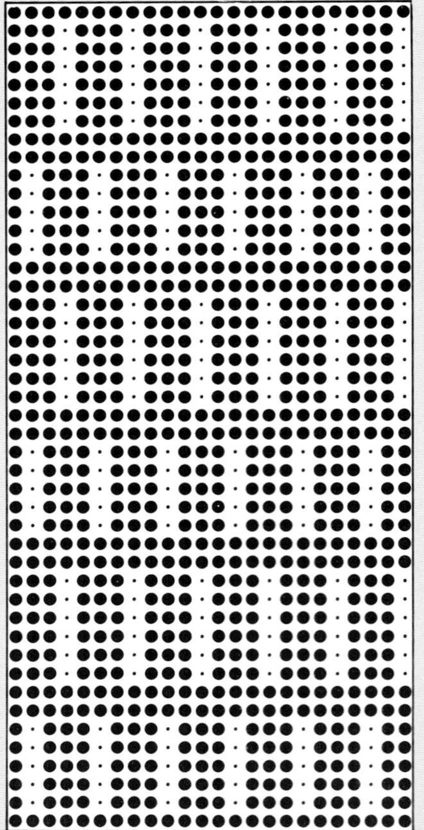

RIGHT SLEEVE

Push 51 needles at left and 1 needle at right of centre 0 to WP (52 needles). With carriage at right and using yarn G, cast on using the hand wound method. Insert punchcard and lock on first row. Set carriage for pattern. Set RC at 000. Using MT, knit 1 row. Release card and continue in tuck stitch. K 7 rows G. Using I, cast on 10 sts at beginning of next row. K 6 rows F, K 1 row H. Cast on 10 sts at right edge. K 7 rows A, K 1 row I. Cast on 10 sts at right edge. K 6 rows E. Using H, cast on 10 sts at beginning of next row. K 7 rows G. Using I, cast on 10 sts at beginning of next row. K 6 rows B. K 1 row H. Cast on 10 sts at right edge. K 7 rows F. K 1 row I. Cast on 10 sts at right edge. K 6 rows D. Using H, cast on 10 sts at beginning of next row (132 sts). K 7 rows C, 1 row I, 6 rows G, 1 row H, 7 rows D, 1 row I, 6 rows A and 1 row H. Work as for body from * to ** once, then from *** to **** once. K 1 row H, 7 rows A, 1 row I, 6 rows D, 1 row H, 7 rows G, 1 row I and 6 rows C. Using H, cast off 10 sts at the beginning of the next row. K 7 rows D. Using I, cast off 10 sts at the

SHAPE GUIDE

All measurements are given in centimetres.

7
57
BACK
20
57
46·5
FRONT
7

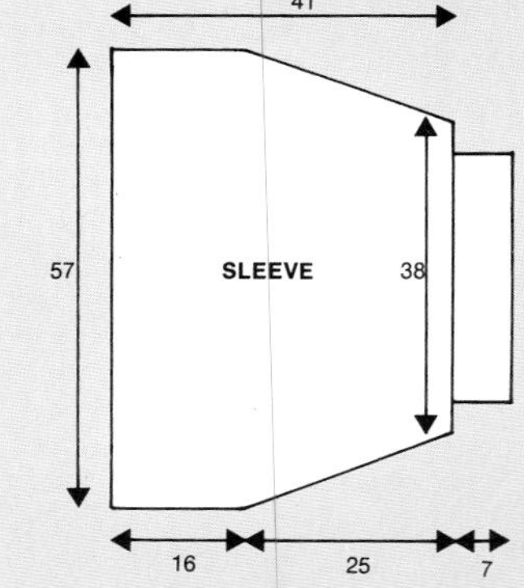

beginning of the next row. K 6 rows F. K 1 1 row H. Cast off 10 sts at right edge. K 7 rows B. K 1 row I. Cast off 10 sts at right edge. K 6 rows G. Using H, cast off 10 sts at the beginning of the next row. K 7 rows E. Using I, cast off 10 sts at the beginning of the next row. K 6 rows A. K 1 row H. Cast off 10 sts at right edge. K 7 rows F. K 1 row I. Cast off 10 sts at right edge (52 sts). K 7 rows G. RC shows 361. Cast off.

LEFT SLEEVE

Work as for right sleeve, reversing shapings by reading left for right and right for left.

WELTS

Machines with ribber
With ribber in position, set machine for 1 × 1 rib. Using yarn A, cast on 150 sts in 1 × 1 rib. * Work 5 tubular/circular rows. Set carriage for 1 × 1 rib knitting. Set RC at 000. Using MT – 2/MT – 2, work 2 rows. Work 2 rows yarn E and 26 rows yarn A. Transfer sts to main bed *.

Machines without ribber
Using $2\frac{1}{4}$mm needles and yarn A, cast on 150 sts. * Working in k1, p1 rib, work 4 rows yarn A, 2 rows yarn E, then continue in yarn A until work measures 7cm *. Push 150 needles to WP. Transfer sts to machine needles.

All machines
With purl side of body facing, pick up sts below waste yarn, place on to needles. Cast off.

CUFFS

Machines with ribber
With ribber in position, set machine for 1 × 1 rib. Using yarn A, cast on 60 sts in 1 × 1 rib. Work as for welts from * to *.

Machines without ribber
Using $2\frac{1}{4}$mm needles and yarn A, cast on 60 sts. Work as for welts from * to *. Push 60 needles to WP. Transfer sts to machine needles.

All machines
With purl side of lower edge of sleeve facing, pick up 60 sts and place on to needles. Cast off.

COLLAR

The collar is made in two pieces.

Machines with ribber
With ribber in position, set machine for 1 × 1 rib. Using yarn A, cast on 152 sts in 1 × 1 rib. Work 5 tubular/circular rows. Set carriage for 1 × 1 rib knitting. Set RC at 000. Using MT – 2/MT – 2, work 2 rows. * Work 2 rows E, 2 rows A, 2 rows D, 2 rows A, 2 rows G, 2 rows A, 2 rows F and 2 rows A. Repeat from * 3 times more. Work 2 rows E, 2 rows A and 2 rows D. Cast off. Make another collar piece to match.

Machines without ribber
Using $2\frac{1}{4}$mm needles and yarn A, cast on 152 sts. Working in k1, p1 rib, work 4 rows A. * Work 2 rows E, 2 rows A, 2 rows D, 2 rows A, 2 rows G, 2 rows A, 2 rows F and 2 rows A. Repeat from * 3 times more. Work 2 rows E, 2 rows A and 2 rows D. Cast off in rib. Make another collar piece to match.

FINISHING

With knit side of work facing, block each piece by pinning out to correct measurements. Dampen with cold, clean water and leave to dry naturally. Sew sleeves to body, matching pattern. Join side, sleeve and collar seams. Sew collar in position.

TUCK·STITCH·VARIATION

The tuck stitch used here produces a fabric with a quilted effect similar to that of the first tuck stitch sweater. By being inventive with the use of colour, a totally different-looking fabric is achieved. We have made up the garment in two different colourways, and finished one of the sweaters with milling and brushing.

Quilted effects
A quilted surface is one of the easiest to produce with tuck stitch. The great advantage of tuck stitch quilting over conventional quilting is that the raised effect is produced without any padding, so the resulting fabric can be lightweight.

Experimenting with colour
A further development of the tuck stitch technique is to introduce different colours or textures of yarns into each "bubble", rather than working each row of bubbles in one solid colour. By using different thicknesses of yarn, yet keeping the same tension, slightly different shaped "bubbles" will be formed.

Fabric finishes
A finish is a process carried out on knitted fabric after removing it from the machine, such as heavy pressing, milling or brushing. Some finishes may distort the knitting or alter its size, so it is important to experiment on samples before trying out a finish on a garment.

Pressing
Since tuck stitch is usually used to produce three-dimensional, textural fabrics, normally you should not press garment pieces after blocking them. However, you may wish to use the iron to deliberately distort the fabric, and produce yet a more unusual effect. If you give tuck stitch a very heavy press the raised quilting will disappear, and the stitch construction will be exposed. This is particularly effective with rayon yarns or loosely knitted fabrics.

Milling and brushing
Milling is a controlled felting effect, achieved by hand washing the garment or garment pieces in very hot water with pure soap flakes. Rub gently until the fibres start to look felted and the stitches merge and lose their distinctive outline. Rinse in hot water, then cold, then hot. Block to shape and dry flat. After drying the knitting can be brushed with a teazle brush. This can be done lightly or roughly, depending on the effect required. It is important to remember that during the milling process the knitting will shrink considerably, so it is essential that the garment is knitted one size larger to compensate for this. There is no magic formula to this finishing process, so you should use it on a garment only after experimenting on samples.

Extremely fluffy fabrics can be produced by milling, but only when using pure wool yarns. If milling is carried out on a jacquard fabric that contains, for example, rayon *and* wool yarns, only the wool will felt. For the inventive knitter, this partial milling technique provides an area of exploration.

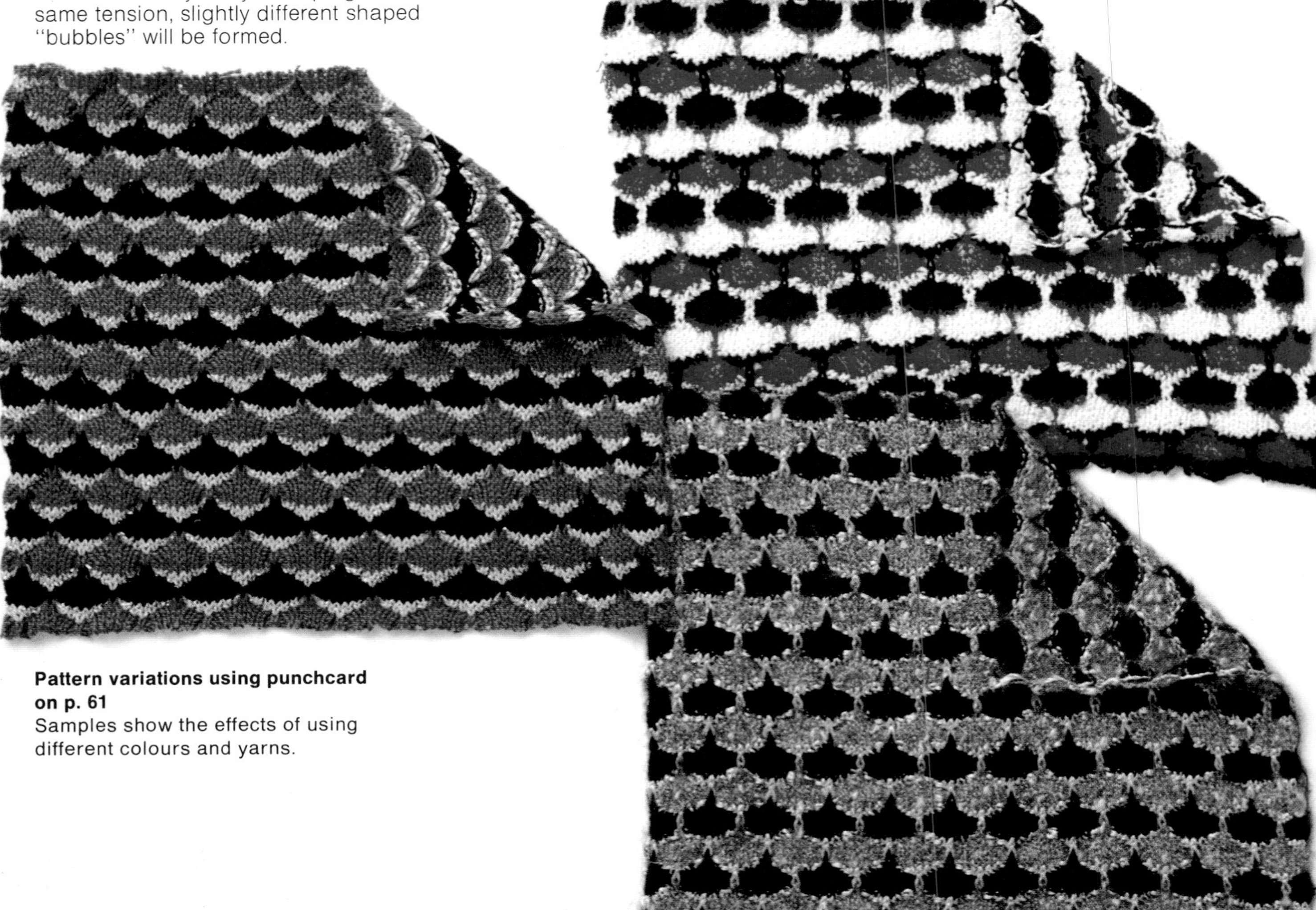

Pattern variations using punchcard on p. 61
Samples show the effects of using different colours and yarns.

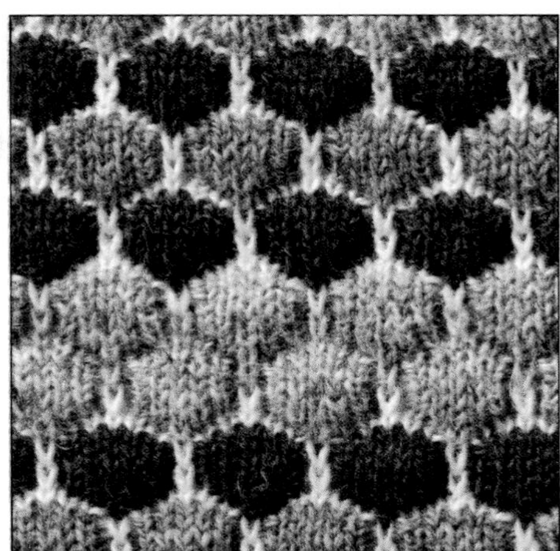

These samples show the same fabric before and after milling.

PATTERN INSTRUCTIONS FOR

CLASSIC CARDIGAN

This comfortable cardigan has been made up in natural shades of Shetland yarn. Before sewing the garment pieces together, mill and brush them to give a soft, yet classic look.

MATERIALS

Yarn

Yarn A 200 (250)g medium-weight Shetland wool (dark brown)
Yarn B 275 (300)g medium-weight Shetland wool (grey)
Yarn C 100 (125)g medium-weight Shetland wool (light brown)
Yarn D 100 (125)g medium-weight Shetland wool (cream)

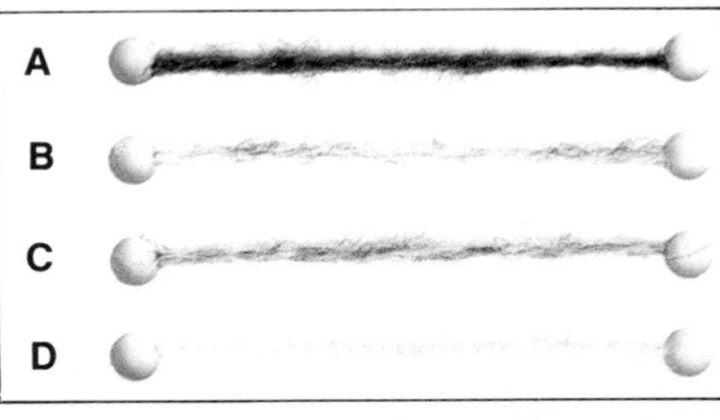

Notions
11 buttons, 1·5cm in diameter
2 stitch holders
Needles
1 pair size 2¾mm

MEASUREMENTS

Before milling: To fit chest 102-107 (112-117)cm (40-42, 44-46in)
Actual chest size 116 (125)cm (45½, 49¼in)
Back length 65 (78·5)cm (25½, 31in)
Sleeve seam 38·5 (43·5)cm (15¼, 17¼in)
After milling: To fit chest 91-97 (102-107)cm (36-38, 40-42in)
Actual chest size 104 (112)cm (41, 44in)
Back length 57·5 (69·5)cm (22¾, 27½in)
Sleeve seam 34·5 (38·5)cm (13½, 15¼in)

MAIN TENSION (MT)

27 sts and 60 rows measure 10cm over pattern (tension dial set at approximately 6). After milling this should result in 30 sts and 68 rows to 10cm.

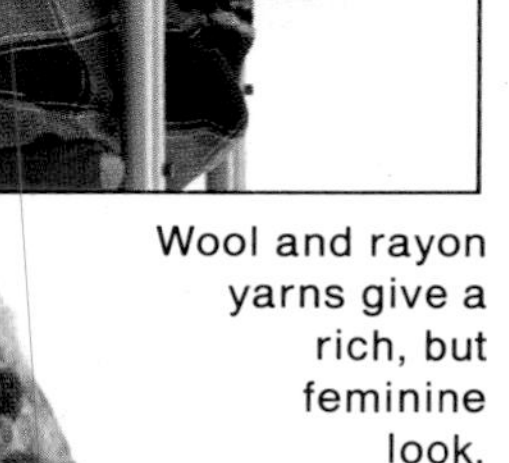

Wool and rayon yarns give a rich, but feminine look.

SPECIAL NOTE

Milling is not a process to be undertaken lightly. It involves the controlled shrinkage of garment pieces, and unless you are very careful you may well end up with an unwearable garment. That is why it is so important to practise the milling and brushing processes on spare samples of knitting before embarking on a garment, taking careful note of the amount of shrinkage in the samples. Remember that you will have to make your garment about one size larger than you require, and that the milling process can only be done on pure wool yarns.

TUCK STITCH STRIPE PATTERN

Knit 1 row yarn D, 6 rows yarn A, 2 rows yarn D, 6 rows yarn C, 2 rows yarn D, 6 rows yarn A, 2 rows yarn D, 14 rows yarn B and 1 row yarn D.

BACK

Using 2¾mm needles and yarn B, cast on 113 (125) sts.
1st rib row: K1, * p1, k1; repeat from * to end.
2nd rib row: P1, * k1, p1; repeat from * to end.
Repeat these two rows 9 times more.
Next row: Rib 13 (19), increase in next st, * rib 1, increase in next st; repeat from * 42 times more, rib to end (157, 169 sts).

Push 79 (85) needles at left and 78 (84) needles at right of centre 0 to WP (157, 169 needles). With carriage at right, transfer sts to machine needles. ** Insert punchcard and lock on first row. Set carriage for pattern. Using MT and yarn D, knit 1 row. Set RC at 000. Release card and continue in tuck stitch stripe pattern **. Knit 213 (281) rows.

Shape armholes: Cast off 6 sts at the beginning of the next 2 rows and 4 sts at the beginning of the next 2 rows, decrease 1 st at each end of every following alternate row until 135 (143) sts remain. Knit 152 (160) rows. RC shows 371 (451). Cast off.

POCKET LININGS (two alike)

Push 19 needles at left and 18 needles at right of centre 0 to WP (37 needles). Using yarn D cast on by hand. Insert punchcard and lock on first row. Set carriage for pattern. Using MT, knit 1 row. Set RC at 000. Release card and continue in tuck stitch stripe pattern. Knit 80 (112) rows. Remove card. Using waste yarn, knit a few rows st st and release from the machine.

RIGHT FRONT

Using 2¾mm needles and yarn B cast on 61 (67) sts. Work 4 rows in rib as given for back.

Next row: Rib 4, cast off 3, rib to end.

Next row: Rib to end, casting on 3 sts over the 3 cast off.

Rib 14 rows.

Next row: Rib 10 and leave these sts on a stitch holder, rib 2 (5), increase in next st, * rib 1, increase in next st; repeat from * 22 times more, rib to end (75, 81 sts). Push 39 needles at left and 36 (42) needles at right of centre 0 to WP (75, 81 needles) ***. With carriage at right, transfer sts to machine needles with stitch holder at left. Work as for back from ** to **. Knit 80 (112) rows.

Place pocket: Lock card. Note position of pattern and needles, using nylon cord, knit 20 sts at left and 18 (24) sts at right by hand taking needles down to NWP. Disconnect RC. Using yarn B, knit 10 rows st st on remaining 37 sts. Cast off, leave needles in WP. With carriage at left and purl side of pocket lining facing replace sts of last row worked in main yarn on to empty needles. Unravel nylon cord over remaining needles bringing needles back to WP. Reconnect RC. Release card and continue tuck stitch stripe pattern 133 (169) rows. RC shows 213 (281).

Shape armhole and front edge: Decrease 1 st at left edge on next and every following 9th row, and at the same time, cast off 4 sts at the beginning of the next row, knit 1 row, decrease 1 st at armhole edge on every following alternate row until 63 (66) sts remain. Continue to decrease at front edge only on every 9th row from previous decrease until 47 (50) sts remain. Knit 13 (16) rows. RC shows 371 (451). Cast off.

LEFT FRONT

Using 2¾mm needles and yarn B, cast on 61 (67) sts. Work 20 rows in rib as given for back.

Next row: Rib 2 (5), increase in next st, * rib 1, increase in next st; repeat from * 22 times more, rib to last 10 sts, turn and leave remaining sts on a stitch holder (75, 81 sts). Push 37 (43) needles at left and 38 needles at right of centre 0 to WP (75, 81 needles). Work as given for right front from *** to end, reversing shapings by reading right for left and left for right.

SLEEVES

Using 2¾mm needles and yarn B, cast on 53 (55) sts. Work 20 rows in rib as given for back.

Next row: Rib 4 (5), increase in next st, * rib 3, increase in next st; repeat from * 10 times more, rib to end (65, 67 sts).

Push 33 (34) needles at left and 32 (33) needles at right of centre 0 to WP (65, 67 needles). With carriage at right transfer sts to machine needles. Work as for back from ** to **. Shape sides by increasing 1 st at each end of every 10th row until there are 103 (109) sts. Knit 23 (31) rows. RC shows 213 (241).

Shape top: Cast off 6 sts at the beginning of the next 2 rows and 4 sts at the beginning of the next 2 rows. Decrease 1 st at each end of the next and every following 8th row until 37 (41) sts remain, then every following alternate row until 13 sts remain. Cast off.

BUTTON BAND

Join shoulder seams. With right side of left front facing and using 2¾mm needles and yarn B, rib across sts on stitch holder working twice into first st (11 sts). Continue in rib until band, when slightly stretched, fits up left front edge and round to centre back neck. Cast off in rib. Tack band in place, with pins mark position of buttons; 1st will be level with buttonhole already worked, 2nd to come level with the beginning of the front shaping, with 9 more spaced evenly between these 2.

BUTTONHOLE BAND

With wrong side of right front facing and using 2¾mm needles and yarn B, rib across sts on stitch holder working twice into first st (11 sts). Continue to match buttonband, working buttonholes as before, to correspond with position of pins.

FINISHING

Without milling

With wrong side of work facing, block each piece by pinning out to correct measurements. Dampen with cold, clean water and leave to dry naturally. Set in sleeves. Join side and sleeve seams. Fold 10 rows at top of pocket to inside and slip stitch in position. Catch down pocket lining on the inside. Sew on front bands, joining at centre back neck *. Sew on buttons.

With milling

Mill all pieces as explained on page 58. Work as above to *. Brush all over carefully using a teazle brush. Sew on buttons.

SHAPE GUIDE

All measurements are given in centimetres. Figures in brackets refer to the larger size. Figures in italics refer to measurements after milling.

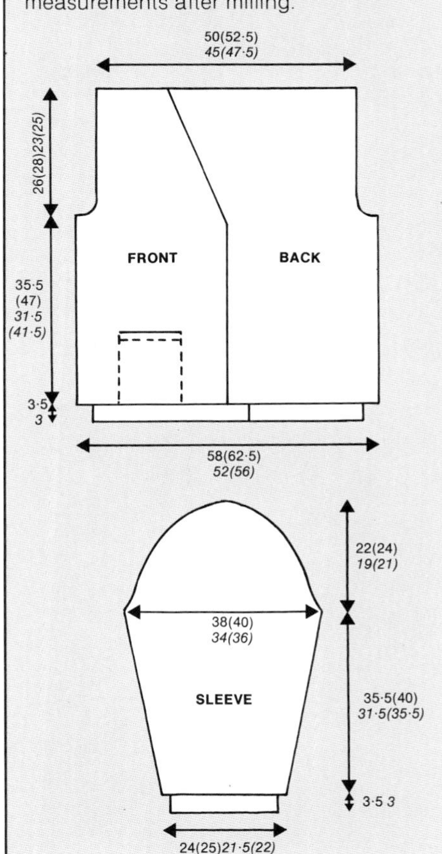

PUNCHCARD

Punch this card before starting to knit.

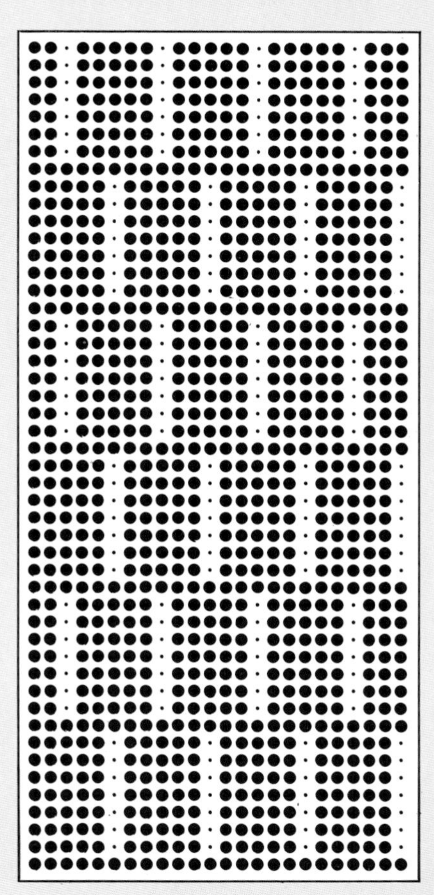

REVERSE·SIDE TUCK·STITCH

The wrong side of tuck stitch fabric can be used as the right side of the garment. With the simple tuck stitch structure as used on *Arabian Nights*, overleaf, the right side of the fabric appears rather dull, while an attractive, textured vertical stripe is produced on the reverse. The small "floats" formed by the tucking bunch together creating tiny bow shapes. The prettiness of these shapes is enhanced by the small holes which give a lacy look to the fabric.

To see the stitch construction, give a sample a heavy press–this stretches the fabric and extends the small holes which have been produced.

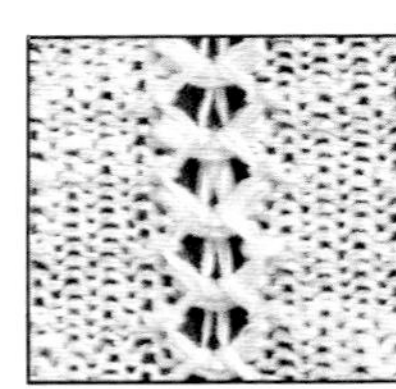

Experimenting with colours and yarns
As shown in the samples on the right, numerous and varied effects can be produced by experimenting with different textures and thicknesses of yarns. Colour can also radically alter the appearance of the design. The use of subtle colours allows the stitch construction to be shown to advantage, while highly textured yarns and similarly toned colours tend to obscure the structural effects.

Reflective yarns work especially well in reverse side tuck stitch. The small floats made around the tucking allow the yarn to twist and twinkle, reflecting the light and providing a shimmering effect.

Experimenting with needle selection
A wide variety of effects can be achieved by changing the spacing of the tucking needles, and the repetition of the tucking. The tucking for this sweater has been done on single needles spaced at regular intervals. The spacing determines the pattern of the vertical stripe. By breaking up the tucking with the minimum number of rows (two), a lightly textured vertical stripe is produced.

During sampling I found that a satisfying way of balancing the vertical stripe formed by the tuck was to introduce horizontal colour stripes. This countered the vertical stripe and developed the fabric into an all-over pattern.

Another way of varying the texture is to tuck on different numbers of rows, or to knit bands of a different stitch construction between the tucking rows.

Pattern variations using punchcard on p. 65
Samples show the effects of using different colours and yarns.

PATTERN INSTRUCTIONS FOR
ARABIAN NIGHTS

The interesting textured effect which is a feature of this evening sweater, has been achieved by using the wrong, "purl" side of the knitting as the right side. The full, puff sleeves are formed by pleating the sleeve head into the armhole.

MATERIALS

Yarn
Yarn A 50 (50)g medium-weight mohair loop (black)
Yarn B 250 (275)g fine-weight mercerised cotton (peach)
Yarn C 250 (275)g fine-weight mercerised cotton (grey)

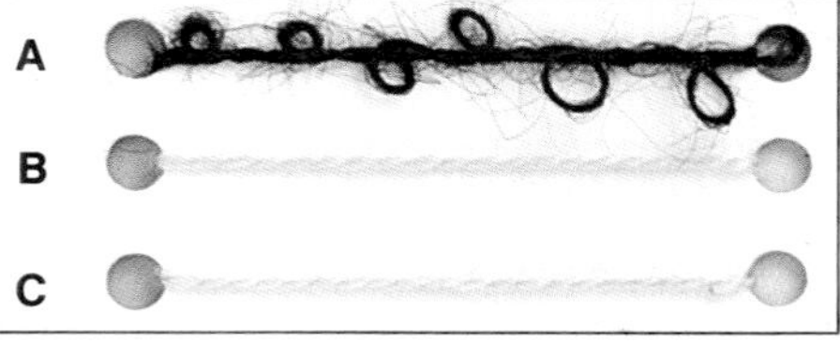

Needles
1 pair size 2¾mm

MEASUREMENTS

To fit chest 81-86 (91-97)cm (32-34, 36-38in)
Actual chest size 97(103)cm (38, 40½in)
Length at centre back 54cm (21¼in)
Sleeve seam 21·5cm (8½in)

MAIN TENSION (MT)

27 sts and 90 rows measure 10cm over tuck stitch pattern (tension dial set at approximately 5)

SPECIAL NOTE

Purl side is used as right side of sweater.

RIB STRIPE PATTERN

Work 2 rows yarn C, 1 row yarn A, 2 rows yarn B and 1 row yarn A.

TUCK STITCH STRIPE PATTERN

Work 8 rows yarn B, 1 row yarn A, 8 rows yarn C and 1 row yarn A.

BACK

With yarn A and 2¾mm needles, cast on 106 (112) sts. Work 26 rows in k1, p1 rib in rib stripe pattern as given above.
Next row: With yarn A, * rib 3, increase 1 in next st; repeat from * to last 2 (0) sts, rib to end (132, 140 sts).
Push 66 (70) needles at left and right of centre 0 to WP (132, 140 needles). With carriage at left, transfer sts to machine needles. Insert punchcard and lock on first row. Set carriage for tuck stitch pattern. Take carriage to right without knitting. Release card and continue in tuck stitch stripe pattern as given above. Set row counter at 000. Using MT, knit 270 rows.

Shape armholes: Cast off 8 sts at beginning of next 2 rows. Decrease 1 st at each end of every following 5th row until 88 (92) sts remain **. Knit 90 (80) rows. Row counter shows 432. Place marker between sts 23 and 24 at left and right of centre 0 for neck edge. Cast off.

FRONT

Work as given for back as far as **. Knit 40 (30) rows.
Shape neck: Using a length of yarn, cast off centre 20 sts. Using nylon cord, knit 34 (36) sts at left by hand taking needles down to NWP. Note pattern row on punchcard. Continue on remaining sts for first side. Knit 1 row. Cast off 3 sts at beginning of next row. Decrease 1 1 st at neck edge on every row until 21 (23) sts remain. Knit 38 rows. Cast off.
With carriage at right, unravel nylon cord over remaining needles bringing needles back to WP. Lock punchcard on number previously noted. Take carriage to left without knitting. Release punchcard and continue in tuck stitch. Finish to correspond with first side, reversing shaping.

SLEEVES

Push 70 needles at left and right of centre 0 to WP (140 needles). Using MT and waste yarn, cast on and knit a few rows ending with carriage at left. Insert punchcard and lock on first row. Set carriage for tuck stitch pattern. Take carriage to right without knitting. Release punchcard and continue in tuck stitch stripe pattern. Set row counter at 000. Knit 162 rows.
Shape top: Cast off 8 sts at beginning of next 2 rows. Decrease 1 st at each end of every following 5th row until 98 sts remain. Knit 42 rows. Decrease 1 st at each end of next and every following 4th row until 70 sts remain. Cast off.
Make another sleeve in the same way.

CUFFS

With purl side facing and using $2\frac{3}{4}$mm needles, pick up 140 sts along lower edge of sleeve. With knit side facing and using yarn A, knit 2 sts together along the row (70 sts). Work 15 rows k1, p1 rib stripe pattern as given on previous page. Cast off very loosely in rib with yarn A.

NECKBAND

Join left shoulder seam taking 5 rows into the seam. With purl side facing, join in yarn A at right shoulder, and using $2\frac{3}{4}$mm needles, pick up and knit 124 sts. Working in k1, p1 rib, work 2 rows yarn B, 1 row yarn A, 2 rows yarn C and 1 row yarn A. Cast off loosely with yarn A.

FINISHING

With purl side of work facing, block each piece by pinning out to correct measurements. Dampen with cold, clean water and leave to dry naturally. Join right shoulder seam, taking 5 rows into the seam. Join neckband, side and sleeve seams. Tack an inverted pleat in top of sleeve and pin centre to shoulder seam. Set in sleeves.

SHAPE GUIDE

All measurements are given in centimetres. Figures in brackets refer to the larger size. Where only one figure is given, it applies to both sizes.

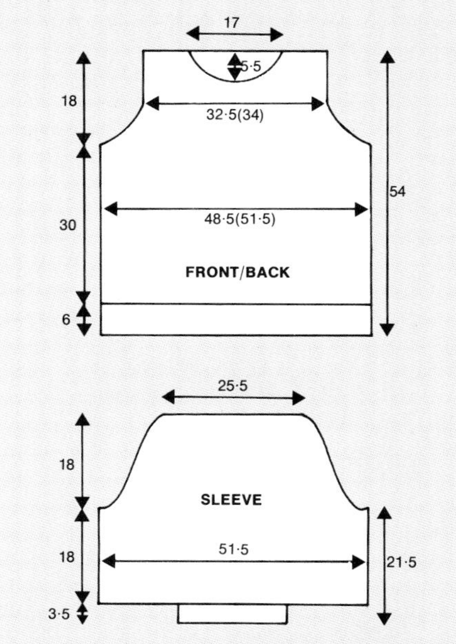

PUNCHCARD

Punch this card before starting to knit.

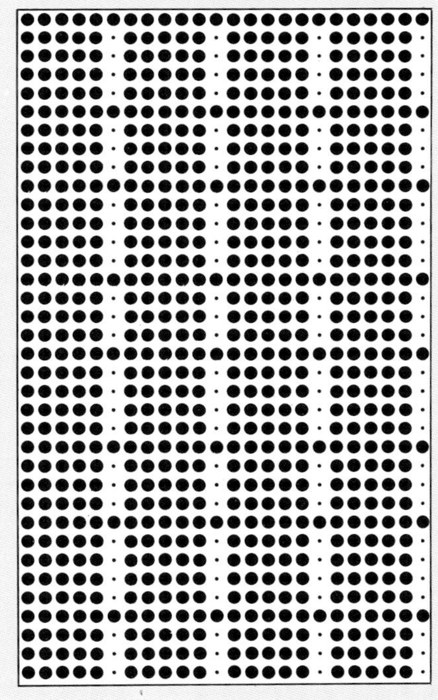

WEAVING

Weaving on a knitting machine is really a combination of knitting and weaving. A knitted base fabric, which is usually stocking stitch (but may be a different stitch construction), is threaded through with another, often thicker, yarn. The technique provides great scope for using thick and heavily textured yarns that may not normally be knitted on a standard gauge knitting machine.

The fabrics that may be achieved with the weaving technique can be quite stunning – unusual textures may be produced, particularly when laying in yarns by hand.

The fabric

The fabric that is produced by this technique is very different from other machine knitted fabrics. Because yarn is woven into the knitting, the fabric does not have much lateral stretch; in fact, it may be just as stable as ordinary softly woven fabrics. When designing a garment that employs this technique, this factor should be taken into account.

Woven fabrics are particularly suitable for making garments using the cut and sew method of making up. There is not enough room here to describe this in detail, but basically it involves knitting lengths of fabric on the knitting machine, and then cutting them into the required shapes before sewing together, rather than shaping them on the machine. Woven fabrics are particularly suitable for this making up method since they tend to fray less than other knitted fabrics.

The technique

There are two different ways of introducing the weaving yarn into the knitted fabric. It may be done semi-automatically, with the assistance of the carriage, or it may be done by hand. This latter weaving technique is known as laying in.

Exact instructions for setting up your machine for the semi-automatic method of weaving will be found in your manual. Usually the machine is threaded so the main or background yarn is fed through the tension unit and into feeder 1/A, as normal. The weaving yarn is placed either on the floor in front of the machine, or through the tension unit. The end of the weaving yarn is put through the weaving yarn guide at the side of the carriage. The needles over which the weaving yarn is to be looped may be selected manually, or with a punch-card. The weaving yarn is controlled by brushes, which must be set so they come in contact with the needle bed. Hold the weaving yarn with the left hand and operate the carriage with the right. For the next row, transfer the weaving yarn to the yarn guide on the other side of the carriage.

Laying in by hand is done by hooking the yarn around the needles in the upper working position.

Pattern variations using punchcard on p. 69

❶-❸ ❺-❼ Selection of yarns and colours altered.

❹ Floats cut after removing knitting from machine.

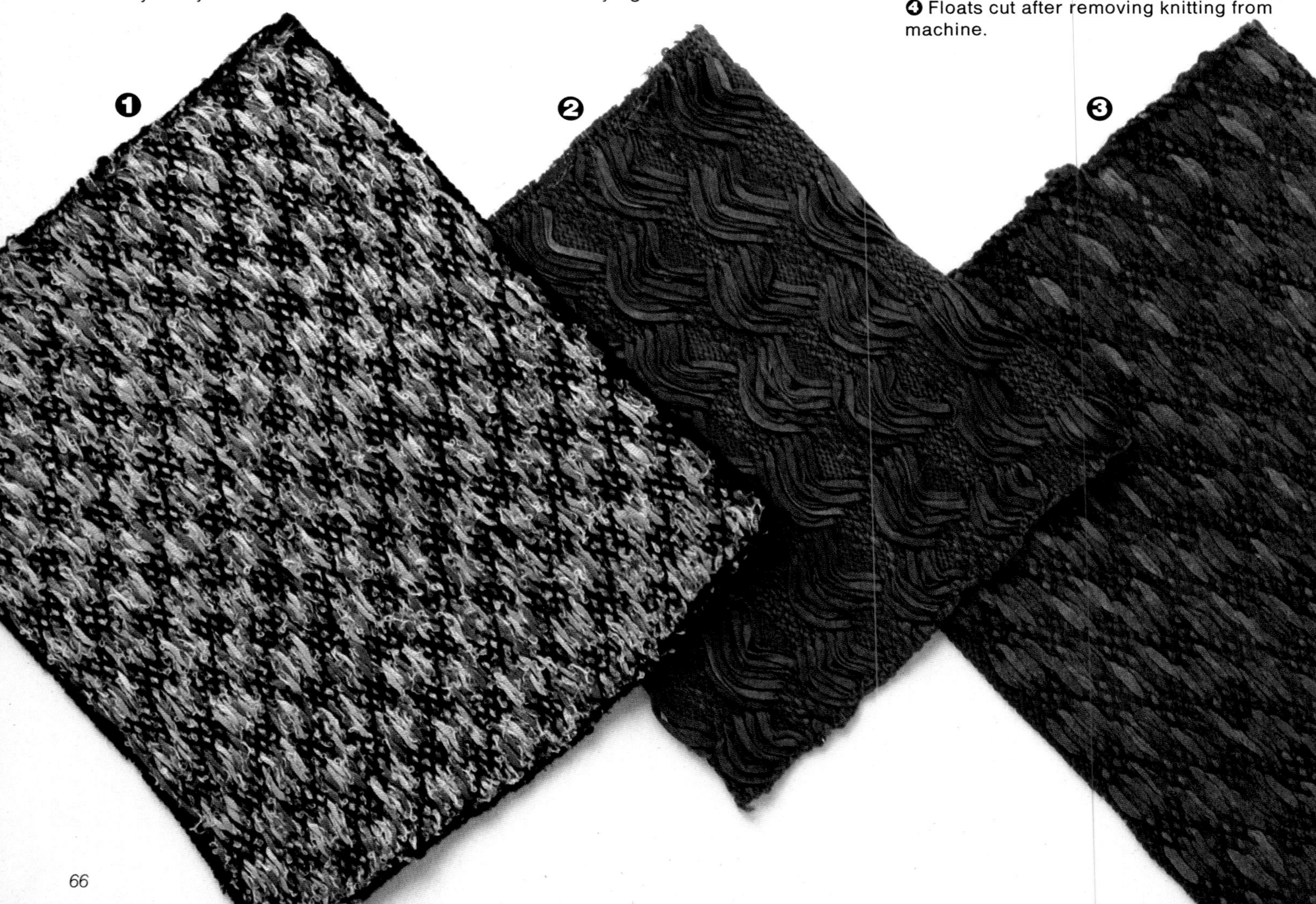

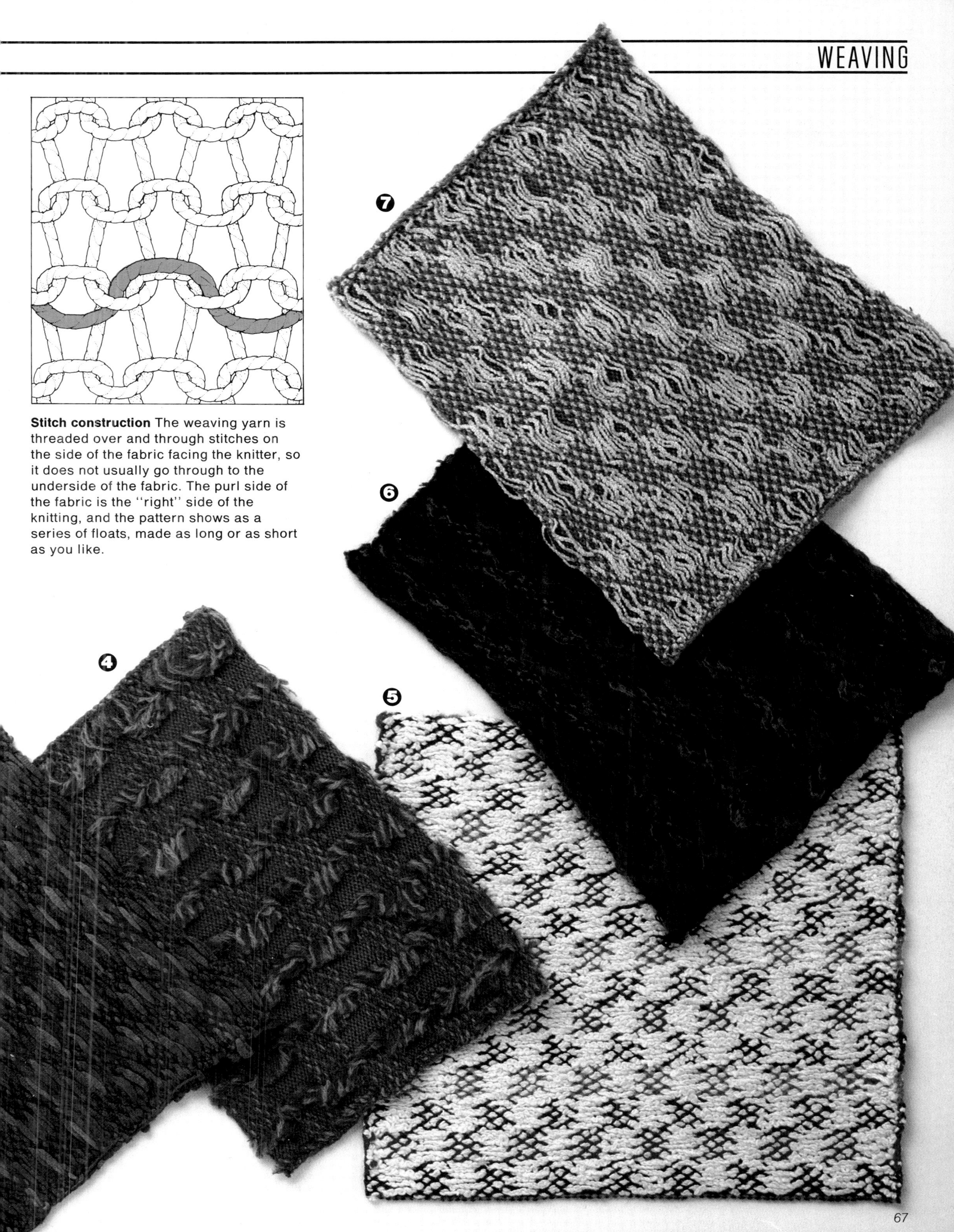

Stitch construction The weaving yarn is threaded over and through stitches on the side of the fabric facing the knitter, so it does not usually go through to the underside of the fabric. The purl side of the fabric is the "right" side of the knitting, and the pattern shows as a series of floats, made as long or as short as you like.

PATTERN INSTRUCTIONS FOR
HEATHER MIST

The subtle colouring on this sweater is achieved by running two fine yarns together for the plain background, and using a multi-coloured tape for the weaving yarn. When sewing together, match the stripes carefully at the armhole seam.

MATERIALS

Yarn

Yarn A 175 (200, 225)g very fine fluffy acrylic yarn (mauve)
Yarn B 175 (200, 225)g fine-weight Botany wool (blue)
Yarn C 100 (125, 150)g thick wool/acrylic mixture tape (multi-colour)

Needles

If you don't have a ribber, you need 1 pair size $2\frac{1}{4}$ mm knitting needles

MEASUREMENTS

To fit chest 81 (86, 91)cm (32, 34, 36in)
Actual chest size 92 (97, 102)cm (36, 38, 40in)
Length to shoulder 57.5cm (22¾in)
Sleeve seam 37.5 (42.5, 42.5)cm (14¾, 16¾, 16¾in)

MAIN TENSION (MT)

28 sts and 48 rows measure 10cm over weaving and stocking stitch stripes (tension dial set at approximately 6)

WEAVING AND STOCKING STITCH STRIPES

Knit 24 rows yarns A and B together, weaving with yarn C. Knit 24 rows yarns A and B together in stocking stitch.

BACK

Machines with ribber
With ribber in position and carriage at right, set machine for 1 × 1 rib. Using yarns A and B together, cast on 130 (136, 144) sts in 1 × 1 rib. Work 5 tubular/circular rows. Set carriage for 1 × 1 rib knitting. Set RC at 000. Using MT-4, knit 32 rows. Transfer sts for st st.
Machines without ribber
Using yarns A and B together and 2¼mm needles, cast on 130 (136, 144) sts. Work 6cm in k1, p1 rib. Push 130 (136, 144) needles to WP. With carriage at right, transfer sts to machine needles.
All machines
Set RC at 000. Using MT, knit 7 rows. Insert punchcard and lock on first row. Set carriage for pattern. Knit 1 row. Release card and continue in weaving and stocking stitch stripe pattern. Knit 144 rows. RC shows 152.
Shape armholes: Cast off 4 sts at the beginning of the next 4 rows. Decrease 1 st at each end of every following alternate row until 104 (108, 114) sts remain *. Knit 82 (80, 78) rows. RC shows 248. Cast off.

FRONT

Work as for back to *. Knit 20 (18, 16) rows. (62 rows less have been worked to shoulder than on back.)
Shape neck: Using a length of yarn, cast off centre 10 sts. Note pattern row on card. Using nylon cord, knit 47 (49, 52) sts at left by hand taking needles down to NWP. Continue on remaining sts for first side. Knit 1 row. Cast off 3 sts at the beginning of the next and following alternate row, knit 1 row. Decrease 1 st at the beginning of the next and every following alternate row until 26 (28, 31) sts remain. Knit 28 rows. Cast off. With carriage at right, unravel nylon cord over remaining needles bringing needles back to WP. Lock card on number previously noted. Set carriage for pattern and take to left without knitting. Release card and continue in weaving and stocking stitch stripe pattern. Finish to correspond with first side reversing shaping.

SLEEVES

Machines with ribber
With ribber in position and carriage at right, set machine for 1 × 1 rib. Using yarns A and B together, cast on 64 (66, 68) sts in 1 × 1 rib. Work 5 tubular/circular rows. Set carriage for 1 × 1 rib knitting. Set RC at 000. Using MT-4, work 32 rows. Using waste yarn, knit a few rows and release from machine.
Machines without ribber
Using yarns A and B together and 2¼mm needles, cast on 64 (66, 68) sts. Work 6cm in k1, p1 rib.
All machines
Push 84 (86, 88) needles to WP. With carriage at right, place sts on to needles as follows: 1 st on to each of first 4 (5, 6) needles, leave 1 needle empty, * 1 st on to each of next 3 needles, leave 1 needle empty; repeat from * across the row ending with 1 st on to each of last 3 (4, 5) needles. Pick up a loop from row below adjacent st and place on to empty needles. Set RC at 000. Using MT, knit 7 (31, 31) rows. Insert punchcard and lock on first row. Set carriage for pattern. Knit 1 row. Release card and continue in weaving and stocking stitch stripe pattern. Shape sides by increasing 1 st at each end of every 8th row until there are 108 (112, 116) sts. Knit 48 (40, 32) rows. RC shows 152 (176, 176).
Shape top: Cast off 4 sts at the beginning of the next 4 rows. Decrease 1 st at each end of every following alternate row until 20 (28, 36) sts remain, then on every row until 12 sts remain. Cast off.

COLLAR

Using yarns A and B together, cast on 174 sts by hand. Set RC at 000. Using MT + 1, knit 55 rows. Cast off.

FINISHING

With purl side of work facing, block each piece by pinning out to correct measurements. Depending on yarn used, press very carefully following instructions on ball or cone band, or dampen with cold, clean water and leave to dry naturally. Join shoulder, side, sleeve and collar seams. Set in sleeves. Sew cast off edge of collar in position.

SHAPE GUIDE
All measurements are given in centimetres. Figures in brackets refer to the larger sizes. Where only one figure is given, it applies to all sizes.

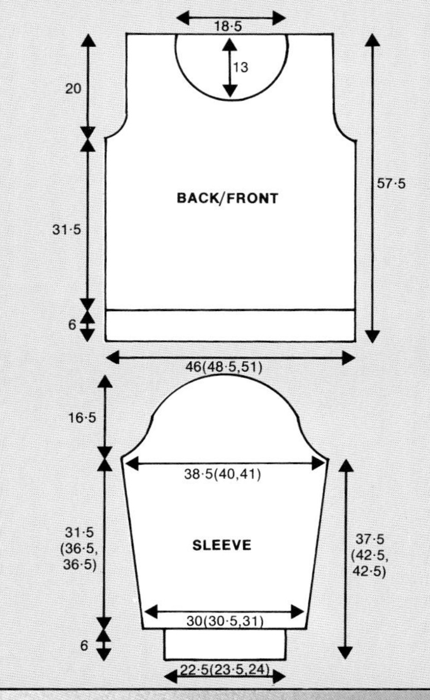

PUNCHCARD
Punch this card before starting to knit.

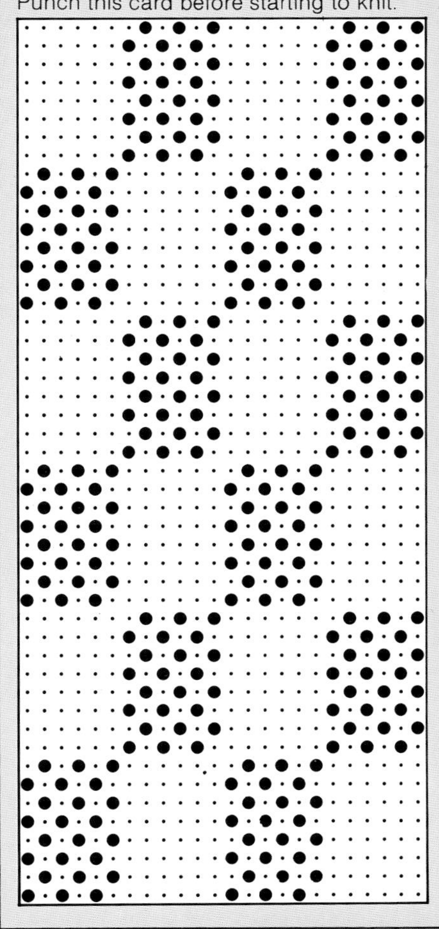

Pattern variations using punchcard on p. 73
❶ ❸ ❺ ❼ Selection of yarns and colours altered
❻ Weaving and stocking stitch sequence altered
❷ ❽ ❾ Some floats left as loops
❹ Weaving and stocking stitch sequence altered, some floats left as loops

CUTTING·FLOATS

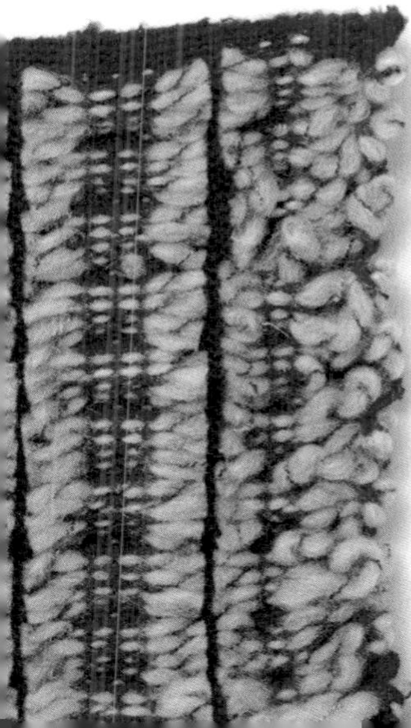

The subject of finishes – those different processes applied to your knitting after removing it from the machine – has already been introduced with milling and brushing in the Tuck Stitch section. However, woven fabrics offer further scope for achieving different finishes. By cutting the floats extraordinary textural surfaces can be produced.

The technique
Obviously, floats that are to be cut must be long enough to allow for cutting, and they must also be knitted in over enough needles so that the cut floats are held firmly in place. Hairy yarns such as wool stay in place best, but with a little experience you will discover that a wide range of yarns can be used.

You will find cutting floats is easier if the fabric is stretched taut. While it is simpler to cut floats which fall in vertical stripes, this type of patterning is not essential, interesting staggered effects may also be produced.

Experimenting with colours and yarns
By working with this technique you will learn that different yarns behave in different ways when they are cut. Rayon drops, and hangs in fringes. If a lightly spun cotton is used, the ends may be burst into fluffy bobbles by heavy steaming. Slippery yarns should only be worked on by the experienced, but when knitted successfully very unusual fabrics may be created.

The appearance of woven fabrics can be altered dramatically by changing the colour sequence used in the repeat. Other variations may be explored when using random dyed yarns, or by combining matt and shiny yarns. Also, remember that by cutting the floats, the background colour is revealed – this presents another opportunity for experimenting with colour.

Milling
Another variation of the float-cutting process is to mill the woven fabric *before* cutting the floats. If wool has been used for the weaving yarn the floats will felt together. Cut them, and open them out to make tabs, either all over the fabric, or in selected areas. Since the fabric may shrink considerably during the milling process, this technique should be practised on samples before it is used on a garment.

8

9

PATTERN INSTRUCTIONS FOR

COCOON

The unusual textured effect featured on this jacket is formed by carefully cutting the floats after knitting each garment piece. For added design interest the stand-up collar has been gently teazle brushed.

MATERIALS

Yarn

Yarn A 225 (300)g medium-weight Shetland wool (black)
Yarn B 250 (325)g medium-weight Shetland wool (grey)
Yarn C 525 (600)g chunky wool (brown multi-colour)

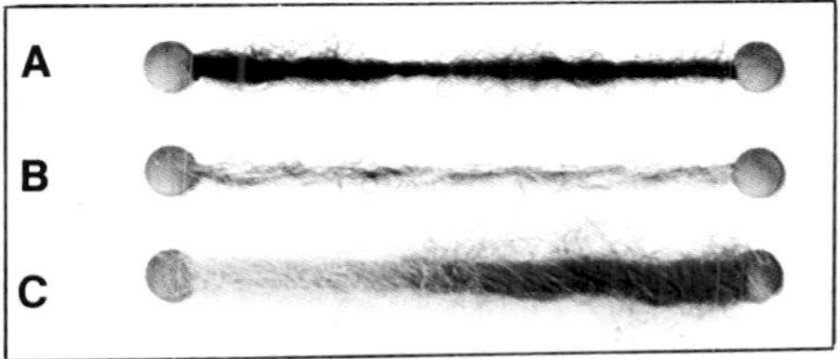

Notions

50cm of narrow elastic for cuffs
1 button 2.5cm in diameter

MEASUREMENTS

To fit chest 81-86 (91-97)cm (32-34, 36-38in)
Actual chest size 141 (157)cm ($55\frac{1}{2}$, $61\frac{3}{4}$in)
Length to shoulder 75cm ($29\frac{1}{2}$in)
Sleeve seam 54·5cm ($21\frac{1}{2}$in)

MAIN TENSION (MT)

21 sts and 35 rows measure 10cm over weaving and stocking stitch stripes (tension dial set at approximately 9)

SPECIAL NOTE

Purl side is used as right side of jacket.

WEAVING AND STOCKING STITCH STRIPES

Knit 4 rows yarn A, weaving with yarn C. Knit 1 row yarn A. Knit 1 row yarn B. Knit 4 rows yarn B, weaving with yarn C. Knit 1 row yarn B. Knit 1 row yarn A.

BACK

Using yarn A, cast on 149 (165) sts by hand. * Set RC at 000. Using MT, knit 12 rows. Insert punchcard and set to first row. Set carriage for pattern. Knit 1 row. Set RC at 000. Release card and continue in weaving and stocking stitch stripe pattern **. Knit 186 (180) rows *. Place marker at each end. Knit 78 (84) rows. RC shows 264. Cast off.

LEFT FRONT

With carriage at right and using yarn A, cast on 76 (84) sts by hand. Work as for back from * to *. Place marker at right edge. Knit 42 (48) rows. RC shows 228.

Shape neck: Cast off 10 sts at the beginning of the next row. Decrease 1 st at neck edge on the next and every following alternate row until 52 (60) sts remain. Knit 8 rows. RC shows 264. Cast off.

RIGHT FRONT

Work as for left front, reversing shaping, by reading left for right.

SLEEVES

Using yarn A, cast on 93 (101) sts by hand. Work as for back from * to **. Knit 192 rows. Cast off loosely.

COLLAR

Using yarn A, cast on 111 sts by hand. Insert punchcard and set to first row. Set carriage for pattern. Knit 1 row. Set RC at 000. Release card and continue in weaving and stocking stitch stripe pattern. Knit 48 rows. Cast off loosely.

SHAPE GUIDE

All measurements are given in centimetres. Figures in brackets refer to the larger size. Where only one figure is given, it applies to both sizes.

24·5(28·5)
22 (24)
75
BACK
FRONT
53 (51)
36(40)
4
70·5(78·5)
54·5
SLEEVE
4
44(48)
14
COLLAR
52·5

FINISHING

With purl side of work facing, block each piece by pinning out to correct measurements. Dampen with cold, clean water and leave to dry naturally. Cut butterflies all over back, fronts and sleeves, starting from centre and working outwards. Using the blunt edge of the blade against the work, twist scissors up and down and over and back under the thick yarn to make sure no threads are caught. Cut 0.5cm from holding stitch. Before cutting a new line, double check that you will cut correctly. Working from right to left, cut against a left side of first holding block, * miss a block, cut each side of next block; repeat from * across work. Join shoulder seams. Tack and sew pleats from shoulder seams to 5cm above armhole markers, taking in the line of blocks between butterflies until edges of butterflies meet. Make pleats right across both fronts and back, including neck. Set in sleeves between markers. Join side and sleeve seams. Fold collar in half lengthwise and join ends. Sew open edge to neck. Turn up 12 rows of st st in yarn A to form hems around cuff edge of sleeve and slip stitch in place, then thread elastic through sleeve hems. With teazle brush collar. Sew button to neck edge on left front and make a loop on right front to correspond. Press seams and hems carefully following instructions on ball or cone band.

PUNCHCARD

Punch this card before starting to knit.

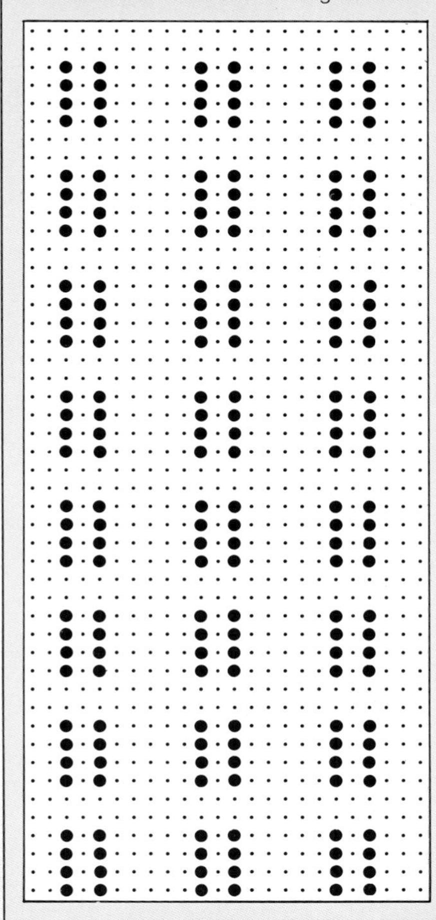

MANIPULATION OF·FLOATS

The weaving technique can be manipulated so that loops are formed from the floats on the purl side of the fabric. The samples and sweaters in this section show two different ways of producing this three-dimensional surface interest.

Tight background tension
If the background yarn is knitted on a tight tension, after removing the work from the machine the background will contract, leaving the woven yarn to form loops. This method is used on the *Turkish Delight* sweater, overleaf. One advantage of this method is that it is not particularly time consuming, however the resulting fabric is stiff, and therefore not suitable for many types of garments.

Manual manipulation
This method, although slightly more laborious, is much more versatile than the technique described above. Depending on the type of machine you have, the needles the yarn is to be hooked around may be selected manually, or with a punchcard. To make the floats the weaving yarn is hooked over each single needle in the upper working position. The floats between the needles are then gently pulled to form loops, before taking the carriage across the knitting. When knitting the next row make sure the loops lay flat and do not get caught up in the knitting. After a few more rows of stocking stitch pick up all the loops and hook them on to single needles in the upper working position.

Variations
Peaches and Cream and *Turkish Delight* show some ways of varying this technique:
- Use a striped background.
- Position the weaving yarns close together.
- Position the weaving yarns far apart.
- Combine stripes of a different stitch construction with stripes of loops.

Or, explore other variations such as:
- Use blocks or stripes of loops on selected parts of a garment, rather than all over.
- Use different stitch constructions for the background.
- Weave different colours in the same row. This variation, multi-coloured weaving, is explored further on page 80.

Pattern variations of weaving design featured on *Turkish Delight* **and** *Peaches and Cream*
Samples show the effects of using different colours and yarns, and altering the weaving sequence

PATTERN INSTRUCTIONS FOR

TURKISH DELIGHT

By working the stocking stitch background in a very tight tension the weaving yarn forms loops when the work is removed from the machine.

MATERIALS

Yarn
Yarn A 175g fine-weight wool (blue)
Yarn B 75g fine-weight wool (orange)
Yarn C 75g fine-weight wool (green)
Yarn D 75g fine-weight wool (pink)
Yarn E 200g chunky wool (multi-colour)

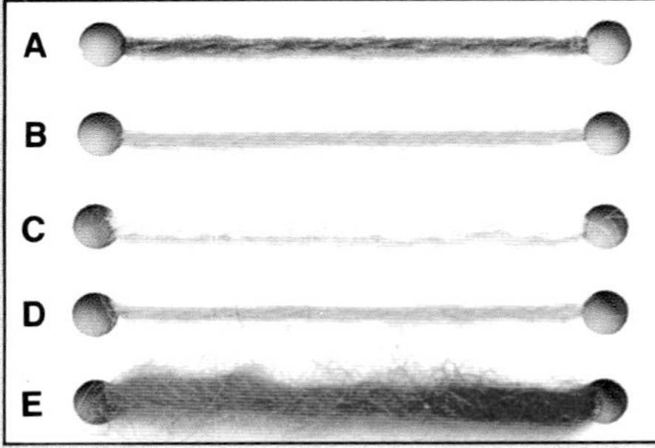

Notions
4 buttons
Needles
If don't have a ribber, you need 1 pair size $2\frac{3}{4}$mm knitting needles

MEASUREMENTS

To fit chest 87-92cm (34-36in)
Actual chest size 126·5cm ($49\frac{3}{4}$in)
Length 63·5cm (25in)

MAIN TENSION (MT)

34 sts and 60 rows measure 10cm over weaving (tension dial set at approximately 2)

WEAVING PATTERN

Knit 3 rows yarn A, 1 row yarn A and weave yarn E. Knit 3 rows yarn B, 1 row yarn B and weave yarn E. Knit 3 rows yarn D, 1 row yarn D and weave yarn E. Knit 3 rows yarn C, 1 row yarn C and weave yarn E.

BACK

Push 100 needles at left and 24 needles at right of centre 0 to WP (124 needles). With carriage at right and using yarn A, cast on by hand. Insert punchcard and set to first row without locking. Set carriage for pattern. Set RC at 000. Using MT, continue in weaving pattern. Knit 36 rows.
Shape armhole: Cast on 76 sts at the beginning of the next row (200 sts). Knit 303 rows. RC shows 340.
Shape armhole: Cast off 76 sts at the beginning of the next row (124 sts). Knit 35 rows. RC shows 376. Cast off.

RIGHT FRONT

Push 24 needles at left and 100 needles at right of centre 0 to WP (124 needles). With carriage at left and using yarn A, cast on by hand. Insert punchcard and set to first row without locking. Set carriage for pattern. Set RC at 000. Using MT, continue in weaving pattern. Knit 40 rows.
Shape armhole: Cast on 76 sts at the beginning of the next row (200 sts). Knit 99 rows. RC shows 140.
Shape neck: Cast off 8 sts at the beginning of the next row. Knit 3 rows. Cast off 2 sts at the beginning of the next and every following 4th row until 186 sts remain. Knit 3 rows. Decrease 1 st at the beginning of the next and following 4th row (184 sts). Knit 31 rows. RC shows 192. Cast off.

LEFT FRONT

Work as for right front reversing shapings and reading left for right and right for left.

NECKBAND

Machines with ribber
With ribber in position, set machine for full needle (double) rib. Push 108 needles on knitter and ribber to WP. Using yarn A, cast on. Work 5 tubular/circular rows. Set carriage for full needle (double) rib knitting. Set RC at 000. Using MT, decrease 1 st on each bed at each end of the next and following 6 alternate rows. Work 1 row. Using waste yarn, work a few rows and release from machine.
Machines without ribber
Using $2\frac{3}{4}$mm needles and yarn A, cast on 172 sts. Working in k1, p1 rib, decrease 1 st at each end of the next 10 rows. Cast off.

WELT

Machines with ribber
With ribber in position, set machine for full needle (double) rib. Push 190 needles on knitter and ribber to WP. Using yarn A, cast on. Work 5 tubular/circular rows. Set carriage for full needle (double) rib knitting. Set RC at 000. Using MT, decrease 1 st on each bed at each end of the next and every following 4th row until 174 sts remain on each bed. Work 1 row. Using waste yarn work a few rows and release from machine.
Machines without ribber
Back welt: Using $2\frac{3}{4}$mm needles and yarn A, cast on 184 sts. Work 20 rows in k1, p1 rib. Cast off in rib.
Right front welt: Using $2\frac{3}{4}$mm needles and yarn A cast on 102 sts.
1st row: * K1, p1; rep from * to last 2 sts, k2tog.
2nd row: P1, * k1, p1; rep from * to end.
3rd row: Rib to last 2 sts, k2tog.
4th row: Rib to end.
Repeat these 4 rows 4 times more. Cast off.
Left front welt: Using $2\frac{3}{4}$mm needles and yarn A, cast on 102 sts.
1st row: K2tog, * k1, p1; rep from * to end.
2nd row: K1, * p1, k1; rep from * to end.
3rd row: K2tog, rib to end.
4th row: Rib to end.
Repeat these 4 rows 4 times more. Cast off.

BUTTONHOLE BAND

Machines with ribber
With ribber in position, set machine for full needle (double) rib. Push 161 needles on knitter and ribber to WP. Using yarn A, cast on. Work 5 tubular/circular rows. Set carriage for full needle (double) rib knitting. Set RC at 000. Using MT, * decrease 1 st on each bed at each end of next row. Decrease 1 st on each bed at right edge on next row. * Repeat from * to * twice more. Counting from right edge, make buttonholes over 5th, 6th; 22nd, 23rd; 39th, 40th; 56th and 57th sts on each bed. Repeat from * to * 4 times more. Using waste yarn, work a few rows and release from machine.
Machines without ribber
Using $2\frac{3}{4}$mm needles and yarn A, cast on 246 sts.
1st row: * K1, p1; rep from * to last 2 sts, k2tog.
2nd row: K2tog, p1, * k1, p1; rep from * to last 2 sts, k2tog.
3rd row: Cast off 4 sts, rib to last 2 sts, k2tog.
4th row: K2tog, rib to last 2 sts, k2tog.
5th row: Cast off 4 sts, rib 23, cast off 3 sts, rib 23. Cast off 3 sts, rib 23, cast off 3 sts, rib to last 2 sts, k2tog.
6th row: K2tog, rib to last 2 sts casting on 3 sts over cast off sts, k2tog.
7th row: Cast off 4 sts, rib to last 2 sts, k2tog.
8th row: K2tog, rib to last 2 sts, k2tog.
9th row: Cast off 4 sts, rib to last 2 sts, k2tog.
10th row: K2tog, rib to end.
Cast off in rib.

BUTTON BAND

Machines with ribber
Work as for buttonhole band, reversing shaping, reading left for right and omitting buttonholes.
Machines without ribber
Using $2\frac{3}{4}$mm needles and yarn A, cast on 246 sts.
1st row: K2tog, * p1, k1; rep from * to end.
2nd row: K2tog, p1, * k1, p1; rep from * to last 2 sts, k2tog.
3rd row: K2tog, rib to last 2 sts, k2tog.
4th row: Cast off 4 sts, rib to last 2 sts, k2tog.
5th row: K2tog, rib to last 2 sts, k2tog.
6th row: Cast off 4 sts, rib to last 2 sts, k2tog.
7th row: K2tog, rib to last 2 sts, k2tog.
8th row: Cast off 4 sts, rib to last 2 sts, k2tog.
9th row: K2tog, rib to last 2 sts, k2tog.
10th row: Cast off 3 sts, rib to last 2 sts, k2tog.
Cast off in rib.

UNDERARM BANDS (two alike)

Machines with ribber
With ribber in position, set machine for full needle (double) rib. Push 32 needles on knitter and ribber to WP. Using yarn A, cast on. Work 5 tubular/circular rows. Set carriage for full needle (double) rib knitting. Set RC at 000. Using MT, work 14 rows. Using waste yarn, work a few rows and release from machine.
Machines without ribber
Using $2\frac{3}{4}$mm needles and yarn A, cast on 52 sts. Work 10 rows in k1, p1 rib. Cast off.

ARMHOLE BANDS (four pieces)

First Two Pieces
Machines with ribber: With ribber in position, set machine for full needle (double) rib. Push 64 needles on knitter and ribber to WP. Using yarn A, cast on. Work 5 tubular/circular rows. Set carriage for full needle (double) rib knitting. Set RC at 000. Using MT, decrease 1 st on each bed at right edge on next and following 6 alternate rows. Work

1 row. Using waste yarn, work a few rows and release from machine.

Machines without ribber: Using $2\frac{3}{4}$mm needles and yarn A, cast on 98 sts.

1st row: * K1, p1; rep from * to last 2 sts, k2tog.

2nd row: K2tog, p1 * k1, p1; rep from * to end.

Repeat these 2 rows 4 times more. Cast off.

Second Two Pieces

Machines with ribber: Work as for first 2 pieces, reversing shaping by reading left for right.

Machines without ribber: Using $2\frac{3}{4}$mm needles and yarn A, cast on 98 sts.

1st row: K2tog, * p1, k1; rep from * to end.

2nd row: P1 * k1, p1; rep from * to last 2 sts, k2tog.

Repeat these 2 rows 4 times more. Cast off.

FINISHING

With knit side of work facing, block each piece by pinning out to correct measurements. Dampen with cold, clean water and leave to dry naturally. Join shoulder and side seams. For all the machine knit ribs, where necessary backstitch through open loops of last row worked in yarn A. Sew neckband, buttonhole band, buttonband and welts into position stretching welt to pull in lower edge. For hand knit ribs, join mitred corners and welt seams leaving an opening in the mitred corners of right front welt for 4th buttonhole. Sew underarm bands into position. Sew armhole bands into position overlapping the straight edge over underarm bands and overlapping front mitre over back mitre at shoulder. Sew mitred ends and straight ends into position. Finish buttonholes and sew on buttons.

PUNCHCARD

Punch this card before starting to knit.

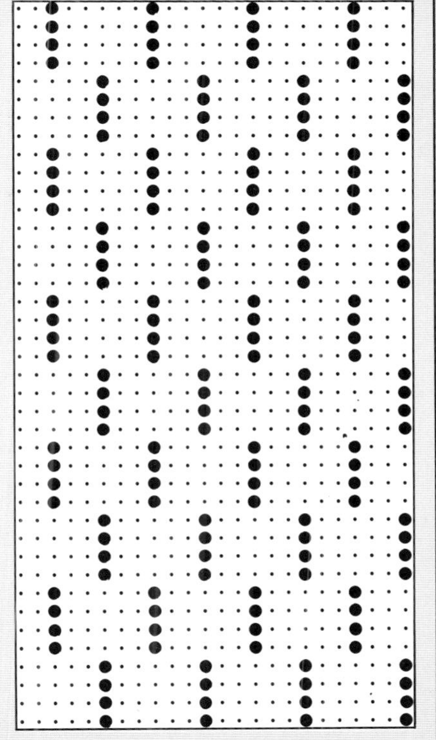

SHAPE GUIDE

All measurements are given in centimetres.

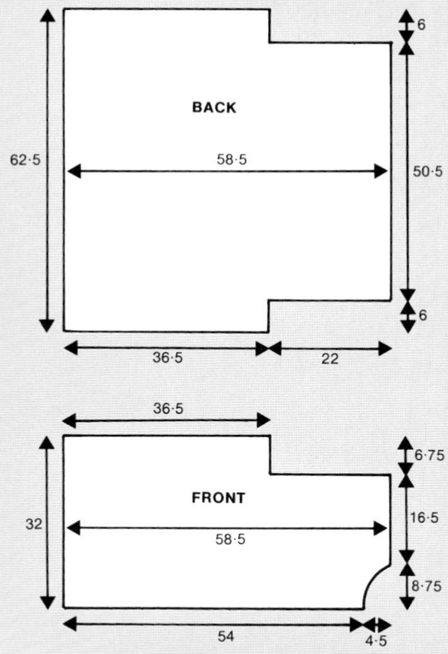

BACK
62·5
58·5
50·5
6
6
36·5
22

FRONT
36·5
32
58·5
6·75
16·5
8·75
54
4·5

PATTERN INSTRUCTIONS FOR
PEACHES AND CREAM

An interesting combination of colours, yarns and stitch construction produces an unusual, but very pretty summer cardigan. Make sure you pull the loops of the weaving yarn evenly.

MATERIALS

Yarn
Yarn A 200 (250)g medium-weight cotton gimp (cream)
Yarn B 100 (125)g medium-weight acrylic gimp (peach)
Yarn C 100 (125)g fine-weight mercerised

A
B
C
D

cotton (turquoise)
Yarn D 50 (75)g chunky wool (multi-colour)
Notions
2 buttons, 1cm in diameter
2 stitch holders
Needles
1 pair size 2¾mm

MEASUREMENTS

To fit chest 81-86 (86-91)cm (32-34, 34-36in)
Actual chest size 97 (103)cm (38½, 40½in)
Length to shoulder 50.5 (60)cm (20, 23¾in)
Sleeve seam 47.5cm (18¾in)

MAIN TENSION (MT)

28 sts and 56 rows measure 10cm over pattern (tension dial set at approximately 6)

RIB STRIPE PATTERN

Knit 2 rows yarn A, 2 rows yarn C, 2 rows yarn A and 2 rows yarn B. These 8 rows form one complete pattern repeat.

WEAVING AND TUCK STITCH PATTERN

* Knit 1 row yarn A and weave with yarn D. Pull woven loops down (loops to measure approximately 3.75cm). Knit 6 rows yarn A (st st). Pick up woven loops and place on to centre needles, coloured red on the punchcard. Knit 1 row yarn A (st st) *. Continue in tuck stitch. Knit 4 rows yarn C, 4 rows yarn A and 4 rows yarn B. ** Repeat from * to *. Continue in tuck stitch. Knit 4 rows yarn B, 4 rows yarn A and 4 rows yarn C. These 40 rows form one complete pattern repeat.

BACK

Using yarn A and 2¾mm needles, cast on 110 (118) sts. Continue in rib stripe pattern and work 21 rows in k1, p1 rib.
Next row: Rib 3 (7), increase in next st, * rib 3, increase in next st; repeat from * to last 2 (6) sts, rib to end (137, 145 sts). Push 72 needles at left and 65 (73) needles at right of centre 0 to WP (137, 145 needles). With carriage at right, transfer sts to machine needles. Insert punchcard and lock on first row. Set carriage for pattern. Set RC at 000. Using MT and yarn A, knit 1 row. Release card and continue in weaving and tuck stitch pattern. Knit 140 (180) rows. RC shows 141 (181).
Shape armholes: Cast off 16 sts at the beginning of the next 2 rows (105, 113 sts). Knit 114 (126) rows. RC shows 257 (309). Cast off.

RIGHT FRONT

Using yarn A and 2¾mm needles, cast on 60 (64) sts. Continue in rib stripe pattern and work 5 rows in k1, p1 rib.
Buttonhole row: Rib to last 5 sts, yfwd, k2tog, rib to end.
Work 13 rows in k1, p1 rib.
Buttonhole row: Rib to last 5 sts, yfwd, k2tog, rib to end.
Work 1 row in k1, p1 rib.
Next row: Rib 3 (7), increase in next st, * rib 3, increase in next st; repeat from * to last 8 sts. Slip last 8 sts on to a stitch holder for border (65, 69 sts).
Push 40 needles at left and 25 (29) needles at right of centre 0 to WP. ** 65 (69) needles. With carriage and stitch holder at right, transfer sts to machine needles. Insert punchcard and lock on first row. Set carriage for patttern. Set RC at 000. Using MT and yarn A, knit 1 row. Release card and continue in weaving and tuck stitch pattern.
Shape front edge: Decrease 1 st at right edge on every 10th row until 51 sts remain. RC shows 141 (181).
Shape armhole: Cast off 16 sts at the beginning of the next row (35 sts). Continue to decrease at front edge on every 10th row from previous decrease until 30 sts remain. Knit 66 (78) rows. RC shows 257 (309). Cast off **.

LEFT FRONT

Using yarn A and 2¾mm needles, cast on 60 (64) sts. Continue in rib stripe pattern and work 20 rows in k1, p1 rib.
Next row: Rib to last 8 sts, slip last 8 sts on to a stitch holder for border.
Next row: Increase in first st, * rib 3, increase in next st; repeat from * to last 3 (7) sts, rib to end (65, 69 sts).
Push 24 (28) needles at left and 41 needles at right of centre 0 to WP. Work as for right front from ** to ** reversing shapings by reading left for right.

SLEEVES

Push 52 (60) needles at left and 45 (53) needles at right of centre 0 to WP (97, 113 needles). Using yarn A, cast on by hand. Insert punchcard and lock on first row. Set carriage for pattern. Set RC at 000. Using MT, knit 1 row. Release card and continue in weaving and tuck stitch pattern (starting at **). Knit 237 rows. RC shows 238. Place marker at each end. Knit 31 rows. RC shows 269. Cast off very loosely.

CUFFS

With purl side facing, join in yarn A and using 2¾mm needles, pick up and knit 64 sts along cuff edge. Continue in rib stripe pattern and work 22 rows in k1, p1 rib. Cast off in rib.

FRONT BAND

Join shoulder seams. With knit side of right front facing, join in yarn A, and using 2¾mm needles, pick up and rib 8 sts from stitch holder. Keeping rib stripe pattern correct, work until strip, when slightly stretched, fits up right front edge, across back neck and down left front edge, matching stripes and ending with one row in yarn A. Leave sts on a spare needle.

FINISHING

With knit side of work facing, block each piece by pinning out to correct measurements. Dampen with cold, clean water and leave to dry naturally. Set in sleeves stretching tops slightly and sewing rows above markers to cast off stitches on back and fronts. Join side and sleeve seams. Sew front band in position, matching stripes. Graft end of front band to stitches on stitch holder. Sew on buttons.

SHAPE GUIDE
All measurements are given in centimetres. Figures in brackets refer to the larger size. Where only one figure is given, it applies to both sizes.

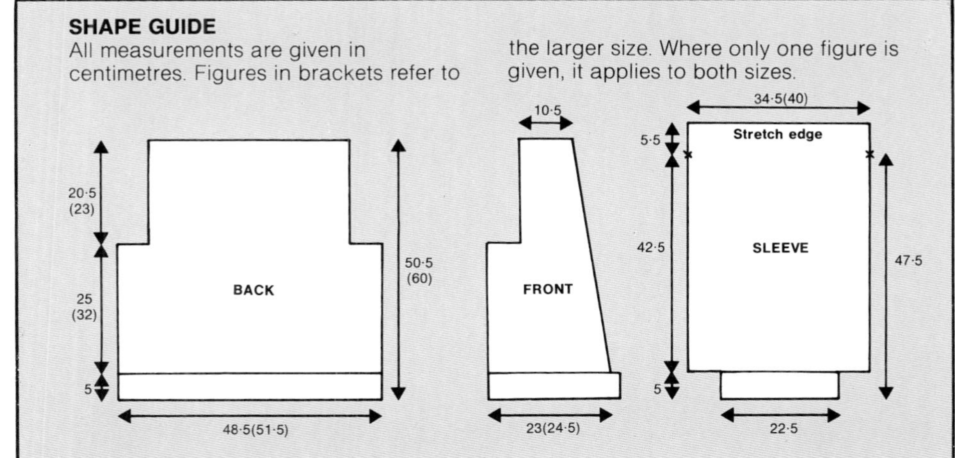

PUNCHCARD
Punch this card before starting to knit.

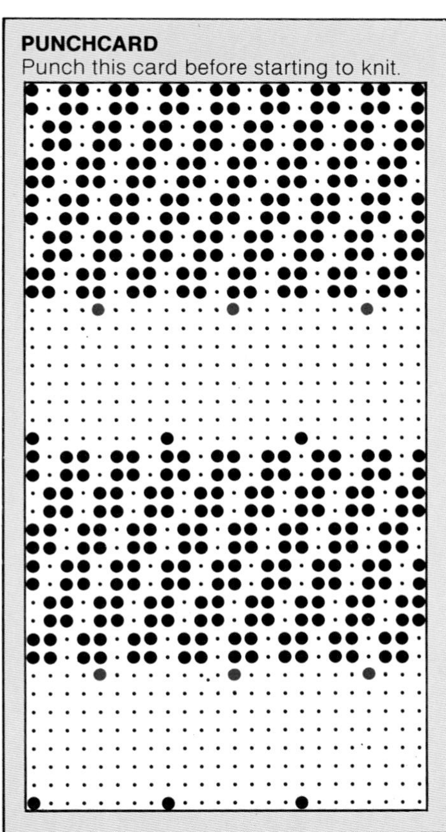

MULTI-COLOURED·WEAVING

An interesting weaving variation is the use of more than one colour in each row. This method can be time-consuming since the weaving yarns have to be laid in by hand, but very attractive fabrics can be produced. In the samples shown here, the needles have been arranged into blocks, and instead of the weaving yarn being knitted from just one cone of yarn (which would produce floats joining each block, as in *Heather Mist*) a separate ball or cone of yarn is used for each block. This technique of individually feeding the yarn into the knitting allows different yarns and colours to be used on each block or set of needles.

The technique

The weaving yarn is laid across selected needles in the upper working position by hand. On some punchcard machines the pattern needles come out to the upper working position as the carriage is taken across the knitting. On others the needles will have to be manually pushed to the upper working position.

Whichever fancy yarn you choose for the laying in, it has to be divided into as many small balls as there are blocks of needles in the width of the knitting. These small balls of yarn should be fed into the work from the floor in front of the machine. One way of preventing the yarns from becoming tangled is to put each ball into an empty plant pot or other container.

In the *Batwing* sweater shown overleaf just two colours of fancy yarns have been used as the weaving yarn, on alternate sets of needles. However, you could use a different yarn on each set of needles. This is shown in samples 1 and 2.

During the initial stages this technique may seem rather laborious, but with experience the speed at which you lay the weaving yarn over the different sets of needles will increase. The important point to note before beginning knitting is to ensure the tension is correct. It is advisable to make test samples; too tight a tension not only produces a stiff, heavy fabric,

1

2

but may also make it difficult to take the carriage carrying the background yarn across the knitting.

Experimenting with colours, yarns and needle selection

This particular design offers great scope for the inventive knitter. The most obvious pattern development is to use different colours of yarn for different sets of needles – this produces a stepped stripe running vertically up the knitting (sample 1). Another development is to take the colour used at the left hand side of the knitting at the end of the repeat and introduce it on the extreme right of the knitting, ready for the next repeat. This movement of colours gives a stepped diagonal stripe pattern (sample 2).

Depending on how you move the yarn from one set of needles to another, you may produce a float, which can be used for additional decorative effect (sample 2).

Although, when using a punchcard, certain needles will come forward, you don't have to lay the weaving yarn over them every single time. By selective laying in, using only specific sets of needles, all manner of different effects may be achieved with the same punchcard (see samples 4 and 6).

The use of a textured yarn for the background can produce a very different fabric from the use of a straight yarn. Mohair used as the weaving yarn may later be brushed to produce attractive fluffy shapes in the fabric. However, fine yarns used as the weaving yarn will tend to disappear into the background knitting.

Pattern variations using punchcard on p. 83

❸ ❺ Selection of yarns and colours altered

❶ ❷ Different colours of yarn used on each set of needles

❹ ❻ Yarn laid over selected sets of needles

PATTERN INSTRUCTIONS FOR
BATWING

The use of a fancy fluffy yarn creates a dramatic sweater suitable for special occasions. A more casual look may be produced if alternative yarns and colours are chosen.

WEAVING CHART

Repeat these 28 rows throughout.

						C		C		C								B		B		B	
							C		C		C								B		B		B
						C		C		C								B		B		B	
							C		C		C								B		B		B
						C		C		C								B		B		B	
							C		C		C								B		B		B
						C		C		C								B		B		B	
B		B		B								C		C		C							
	B		B		B								C		C		C						
B		B		B								C		C		C							
	B		B		B								C		C		C						
B		B		B								C		C		C							
	B		B		B								C		C		C						
B		B		B								C		C		C							
						B		B		B								C		C		C	
							B		B		B								C		C		C
						B		B		B								C		C		C	
							B		B		B								C		C		C
						B		B		B								C		C		C	
							B		B		B								C		C		C
						B		B		B								C		C		C	
C		C		C								B		B		B							
	C		C		C								B		B		B						
C		C		C								B		B		B							
	C		C		C								B		B		B						
C		C		C								B		B		B							
	C		C		C								B		B		B						
C		C		C								B		B		B							

Repeat this sequence across full width of knitting.

MATERIALS

Yarn A 300 (350)g fine-weight wool (black)
Yarn B 100 (125)g thick fluffy acrylic/wool gimp (multi-colour blue)
Yarn C 100 (125)g thick fluffy acrylic/wool gimp (multi-colour brown)

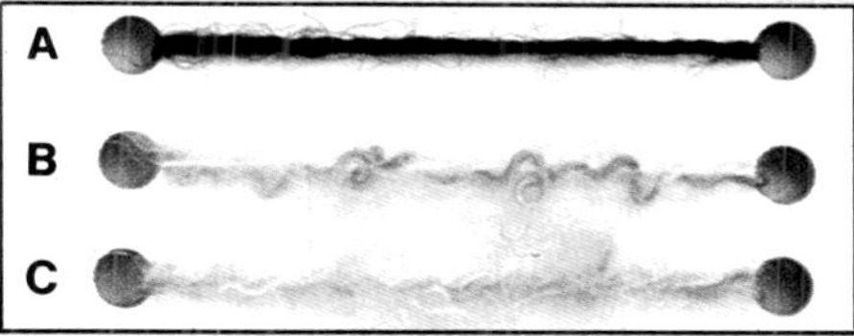

Needles
If you don't have a ribber, you need 1 pair size 2¾mm knitting needles

MEASUREMENTS

To fit chest 86 (91)cm (34, 36in)
Actual chest size 91 (96)cm (35¾, 37¾in)
Length at centre back 62.5cm (24¾in)
Sleeve seam 53.7cm (21¼in)

MAIN TENSION (MT)

28 sts and 54 rows measure 10cm over weaving and stocking stitch squares (tension dial set at approximately 3)

SPECIAL NOTE

These instructions are written for punchcard machines whose pattern needles come out to Upper Working Position.
However, the sweater can be made on other machines by following the weaving chart.
Before starting to knit, wind yarn B and yarn C into seven separate balls.

WEAVING AND STOCKING STITCH SQUARES

Punchcard machines whose pattern needles come out to UWP
Knit 1 row yarn A, weaving with 1 ball yarn B over first 6 selected needles, 1 ball yarn C over next 6 selected needles, 2nd ball yarn B over next 6 selected needles, 2nd ball yarn C over next 6 selected needles and so on across the row, alternating yarns B and C.
* Knit 6 more rows in the same way, keeping the colours as set and noting that weaving yarn lays across needles in opposite direction on every other row. Continue as follows: knit 7 rows yarn A, weaving with yarns B and C as before, but this time move each ball to the next set of selected needles to the left, thus breaking off and joining in a new ball of yarn as required at edges of work. To avoid breaking off the weaving yarn for each square, start the weaving at the bottom right hand corner of each square.
Other machines
With yarn A in feeder 1 throughout, push all needles to HP. Working from weaving chart, using separate balls of yarns B and C for each set of needles, lay weaving yarn B over needles marked B and under the adjacent unmarked needles. Lay weaving yarn C over needles marked C and under the adjacent unmarked needles and knit the row.
Continue as for punchcard machines whose pattern needles come out to UWP, above, from *.

BACK AND FRONT (alike)

Push 48 needles at extreme left of machine to WP. With carriage at left and using yarn A, cast on by hand. Insert punchcard and set to first row. Set carriage for pattern. Using MT, knit 1 row. Set RC at 000. Release card and continue in weaving and stocking stitch squares pattern. Increase 1 st at right edge on every 3rd row until there are 132 sts. RC shows 252.
Shape body: Cast on 24 sts at the beginning of the next row (156 sts). Knit 245 (259) rows. RC shows 498 (512).
Shape sleeve: Cast off 24 sts at the beginning of the next row (132 sts). Decrease 1 st at right edge on next and every following 3rd row until 48 sts remain. RC shows 749 (763). Remove card and knit 1 row yarn A in st st. Cast off.

WELTS

Machines with ribber
Push 147 (157) needles to WP. With knit side facing, pick up 147 (157) sts evenly along lower edge and place on to needles. * With ribber in position, set machine and transfer sts for 1 × 1 rib. Set RC at 000. Using MT – 1/ MT – 1 and 2 strands of yarn A together, knit 30 rows. Cast off *.
Machines without ribber
With purl side facing, using 2 strands of yarn A together and 2¾mm needles, pick up and knit 147 (157) sts evenly along lower edge.
1st rib row: P1 * k1, p1; repeat from * to end.
2nd rib row: K1, * p1, k1; repeat from * to end.
Repeat these two rows for 7cm ending with a 1st rib row. Cast off in rib.

CUFFS

Join upper sleeve seams, leaving approximately 28cm open for neck.
Machines with ribber
Push 61 needles to WP. With knit side facing, pick up 61 sts evenly along lower edge of sleeve and place on to needles. Work as for welts from * to *.
Machines without ribber
With purl side facing, join in 2 strands of yarn A together and using 2¾mm needles, pick up and knit 61 sts evenly along lower edge of sleeve. Work 7cm in rib as given for welt, ending with a 1st rib row. Cast off.

NECK FACINGS

Push 82 needles to WP. With knit side facing, pick up 82 sts evenly along neck edge and place on to needles. Set RC at 000. Using MT and yarn A, knit 20 rows. Cast off loosely.

FINISHING

With purl side of work facing, block each piece by pinning out to correct measurements. Dampen with cold, clean water and leave to dry naturally. Join side and sleeve seams. Fold neck facing to inside and slip stitch in position. Join upper sleeve seams for a further 1cm each side of neck.

PUNCHCARD
Punch this card before starting to knit

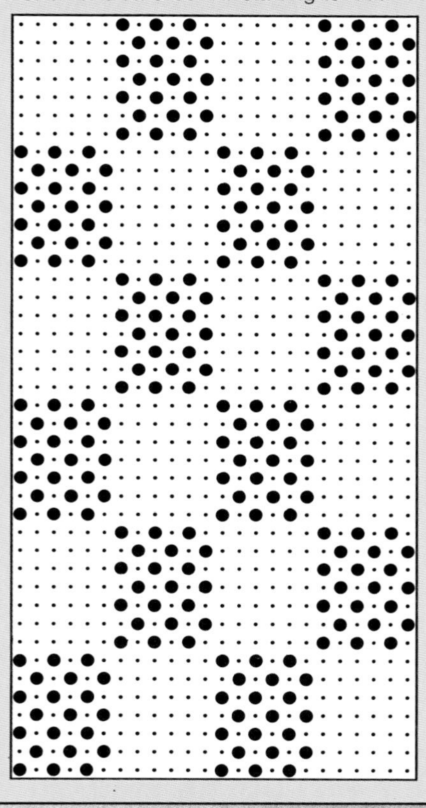

SHAPE GUIDE
All measurements are given in centimetres. Figures in brackets refer to the larger size. Where only one figure is given it applies to both sizes.

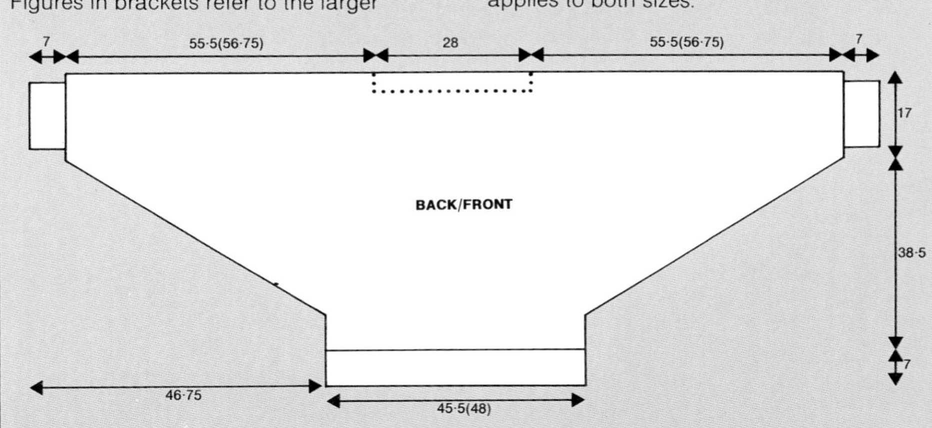

INTARSIA

Considering the great variety of shapes and images that can be produced by the intarsia method, it is surprising how little it is used. Intarsia is a technique in which colour changes can be made at any point in the knitted row, without having the second yarn floating along the back of the

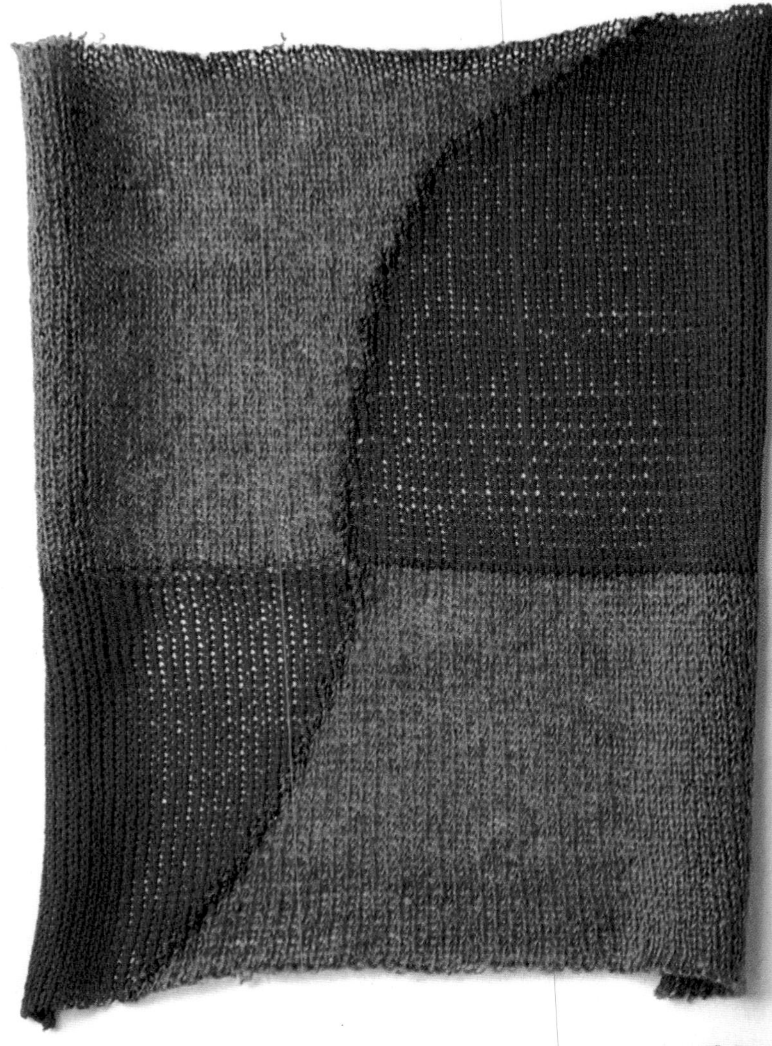

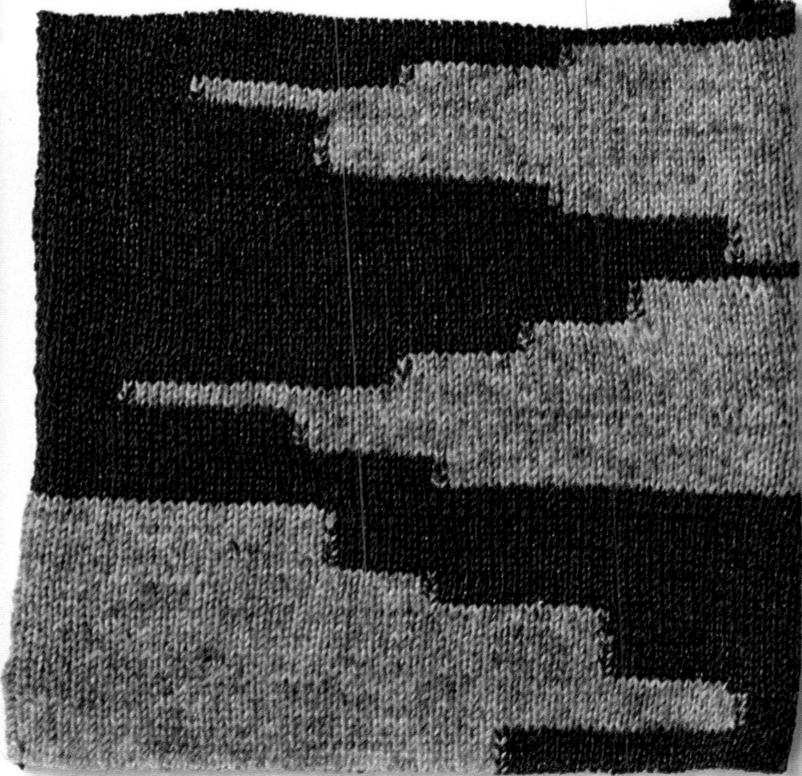

fabric. Using this technique, there is no limit to the number of colours that may be knitted in one row, and because there are no floats, large or small motifs may be knitted. The beauty of intarsia is the dramatic design statements which can be knitted and the ease with which large scale motifs can be created. With careful use of colour, intarsia designs do not have to be complicated, quite simple ideas can work well.

The technique
Different coloured yarns are laid across the open latches of the needles in the order required; at the point where two yarns meet, the adjoining yarns are crossed over the same needle. In many basic machines you just have to take the ordinary carriage across the needles to knit the row. Generally, with the more sophisticated punchcard and electronic machines you must use a special intarsia carriage. Whichever sort of machine you have, feed the yarn into the needle bed from the floor, not from the tension unit. You may find this technique time-consuming to begin with, since the yarns have to be manually looped around the needles in the order required for each row. However, with a little practice you will become proficient, and able to produce the most complicated pictorial sweaters.

Working out Intarsia designs
The range of designs open to the knitter using this structure is enormous. It is advisable to start on simple straight line patterns before going on to more complicated designs and curved shapes. To start with use only two colours, involving just one yarn change and then, as you gain confidence, introduce more colour changes. Remember that you will need a separate ball of yarn for each shape you knit.

A very basic intarsia design is the chequerboard, or quarter sweater. This is formed by dividing the front of a sweater into quarters. Using the chequerboard as a starting point, a variety of intarsia designs may be developed. The chequerboard idea has been used in the intarsia sweater shown overleaf. It has been made more interesting by breaking the front and back panels of the sweater into nine colour areas, and using a zig zag line at the point where the colours change.

Intarsia is one of the few knitting techniques which can be sampled simply on paper. By cutting sheets of paper to the shape of your sweater, intarsia designs can be drawn and coloured in quickly and easily. Do not be discouraged if you feel you are not very good at drawing. These are simply meant to be working sketches to help you become more adventurous and inventive.

Before starting to knit, designs should be worked out to scale. This can be done with a full-size graphed pattern, or by using your sketched pattern idea in conjunction with mathematical calculations. The styling details of the neck and arm insets should be carefully considered in relation to the intarsia pattern, too. Thinking out detailing carefully can make all the difference between a truly stylish sweater, and a slightly confused garment.

Experimenting with colours and yarns
Colour is very important in all intarsia work and should be thought about carefully and practically before a garment is embarked upon. Yarns can look very different when knitted, compared to how they look on their cone, especially when combined with other colours.

Traditionally, fancy yarns are not used much in intarsia work, but there is no reason why they shouldn't be tried; attractive effects can be obtained with interesting yarns. When using textured yarns, extra care should be taken that stitches do not jump off the needles, particularly at the point where the colours and yarns change. This can easily happen if the carriage is taken across quickly without care. Weighting the knitting will help to prevent this problem.

PATTERN INSTRUCTIONS FOR PATCHES

Soft pastel shades or bright eye-catching colours look equally good on this lightweight sweater. The zigzag stripes that separate the squares of colour on the front and back are echoed in the picot-edge neckline.

MATERIALS

Yarn
Yarn A 125 (150, 175)g medium-weight Shetland wool (blue)
Yarn B 125 (150, 175)g medium-weight Shetland wool (pink)
Yarn C 125 (150, 175)g medium-weight Shetland wool (green)

Needles
If you don't have a ribber you need 1 pair size 2¾mm knitting needles

MEASUREMENTS

To fit chest 86 (91, 97)cm (34, 36, 38in)
Actual chest size 94 (98, 103)cm (37, 38½, 40½in)
Length to shoulder 62cm (24½in)
Sleeve seam 14cm (5½in)

MAIN TENSION (MT)

34 sts and 40 rows measure 10cm over stocking stitch (tension dial set at approximately 5)

SPECIAL NOTE

Needles in NWP are counted as sts throughout

BACK AND FRONT (alike)

Machines with ribber
With ribber in position and carriage at right, set machine for 1 × 1 rib. Using yarn A, cast on 159 (167, 175) sts in 1 × 1 rib. Knit 5 tubular/circular rows. Set carriage for 1 × 1 rib knitting. Set RC at 000. Using MT—1/MT—1, knit 30 rows. Transfer sts for st st. Increase 1 st (160, 168, 176 sts).
Machines without ribber
Using yarn A and 2¾mm needles, cast on 159 (167, 175) sts.
1st rib row: K1 * p1, k1; rep from * to end.
2nd rib row: P1 * k1, p1; rep from * to end.
Repeat these 2 rows for 7cm, ending with a 1st rib row. Push 159 (167, 175) needles to WP. With carriage at right, transfer sts to machine needles. Increase 1 st.
All machines
Set RC at 000. Using MT and yarns A, B and C work Intarsia pattern as given on chart, overleaf. Knit 122 rows.
Shape armholes: Cast off 6 sts at the beginning of the next 2 rows. Decrease 1 st at each end of every row until 134 (142, 150) sts remain, then every following alternate row until 128 (134, 140) sts remain. Knit 83 (81, 79) rows. RC shows 220.
Shape shoulders: Cast off 24 (27, 30) sts at the beginning of the next 2 rows (80 sts). Intarsia pattern completed.
Neck facing: Counting from the right edge, the needles are numbered 1 to 80. Transfer the 1st st on to the 2nd needle, the 5th st on to the 4th needle, the 6th st on to the 7th needle, the 10th st on to the 9th needle, and so on across the row. Push the empty needles to NWP, thus leaving 1 needle in NWP, 3 needles in WP, (2 needles in NWP, 3 needles in WP) along the row ending with 1 needle in NWP. Using yarn A, knit 1 row. Transfer the 2nd st on to the 3rd needle, the 4th st on to the 3rd needle, the 7th st on to the 8th needle, the 9th st on to the 8th needle and so on across the row. Push the empty needles to NWP, thus leaving 2 needles in NWP, 1 needle in WP, (4 needles in NWP, 1 needle in WP) along the row

INTARSIA CHART

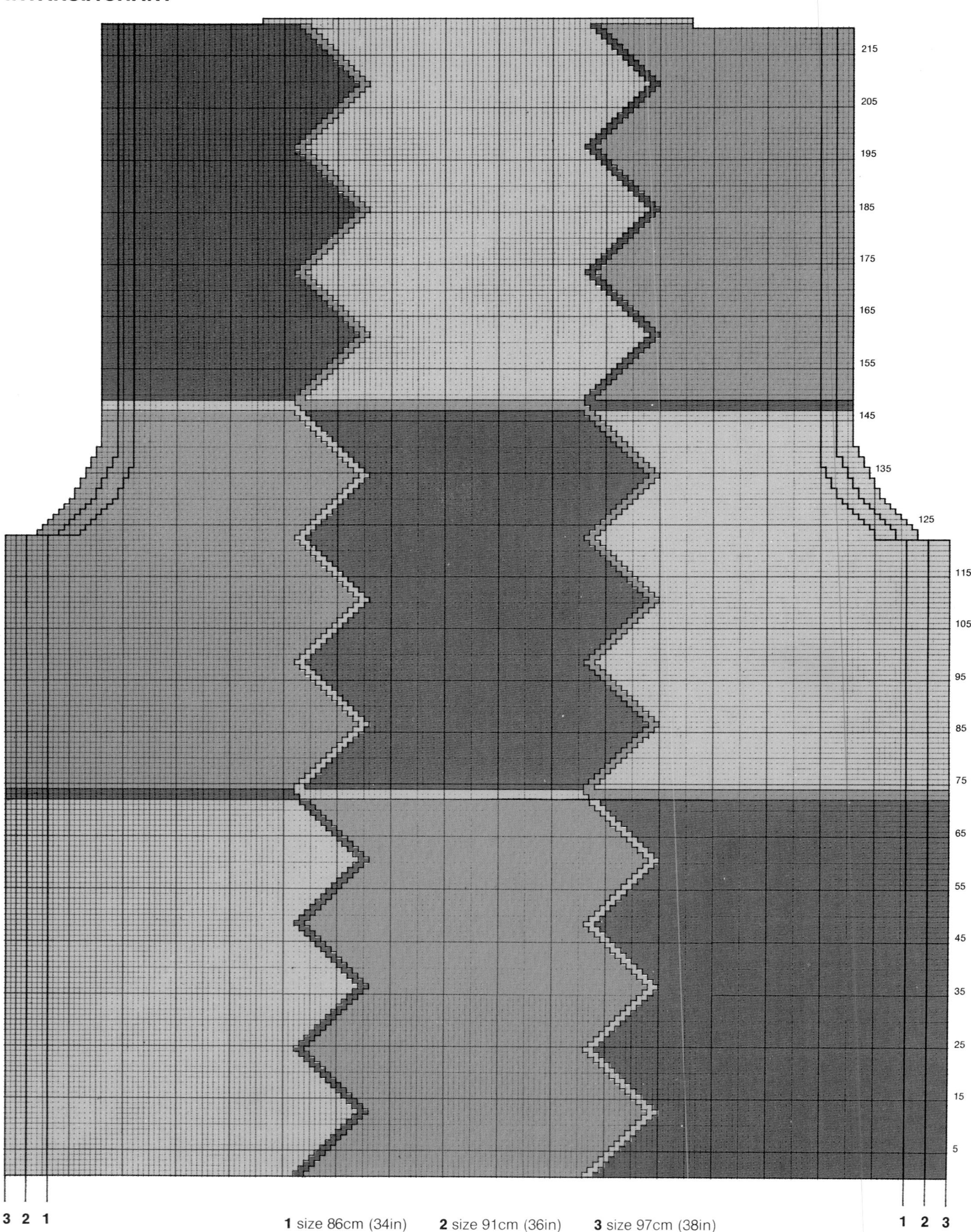

1 size 86cm (34in) **2** size 91cm (36in) **3** size 97cm (38in)

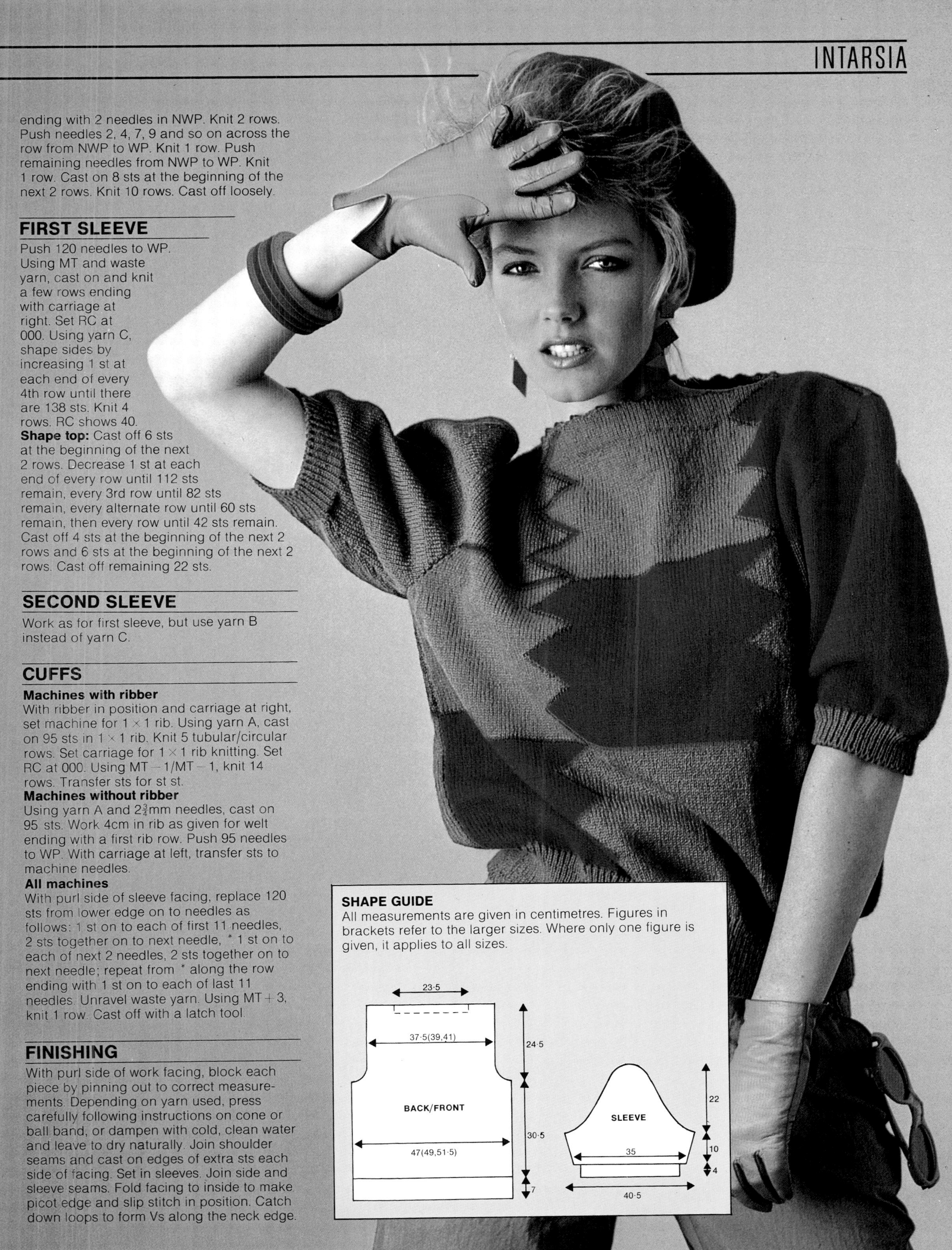

ending with 2 needles in NWP. Knit 2 rows. Push needles 2, 4, 7, 9 and so on across the row from NWP to WP. Knit 1 row. Push remaining needles from NWP to WP. Knit 1 row. Cast on 8 sts at the beginning of the next 2 rows. Knit 10 rows. Cast off loosely.

FIRST SLEEVE

Push 120 needles to WP. Using MT and waste yarn, cast on and knit a few rows ending with carriage at right. Set RC at 000. Using yarn C, shape sides by increasing 1 st at each end of every 4th row until there are 138 sts. Knit 4 rows. RC shows 40.

Shape top: Cast off 6 sts at the beginning of the next 2 rows. Decrease 1 st at each end of every row until 112 sts remain, every 3rd row until 82 sts remain, every alternate row until 60 sts remain, then every row until 42 sts remain. Cast off 4 sts at the beginning of the next 2 rows and 6 sts at the beginning of the next 2 rows. Cast off remaining 22 sts.

SECOND SLEEVE

Work as for first sleeve, but use yarn B instead of yarn C.

CUFFS

Machines with ribber

With ribber in position and carriage at right, set machine for 1 × 1 rib. Using yarn A, cast on 95 sts in 1 × 1 rib. Knit 5 tubular/circular rows. Set carriage for 1 × 1 rib knitting. Set RC at 000. Using MT − 1/MT − 1, knit 14 rows. Transfer sts for st st.

Machines without ribber

Using yarn A and 2¾mm needles, cast on 95 sts. Work 4cm in rib as given for welt ending with a first rib row. Push 95 needles to WP. With carriage at left, transfer sts to machine needles.

All machines

With purl side of sleeve facing, replace 120 sts from lower edge on to needles as follows: 1 st on to each of first 11 needles, 2 sts together on to next needle, * 1 st on to each of next 2 needles, 2 sts together on to next needle; repeat from * along the row ending with 1 st on to each of last 11 needles. Unravel waste yarn. Using MT + 3, knit 1 row. Cast off with a latch tool.

FINISHING

With purl side of work facing, block each piece by pinning out to correct measurements. Depending on yarn used, press carefully following instructions on cone or ball band, or dampen with cold, clean water and leave to dry naturally. Join shoulder seams and cast on edges of extra sts each side of facing. Set in sleeves. Join side and sleeve seams. Fold facing to inside to make picot edge and slip stitch in position. Catch down loops to form Vs along the neck edge.

SHAPE GUIDE

All measurements are given in centimetres. Figures in brackets refer to the larger sizes. Where only one figure is given, it applies to all sizes.

LACE·KNITTING

Lace fabrics can be produced by transferring stitches to a neighbouring needle so that holes appear in the fabric, or by working certain stitch constructions, such as tuck stitch, with fine yarns and a loose tension. This first method is known as stitch transfer lace, and the samples and garments in this section are all made by this method.

Stitches may be transferred by hand, using the transfer tool supplied with all knitting machines, but it can take a long time to transfer a large number of stitches. All the major manufacturers produce special lace carriages which can do the transferring automatically. For some machines, the lace carriage transfers the stitches *and* knits, but others have to be used in addition to the ordinary carriage, i.e. the lace carriage only transfers the stitches, it does not knit them. Consequently, sometimes slightly different punchcards have to be used for the different types of lace carriages. Where this is the case for the lace sweaters in this section, we have shown two different punchcards.

All the sweaters and samples in this section were made using a lace carriage which transfers stitches only. Sometimes it is impossible to produce exactly the same pattern with a lace carriage which transfers stitches and knits them. Where this is the case we have provided a punchcard which produces a very similar pattern to that illustrated.

Transferring stitches
Usually lace patterns incorporate stitches transferred to the left and to the right. If stitches are constantly transferred in only one direction, the fabric will bias. Only single stitches may be selected as pattern stitches – there must be at least one plain stitch on either side of the pattern stitch. There should also be two rows of plain knitting before repeating a lace stitch on the same needle.

Working out lace designs
If you are devising your own lace designs try out your ideas on graph paper before punching a card or drawing a graph. Some knitters plot out their patterns straight on to the graph or punchcard. However, this doesn't allow for possible mistakes and can be wasteful. By planning designs first on paper, a variety of ideas can be worked out, and, if necessary, modified until a satisfactory pattern is achieved. This approach also encourages invention and experimentation before you commit yourself to a punchcard. Actually seeing your idea dotted out may spark off better ideas or modifications which improve your original thought. For example, a lace pattern forming checks and stripes can be sketched in so that it is possible to see the remaining blank areas where, if desired, small lace motifs can be added. These areas can be altered until the best shape and proportion in relation to the check or stripe has been achieved. A little time spent at this stage will be rewarded by more original lace patterns. For hand stitch transfer the same preparation is needed, since a graph is needed for guidance for all but the simplest of designs.

Sampling
Once you have decided on a design and started knitting, it is important to be just as adventurous in sampling lace patterns as with any other knitting technique. Using colour in unusual ways can produce optical effects which create patterns within the lace structure itself. A variety of unique

Stitch construction A stitch is transferred from its needle to the next needle, and the knitting is continued. The empty needle picks up the new yarn and continues to knit, leaving a hole where the stitch was transferred.

Pattern variations using punchcard on p. 91
Samples show the effect of using different colours and yarns.

designs can be produced by introducing plain knitted areas or stripes between the lace knitting.

All-over lace
When using a lace pattern all over a garment, care must be taken to ensure that the lace fabric is not too transparent, otherwise an underment will have to be worn. To produce lace fabrics that are solid enough to be worn without something underneath, the knitted lace must be designed so that solid areas of knitting are interspersed with lace. The all-over lace pattern used on *Northern Lights* is based on a diamond shape. Solid areas of knitting are left between the transferred stitches, this produces a light, drapable fabric, suitable for a variety of sweater styles.

PATTERN INSTRUCTIONS FOR
NORTHERN LIGHTS

A versatile summer top suitable for day and evening has been created from this lovely soft, draping lace fabric. Glass drop beads add elegance to the fluted neckline and the large full sleeves are gathered into the armhole and cuff.

MATERIALS

Yarn
Yarn A 300g medium-weight cotton/acrylic mixture yarn (multi-colour)

A 

Notions
50 drop beads 1cm long
Needles
If you don't have a ribber, you need 1 pair size 2¾mm knitting needles

MEASUREMENTS

To fit chest 86-97cm (34-38in)
Actual chest size 106cm (41¾in)
Length to shoulder 49cm (19¼in)
Sleeve seam 10.5cm (4¼in)

MAIN TENSION (MT)

30 sts and 46 rows measure 10cm over lace pattern (tension dial set at approximately 4)

SPECIAL NOTE

For knitters with a lace carriage which transfers stitches and does not knit them.
This sweater illustrates how pattern variations on a punchcard may be achieved by altering the sequence of the lace and knit carriages. The samples on these pages were made by operating the lace and knit carriages as indicated by the arrows on the side of the punchcard. The sweater illustrated overleaf was made with the same punchcard, but with the following carriage sequence:

Lock punchcard on starting line. Take lace carriage from left to right. Release card and take the lace carriage across three more times (lace carriage is back at left). * Knit two rows with the knit carriage. Take the lace carriage across four times; repeat from * throughout. Sometimes needles will come forward for selection, but they will automatically be knitted back by the knit carriage. Just continue working four rows with the lace carriage and two rows with the knit carriage. You'll find that on two complete revolutions of the card different needles will be selected for patterning. This adds to the intricacy of the design.

For knitters with a lace carriage which transfers stitches and knits them
The lace pattern produced will be slightly different from that shown in the samples and in the sweater.

BACK

Push 80 needles at left and right of centre 0 to WP (160 needles). With carriage at left and using yarn A, cast on by hand. Insert punchcard and lock on first row. Set carriage for pattern. Set RC at 000. Using MT, knit 1 row. Release card and continue in lace pattern. Knit 100 rows. RC shows 101.
Shape armholes: Cast off 8 sts at the beginning of the next 2 rows. Decrease 1 st at each end of every alternate row until 120 sts remain *. Knit 80 rows. RC shows 207.
Shape neck: Using a length of yarn A, cast off centre 34 sts. Note pattern row on card. Using nylon cord, knit 43 sts at left by hand taking needles down to NWP. Continue on remaining sts for first side. Decrease 1 st at neck edge on every row until 24 sts remain. Knit 5 rows. Cast off. With carriage at left, unravel nylon cord over remaining needles bringing needles back to WP. Lock card on number previously noted. Take carriage to right without knitting. Release card and continue in lace pattern. Finish to correspond with first side reversing shapings.

FRONT

Work as for back to *. Knit 62 rows. RC shows 189.
Shape neck: Using a length of yarn A, cast off centre 24 sts. Note pattern row on card. Using nylon cord, knit 48 sts at left by hand taking needles down to NWP. Continue on remaining sts for first side.
Decrease 1 st at neck edge on every row until 36 sts remain, then on every following alternate row until 24 sts remain. Knit 6 rows. Cast off. With carriage at left, unravel nylon cord over remaining needles bringing needles back to WP. Lock card on number previously noted. Take carriage to right without knitting. Release card and continue in lace pattern. Finish to correspond with first side reversing shapings.

SLEEVES

Push 92 needles at left and right of centre 0 to WP (184 needles). With carriage at left and using yarn A, cast on by hand. Insert punchcard and lock on first row. Set carriage for pattern. Set RC at 000. Using MT, knit 1 row. Release card and continue in lace pattern. Shape sides by increasing 1 st at each end of every following 4th row until there are 200 sts. Knit 4 rows. RC shows 37.
Shape top: Cast off 12 sts at beginning of next 2 rows. Decrease 1 st at each end of every 4th row until 124 sts remain, then on every row until 100 sts remain. Cast off 2 sts at beginning of next 4 rows, 4 sts at beginning of next 4 rows and 6 sts at beginning of next 4 rows. Cast off remaining 52 sts.

CUFFS

Machines with ribber
With ribber in position, set machine for full needle (double) rib. Push 48 needles on knitter and ribber to WP. Using yarn A, cast on. Work 5 tubular/circular rows. Set carriage for full needle (double) rib knitting. Set RC at 000. Using MT—1/MT—1, work 12 rows. Transfer ribber sts to knitter. Cast off.
Machines without ribber
Using yarn A and $2\frac{3}{4}$mm needles, cast on 96 sts. Work 2.5cm in k1, p1 rib. Cast off in rib.

NECKBAND

Machines with ribber
With ribber in position, set machine for full needle (double) rib. Push 149 needles on knitter and ribber to WP. Using yarn A, cast on. Work 5 tubular/circular rows. Set carriage for full needle (double) rib knitting. Set RC at 000. Using MT—1/MT—1, work 12 rows. Transfer ribber sts to knitter. Cast off.
Machines without ribber
Using yarn A and $2\frac{3}{4}$mm needles, cast on 298 sts. Work 2.5cm in k1, p1 rib. Cast off in rib.

FINISHING

With purl side of work facing, block each piece by pinning out to correct measurements. Depending on yarn used, press carefully following instructions on ball or cone band, or dampen with cold, clean water and leave to dry naturally. Join shoulder, side and sleeve seams. Set in sleeves gathering tops to fit the armhole. Join ends of cuffs. Gather lower edges of sleeves and sew on cuffs. Turn 1cm at lower edge to inside and catch down. Join ends of neckband. Sew cast off edge of neckband into position. Fold in half to right side and catch down securely with a few stitches at approximately 6cm intervals, to make a fluted neckline. Sew beads at these points, and on the inside at halfway point between these points on the foldline of the neckband. Sew beads at intervals around the lower edge of the sweater.

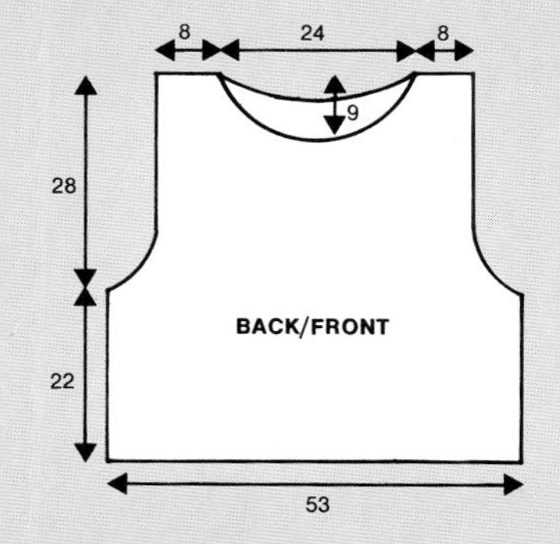

SHAPE GUIDE
All measurements are given in centimetres

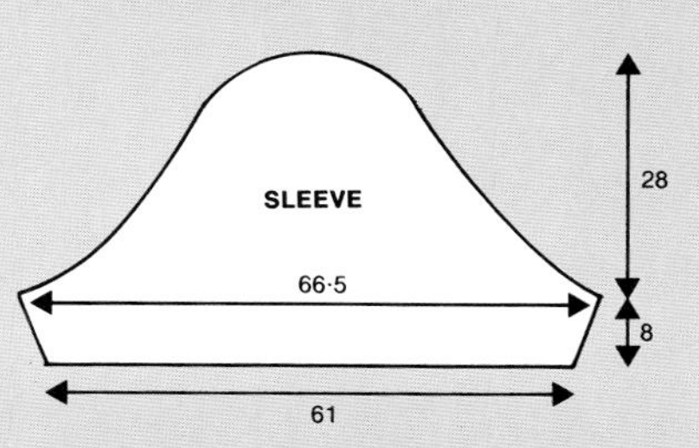

PUNCHCARDS
Depending on whether you have a lace carriage which transfers stitches *and* knits them, or one which just transfers stitches, punch one of these cards before starting to knit

Key
→ Move lace carriage from left to right
← Move lace carriage from right to left
↪ Knit two rows with the knit carriage, if applicable

Punchcard 1
For a lace carriage which transfers stitches and knits them
This will result in a sweater with a diamond lace pattern similar to the samples on page 88.

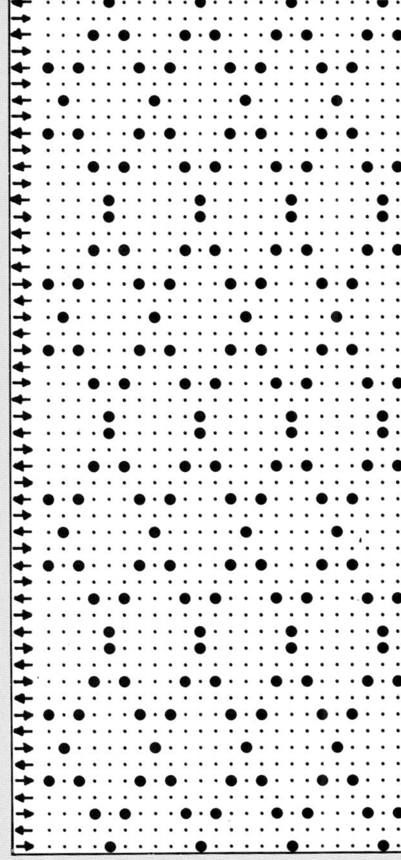

Punchcard 2
For a lace carriage which transfers stitches only
This will result in a sweater with the same diamond lace pattern as shown in the samples on page 88.

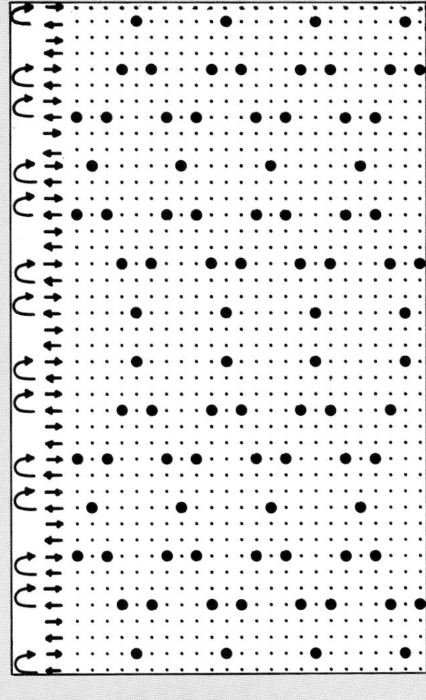

LACE·IN BLOCKS

Lace knitting need not be used only as an all-over fabric, but can also be used as insets, as shown on pages 96-99, or in blocks, as shown here. Using lace knitting in these ways provides textural contrasts in one garment. Also, if your lace fabric is too transparent for a conventional all-over garment, it may be used in selected areas.

Experimenting with lace patterns
When carrying out stitch transfer on relatively small areas of knitting, it is sometimes advantageous to use the hand method, rather than a punchcard or electronic graph in combination with a lace carriage, since hand stitch transfer leaves far more scope for adventurous pattern variations. You can change the lace patterning as you wish, producing randomly-spaced areas of lace over a garment. Using punchcards or graphs fed into the machine can limit the technique. You have to be even more inventive and experimental to create variations from one punchcard lace pattern.

One obvious development is to introduce plain knitting between the lace patterning, as shown in the *Pinstripe* sweater. The plain knitting does not have to be regularly spaced, but can interrupt the lace patterning wherever you wish. It is surprising how different a design can look when the lace patterning is broken up in this way, particularly when colour and fancy yarn changes are also used.

Pattern variations using punchcard on p. 94
Samples show the effect of using different colours and yarns, and varying the number of stocking stitch rows worked.

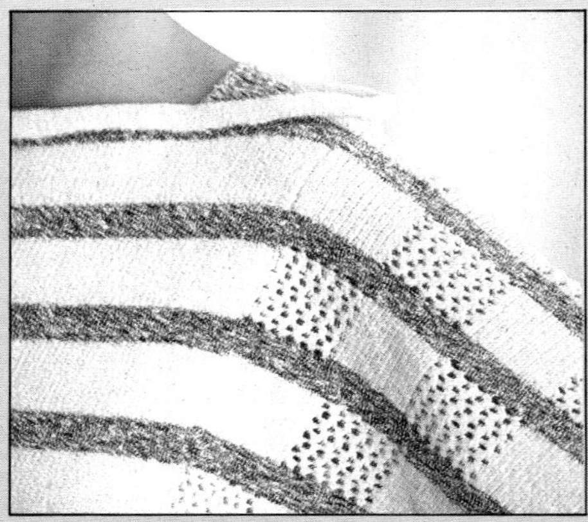

Detail of *Pinstripe* showing roll collar, shoulder gusset and lace blocks.

PATTERN INSTRUCTIONS FOR
PINSTRIPE

This sweater shows how large areas of solid plain knitting may be incorporated with a lace pattern. The basic sweater shape is made from four pieces, when sewing together match the stripes carefully. The addition of the shoulder gussets gives interest to the shoulder line.

MATERIALS

Yarn
Yarn A 350g thick cotton chenille (natural)
Yarn B 100g medium-weight cotton gimp/ knop (black/white)

Needles
If you don't have a ribber, you need one pair size 2¾mm knitting needles

MEASUREMENTS

To fit chest 81-91cm (32-36in)
Actual chest size 99cm (39in)
Length to base of neckband 51.5cm (20¼in)

MAIN TENSION (MT)

29 sts and 44 rows measure 10cm over stocking stitch (tension dial set at approximately 6)
26 sts and 44 rows measure 10cm over lace pattern (tension dial set at approximately 6)

SPECIAL NOTE

For knitters with a lace carriage which transfers stitches and knits them
Using the punchcard given overleaf, the lace pattern produced will be slightly different from that shown in the samples and in the sweater. Also, because the stitches are repeatedly transferred in the same direction, depending on the yarn and tension you use, you may find your fabric biases. In order to prevent this, and at the same time match the pattern at the front and back, while working the eight stocking stitch rows take the carriage to the opposite side of the needle bed without knitting a row. Yarn B will have to be broken off and joined in again at the other side. Don't forget to lock your card, then release it, to keep the pattern correct.

PLAIN LACE PATTERN

Knit 18 rows yarn A and 8 rows yarn B.

CENTRE BACK AND CENTRE FRONT PANELS (alike)

Push 86 needles to WP. Using MT and waste yarn, cast on and knit a few rows ending with carriage at right. Set RC at 000. Using yarn A, knit 20 rows. Working in stripes of 8 rows yarn B and 18 rows yarn A, knit 190 rows. RC shows 210.
Shape neck: Cast on 5 sts at beginning of the next 2 rows (96 sts). Knit 10 rows. Cast off

SLEEVE AND SIDE PANELS

Push needles 12 to 37 inclusive at right of centre 0 to WP (26 needles). Using MT and waste yarn, cast on and knit a few rows ending with carriage at right. Set RC at 000. Using yarn A, knit 1 row. Insert punchcard and lock on first row. Set carriage for lace pattern. Knit 1 row. Release card and continue in plain lace pattern. Knit 64 rows. Increase 1 st at left edge on next and every following 3rd row until there are 42 sts. Knit 1 row. Cast on 4 sts at the beginning of the next and every following alternate row until there are 134 sts. Knit 61 rows. RC shows 219. Place marker at right edge. Knit 62 rows. Cast off 4 sts at the beginning of the next and every following alternate row until 42 sts remain. Knit 1 row. Decrease 1 st at left edge on next and every following 3rd row until 26 sts remain. Knit 63 rows. Break off yarn B and continue in yarn A. Knit 2 rows. RC shows 438. Using waste yarn, knit a few rows in st st and release work from machine.

SHOULDER GUSSETS

Using yarn B, cast on 18 sts by hand. Set RC at 000. Using MT, knit 28 rows. Decrease 1 st at each end of the next and every following alternate row until 8 sts remain. Knit 1 row. Cast off. Make two.

CUFFS

Machines with ribber
With ribber in position, set machine for 1 × 1 rib. Using yarn B, cast on 52 sts in 1 × 1 rib. Work 5 tubular/circular rows. Set carriage for 1 × 1 rib knitting. Set RC at 000. Using MT – 1, work 20 rows. Transfer sts to main bed. With purl side of sleeve facing, pick up 52 sts and place on to needles. Cast off.

Machines without ribber
With knit side facing, using 2¾mm needles and yarn B, pick up 52 sts from sleeve. Work in k1, p1 rib until work measures 4cm. Cast off in rib.

WELTS

Matching stripes, join centre back and centre front panels to side panels. Join neckband extensions to side panels up to markers. Join neckband seams.

Machines with ribber
With ribber in position, set machine for 1 × 1 rib. Using yarn B, cast on 118 sts in 1 × 1 rib. Work 5 tubular/circular rows. Set carriage for 1 × 1 rib knitting. Set RC at 000. Using MT – 1, work 20 rows. Transfer sts to main bed. With purl side facing, pick up 138 sts from lower edge and place on to needles as follows: 1 st on to each of first 2 needles, 2 sts together on to next needle, * 1 st on to each of next 5 needles, 2 sts together on to next needle; repeat from * along the row ending with 1 st on to last needle. Unravel waste yarn. Cast off.

Machines without ribber
With purl side facing, using 2¾mm needles pick up 138 sts from lower edge. With knit side facing, using yarn B, k 2 sts, k2tog, * k 5 sts, k2tog; repeat from * to last st, k 1 st (118 sts). Work in k1, p1 rib until work measures 4cm. Cast off in rib.

SHAPE GUIDE
All measurements are given in centimetres.

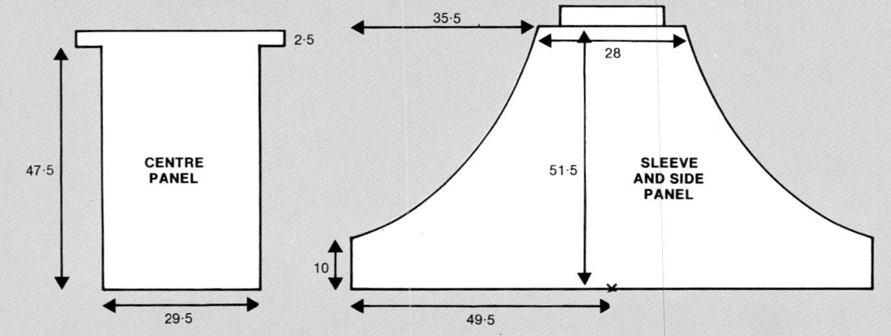

PUNCHCARDS
Depending on whether you have a lace carriage which transfers stitches *and* knits them, or one which just transfers stitches, punch one of these cards before starting to knit.

Key
→ Move lace carriage from left to right
← Move lace carriage from right to left
↪ Knit two rows with yarn A with the knit carriage, if applicable
8 Knit 8 rows with yarn B with the knit carriage, if applicable

Punchcard 1
For a lace carriage which transfers stitches and knits them. This will result in a sweater with a square pattern similar to the one shown.

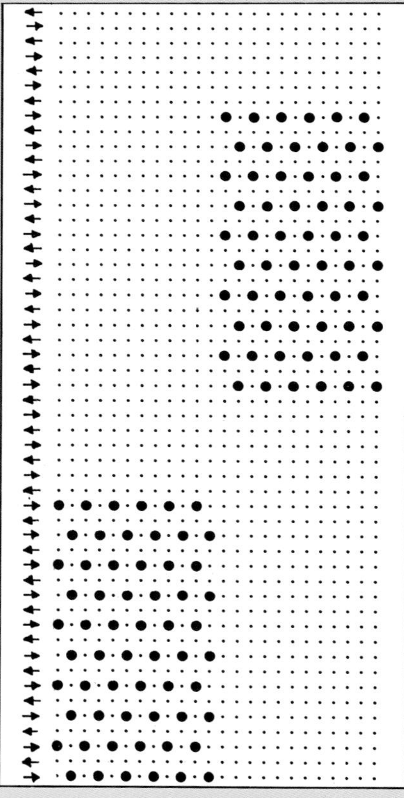

Punchcard 2
For a lace carriage which transfers stitches only. This will result in a sweater with a square pattern the same as the one shown.

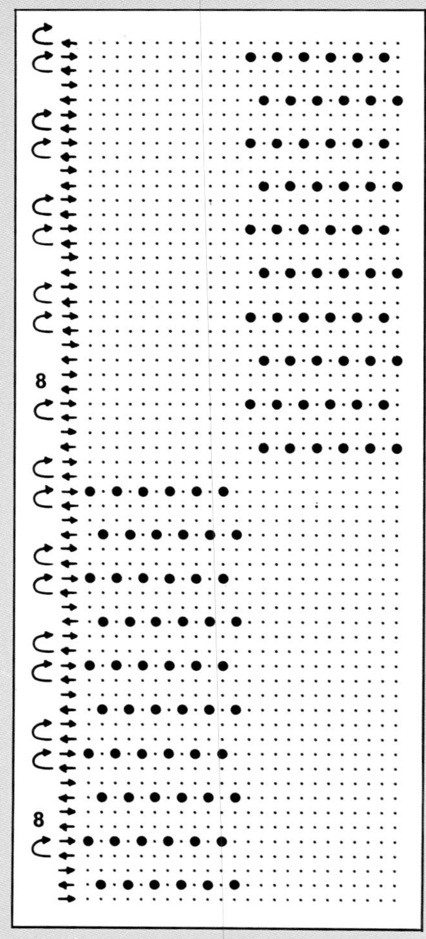

FINISHING

With purl side of work facing, block each piece by pinning out to correct measurements. Depending on yarn used, press very carefully (omitting neck edge which should be allowed to roll) or dampen with cold, clean water and leave to dry naturally. Join side and sleeve seams. Sew shoulder gussets into position under neckband.

LACE·INSETS

Whereas the previous sweater demonstrated the use of small areas of lace, the lace sweater on the next page shows one way of using lace patterns for specific parts of a garment. Since lace fabrics are so different in appearance and handling from other types of fabric, lace is an excellent stitch pattern to use in large or small areas to create contrast.

Working out designs
Garments may be designed in which the various areas of different stitch constructions are knitted separately, then sewn together. Thus, fabric can be inserted at the sewing together stage, or, with clever planning, you may be able to knit the plain areas and the lace in one piece. Once again, sketching your ideas before knitting will help you create original garments. The more you play around with the sweater shape and the different areas of lace, the more you will realise just how many options are open to you.

One important point to remember is that lace fabrics hang differently from more solidly knitted fabrics. They are usually fairly fine, and drape well. This can be used as a design feature; for example, you could create a very unusual sweater with a solid front, and a lace back.

Experimenting with colours and yarns
Lace patterns can become more exciting when different types of yarns are combined. For instance, if you alternate stripes of lace knitted in a fluffy yarn with stripes of lace knitted in straight yarn, you will find that the fluffy yarn conceals the holes while the straight yarn reveals them. Fine glitter yarn mixed with straight cotton yarn will produce a spider's web effect. As with any other stitch construction, however, you should experiment with many types of yarn. For example, lace patterns can look very effective when worked in thick yarns on a chunky machine.

Pattern variations using punchcard on p. 98
❶ ❸ Selection of colours and yarns altered
❷ ❹ ❺ Plain stripes introduced into the lace design

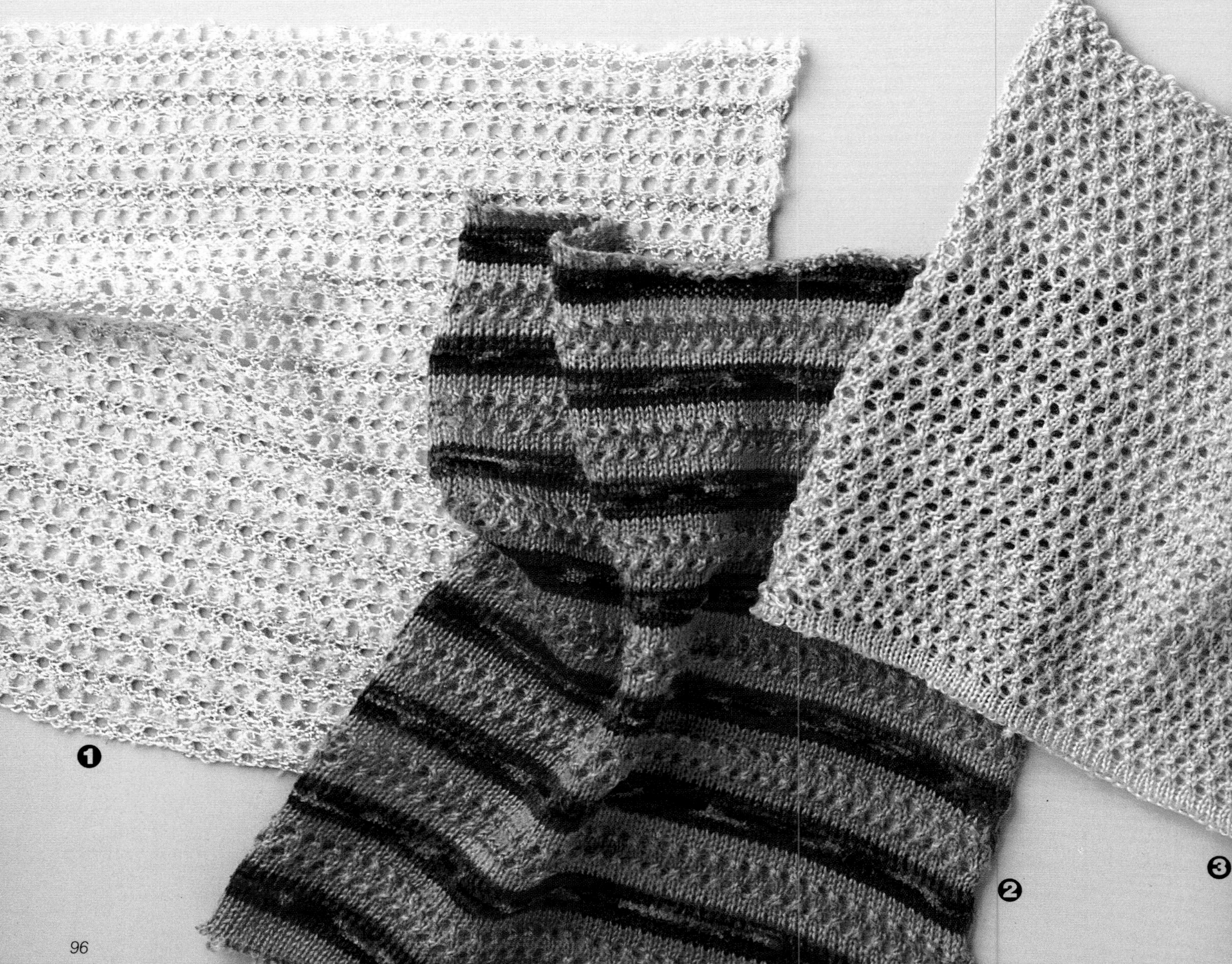

PATTERN INSTRUCTIONS FOR
GUINIVERE

Two different stitch techniques, lace stitch and tuck stitch, have been combined in this long-sleeved, high-necked sweater. Dress it up for a glamorous evening look, or keep it simple for daytime wear.

MATERIALS

Yarn

Yarn A 550 (575)g medium-weight cotton/acrylic mixture yarn (multi-colour)
Yarn B 100 (125)g fine-weight mercerised cotton (pink)

Needles

1 pair size $2\frac{3}{4}$mm

MEASUREMENTS

To fit chest 81 (91)cm (32, 36in)
Actual chest size 90 (98)cm ($35\frac{1}{2}$, $38\frac{1}{2}$in)
Length to shoulder 52.5 (57.5)cm ($20\frac{3}{4}$, $22\frac{3}{4}$in)
Sleeve seam 39 (43)cm ($15\frac{1}{2}$, 17in)

MAIN TENSION (MT)

30 sts and 112 rows measure 10cm over tuck stitch pattern on MT (tension dial set at approximately 4)
28 sts and 48 rows measure 10cm over lace pattern on MT+2 (tension dial set at approximately 6)

SPECIAL NOTE

If you have a lace carriage which transfers stitches and knits them, the lace pattern produced with punchcard 2 will differ slightly from that shown in the samples and in the sweater.

TUCK STITCH PATTERN

Knit 6 rows yarn B and 2 rows yarn A.

BACK

Using yarn A and $2\frac{3}{4}$mm needles, cast on 136 (148) sts. Work 5cm in k1, p1 rib. Push 136 (148) needles to WP. With carriage at left, transfer sts to machine needles. Insert punchcard 1 and lock on first row. Set carriage for pattern. Take carriage to right without knitting. Release card and continue in tuck stitch pattern. Set RC at 000. Using MT, knit 296 (328) rows.

Shape armholes: Cast off 4 sts at the beginning of the next 2 rows and 3 sts at the beginning of the following 2 rows. Decrease 1 st at each end of every row until 112 (120) sts remain, then on every following alternate row until 108 (116) sts remain. Knit 63 (61) rows. RC shows 372 (404). Remove card. Using waste yarn, knit a few rows in st st and release from machine leaving needles in WP. With carriage at left and knit side facing, replace sts on to needles. Unravel waste yarn. Insert punchcard 2 and lock on first

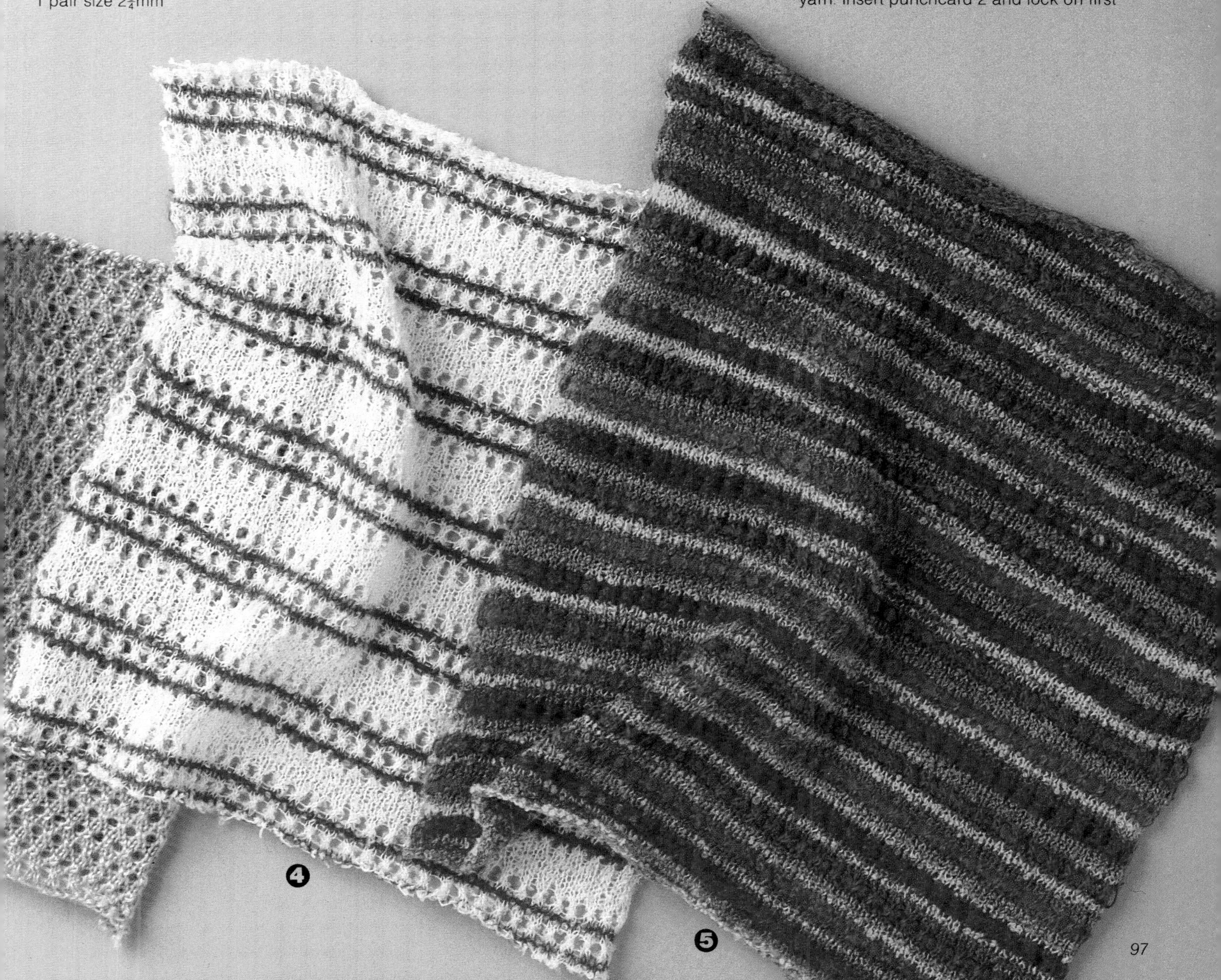

4

5

row. Set carriage for pattern. Set RC at 000. Using MT+2 and yarn A, knit 1 row. Release card and continue in lace pattern *. Knit 56 (66) rows. RC shows 57 (67).
Shape neck: Using a length of yarn A, cast off centre 24 sts. Using nylon cord, knit 42 (46) sts at left by hand taking needles down to NWP. Note pattern row on card. Continue on remaining sts for first side. Knit 1 row. Cast off 4 sts at the beginning of the next and following 2 alternate rows, knit 1 row. Cast off 2 sts at beginning of next row (28, 32 sts). Knit 4 rows. Cast off. With carriage at left, unravel nylon cord bringing needles back to WP. Lock card on number previously noted. Set carriage for pattern and take to right without knitting. Release card and continue in lace pattern. Knit 1 row. Finish to correspond with first side, reversing shapings.

FRONT

Work as for back to *. Knit 52 (62) rows.
Shape neck: Using a length of yarn A, cast off centre 24 sts. Using nylon cord, knit 42 (46) sts at left by hand taking needles down to NWP. Note pattern row on card. Continue on remaining sts for first side. Decrease 1 st at neck edge on every row until 30 (34) sts remain, then on every following alternate row until 28 (32) sts remain. Cast off.
With carriage at left, unravel nylon cord over remaining needles bringing needles back to WP. Lock card on number previously noted. Set carriage for pattern and take to right without knitting. Release card and continue in lace pattern. Finish to correspond with first side reversing shapings.

SLEEVES

Using yarn A and 2¾mm needles, cast on 56 (60) sts. Work 3cm in k1, p1 rib.
Next row: Rib 1 (3), increase in next st, * rib 3, increase in next st; repeat from * to last 2 (4) sts, rib to end (70, 74 sts). Push 70 (74) needles to WP. With carriage at left, transfer sts to machine needles. Insert punchcard 2 and lock on first row. Set carriage for pattern. Set RC at 000. Using MT+2, knit 1 row. Release card and continue in lace pattern. Shape sides by increasing 1 st at each end of every 6th row until there are 110 (116) sts. Knit 52 (66) rows. RC shows 173 (193).
Shape top: Cast off 4 sts at the beginning of the next 2 rows and 3 sts at beginning of next 2 rows. Decrease 1 st at each end of every following alternate row until 84 (90) sts remain, then on every following 3rd row until 52 (54) sts remain, then on every following alternate row until 40 sts remain, then on every row until 12 sts remain. Cast off.

NECKBAND

Using yarn A and 2¾mm needles, cast on 184 sts. Work 3.5cm in k1, p1 rib. Cast off.

FINISHING

With knit side of work facing, block each piece by pinning out to correct measurements. Dampen with cold, clean water and leave to dry naturally. Join shoulder, side and sleeve seams. Set in sleeves. Sew neckband in position with ends at centre front.

SHAPE GUIDE
All measurements are given in centimetres. Figures in brackets refer to the larger size. Where only one figure is given, it applies to both sizes.

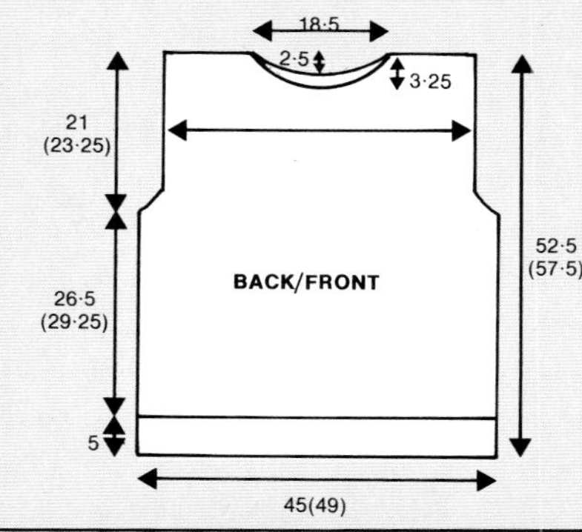

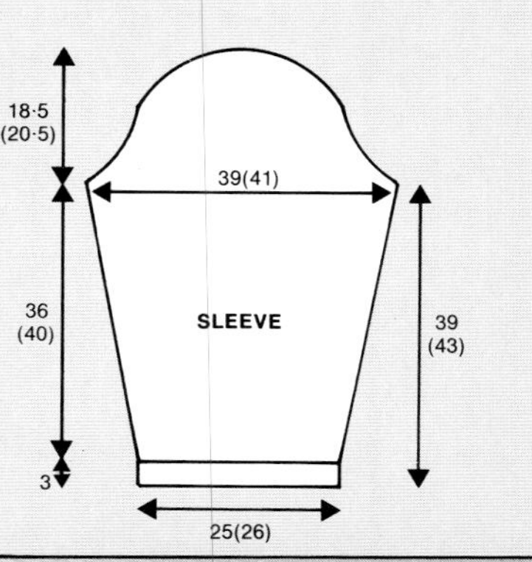

PUNCHCARDS
Punch these two cards before starting to knit.

Key
→ Move lace carriage from left to right
← Move lace carriage from right to left
↪ Knit two rows with the knit carriage, if applicable

Punchcard 1

Punchcard 2

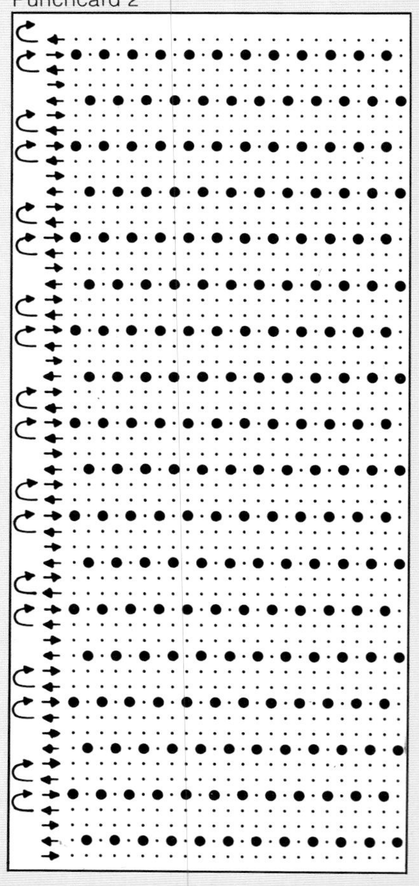

HAND·SELECTED NEEDLE·KNITTING

Whereas the pattern needles for most of the previous sweaters are selected by a punchcard or electronic graph, the pattern needles for the four garments in this section are selected by hand. Patience and care are needed when manually selecting pattern needles, but the resulting fabrics can be exciting and different. There is also more room for individual creative expression, since the pattern may be varied at will, to produce random or uniform designs all over a garment, or in selected areas only.

Partial knitting
The fabrics in this section are all created by using a technique known as "partial knitting". Basically it involves knitting some stitches in a row, while holding others. The technique may be exploited in various ways to produce radically different effects. For example it may be used to achieve small raised areas, or bobbles, dotted at random across the surface of the knitting as shown on pages 108-9, or it can be used to produce regularly patterned raised areas, as demonstrated below and on pages 104-7. It provides yet another different way of making lace fabrics, as on page 112, and can also be used to shape garment pieces.

The technique
In order to use this technique, you must set the controls on your machine so that needles in the holding position will not knit when the carriage is taken across. This control is usually found on the carriage, and the position it should be turned to may be marked either "partial knitting", "holding cam" or "returning". Push the needles you don't want to knit on forwards into holding position. When you want these needles to knit in, push them back to upper working position. The selection of the holding needles and the number of rows worked before knitting in the holding needles determines the characteristics of the pattern produced. In the samples shown below, alternate pairs of needles are held for four rows each, resulting in a mock rib effect on the knit side of the fabric. On the reverse hexagonal shapes are formed. These give the impression of having been tucked.

Experimenting with tension and colour
The appearance of fabrics created with this stitch construction is considerably affected by changing the tension. A loose tension may produce a delicate cobwebby fabric, whereas a firm tension will result in the raised rib effect shown on *Anchors Away*. This is not a true rib as produced in hand knitting or with double bed machines, it has no elasticity, and therefore can not be used in welts or for cuffs. To produce vertical stripes, as shown in *Anchors Away*, work four rows in each colour, changing the yarn colour at the same time as changing the needles selected for holding. Different patterns may be produced if the number of rows worked in each colour is varied.

Pattern variations of the stitch technique featured in *Anchors Away*

PATTERN INSTRUCTIONS FOR
ANCHORS AWAY

Both sides of the fabric produced by this stitch technique are equally attractive – on the knit side a pretty textured stripe is formed, while on the purl side hexagonal shapes, similar in their formation to tuck stitch, are created. To demonstrate the versatility of this fabric we have shown the same sweater twice, in different colours, using the purl and the knit sides for the right side of the sweater.

MATERIALS

Yarn

Yarn A 350 (375, 400)g medium-weight rayon (blue)
Yarn B 225 (250, 275)g medium-weight rayon (white)

Notions

8 glass drop beads (optional)

MEASUREMENTS

To fit chest 87 (91, 97)cm (34, 36, 38in)
Actual chest size 94 (100, 105)cm (37, 39½, 41½in)
Length at centre back 54.5 (57.5, 60.5)cm (21½, 22¾, 23¾in)
Sleeve seam 39.5cm (15½in)

MAIN TENSION (MT)

30 sts and 80 rows measure 10cm over pattern on MT (tension dial set at approximately 8)
30 sts and 45 rows measure 10cm over st st on MT – 2 (tension dial set at approximately 6)

STITCH PATTERN

Set carriage to hold sts. With 1 needle in WP, * 2 needles in HP, 2 needles in WP; repeat from * to last needle, 1 needle in HP. Using yarn A, knit 4 rows. ** Arrange needles carefully by hand making sure no sts fall off. With 1 needle in HP, * 2 needles in UWP; 2 needles in HP; repeat from * to last needle, 1 needle in UWP. Using uarn B, knit 4 rows. With 1 needle in UWP, * 2 needles in HP, 2 needles in UWP; repeat from * to last needle, 1 needle in HP. Using yarn A, knit 4 rows **. Repeat from ** to **.

STRIPE PATTERN FOR SLEEVES AND COLLAR

Working in st st, knit 4 rows yarn B, 12 rows yarn A.

BACK

Push 142 (150, 158) needles to WP. Using MT and waste yarn, cast on and knit a few rows ending with carriage at right. Set RC at 000. Using MT – 6 and yarn A, knit 60 rows. Make a hem by placing loops of first row

worked in yarn A on to corresponding needles. Unravel waste yarn when work is completed. Set RC at 000. Using MT, continue in Stitch pattern, knit 224 (232, 240) rows.
Shape raglan armholes: Cast off 4 sts at the beginning of the next 2 rows *. Decrease 1 st at each end of 2nd and every following 4th row until 52 sts remain.
Shape neck: Using nylon cord, knit 36 sts at left by hand taking needles down to NWP. Continue on remaining sts for first side. Decrease at raglan edge on every 4th row from previous decrease and at the same time, knit 1 row. Cast off 3 sts at the beginning of the next and following alternate row, knit 1 row. Cast off 2 sts at the beginning of the next row, knit 1 row. Decrease 1 st at the beginning of the next and following 2 alternate rows. 2 sts remain. Knit 4 rows. Cast off. With carriage at left unravel nylon cord over 16 needles at left bringing needles back to UWP. Finish to correspond with first side, reversing shapings.
Neckband: With carriage at right, unravel nylon cord over remaining 20 needles bringing needles back to UWP. Push 13 needles at each side to WP. Pick up 13 sts from each side of neck and place on to empty needles (46 sts). ** Set RC at 000. Using MT—6 and yarn A, work 20 rows st st. Cast off loosely.

FRONT

Work as for back to *. Decrease 1 st at each end of the 2nd and every following 4th row until 62 sts remain.
Shape neck: Using nylon cord, knit 41 sts at left by hand taking needles down to NWP. Continue on remaining sts for first side. Decrease 1 st at raglan edge on every 4th row from previous decrease and at the same time, knit 1 row. Cast off 3 sts at the beginning of the next row, knit 1 row. Decrease 1 st at the beginning of the next and every following 4th row 8 times. 2 sts remain. Knit 4 rows. Cast off. With carriage at left unravel nylon cord over 21 needles at left bringing needles back to UWP. Finish to correspond with first side reversing shapings.
Neckband: With carriage at right, unravel nylon cord over remaining 20 needles bringing needles back to UWP. Push 15 needles at each side to WP. Pick up 15 sts from each side of neck and place on to empty needles (50 sts). Work as for back from ** to end.

SLEEVES

Push 50 (52, 54) needles to WP. Using MT and waste yarn, cast on and knit a few rows ending with carriage at right. Set RC at 000. Using MT—6 and yarn A, knit 60 rows. Using waste yarn, knit a few rows and release from machine. Push 60 (62, 64) needles to WP. With purl side facing, replace sts on to needles as follows: 1 st on to each of first 7 (8, 9) needles. Leave 1 needle empty. * 1 st on to each of next 4 needles. Leave 1 needle empty. Repeat from * along the row ending with 1 st on each of last 7 (8, 9) needles. Unravel waste yarn. Make a hem by placing loops of first row worked in yarn A evenly along the row. Unravel waste yarn when work is completed. Set RC at 000. Using MT—2, continue in stripe pattern. Shape sides by increasing 1 st at each end of every following 4th (3rd, 3rd) row until there are 78 (90, 108) sts; then on every following 3rd (3rd, 2nd) row until there are 110 (118, 126) sts. Using MT, continue in stitch pattern and increase 1 st at each end of every following 8th row until there are 114 (122, 130) sts. Knit 104 rows. RC shows 204.
Shape raglan top: Cast off 4 sts at the beginning of the next 2 rows. Decrease 1 st at each end of 2nd and every following 4th row until 18 sts remain. Knit 4 rows. Push needles to UWP.
Neckband: Work as for back from ** to end.

COLLAR BACK

Push 144 needles to WP. * Using MT and waste yarn, cast on and knit a few rows ending with carriage at right. Set RC at 000. Using MT—2 and yarn A, knit 4 rows. Change to yarn B, knit 4 rows. Make a hem by placing loops of first row worked in yarn A on to corresponding needles. Unravel waste yarn when work is completed. Set RC at 004. Continue in stripe pattern (beginning with 12 rows in yarn A) *. Shape sides by decreasing 1 st at each end of the next and every following alternate row until 52 sts remain. Knit 1 row. RC shows 96. Using waste yarn, knit a few rows and release from machine.
Neckband: Push 40 needles to WP. With purl side facing replace sts on to needles as follows: 1 st on to each of first 3 needles, 2 sts together on to next needle. ** 1 st on to each of next 2 needles. 2 sts together on to next needle. Repeat from ** along the row ending with 1 st on each of last 3 needles. Unravel waste yarn, *** Set RC at 000. Using MT—6 and yarn A, knit 30 rows st st. Cast off loosely.

COLLAR FRONT

Push 144 needles to WP. Work as for collar back from * to *. Shape sides by decreasing 1 st at each end of the next and every following alternate row until 60 sts remain. Knit 1 row. RC shows 88.
Shape neck: Using nylon cord, knit 42 sts at left by hand taking needles down to NWP. Continue on remaining sts for first side. Decrease at side edge on every alternate row from previous decrease and at the same time, knit 1 row. Cast off 6 sts at the beginning of the next and following alternate row. Continue to decrease at side edge only on every alternate row from previous decrease until 2 sts remain. Knit 1 row. Cast off. With carriage at left unravel nylon cord over 18 needles at left bringing needles back to WP. Finish to correspond with first side, reversing shapings. With carriage at right unravel nylon cord over remaining 24 needles bringing needles back to WP. Using waste yarn, knit a few rows and release from machine.
Neckband: Push 18 needles to WP. With purl side facing replace sts on to needles as follows: 1 st on to first needle, 2 sts together on to next needle **, 1 st on to each of next 2 needles, 2 sts together on to next needle. Repeat from ** along the row ending with 1 st on last needle. Unravel waste yarn. Push 11 needles at each side to WP. Pick up 11 sts from each side of neck and place on to empty needles (40 sts). Work as for collar back from *** to end.

COLLAR SIDE PANELS

Push 114 needles to WP. Work as for collar back from * to *. Shape sides by decreasing 1 st at each end of the next and every following alternate row until 22 sts remain. Knit 1 row. RC shows 96. Using waste yarn, knit a few rows and release from machine.
Neckband: Push 18 needles to WP. With purl side facing, replace sts on to needles as follows: 1 st on to first needle, 2 sts together on to next needle, ** 1 st on to each of next 4 needles, 2 sts together on to next needle. Repeat from ** along the row ending with 1 st on last needle. Unravel waste yarn. Work as for collar back from *** to end.

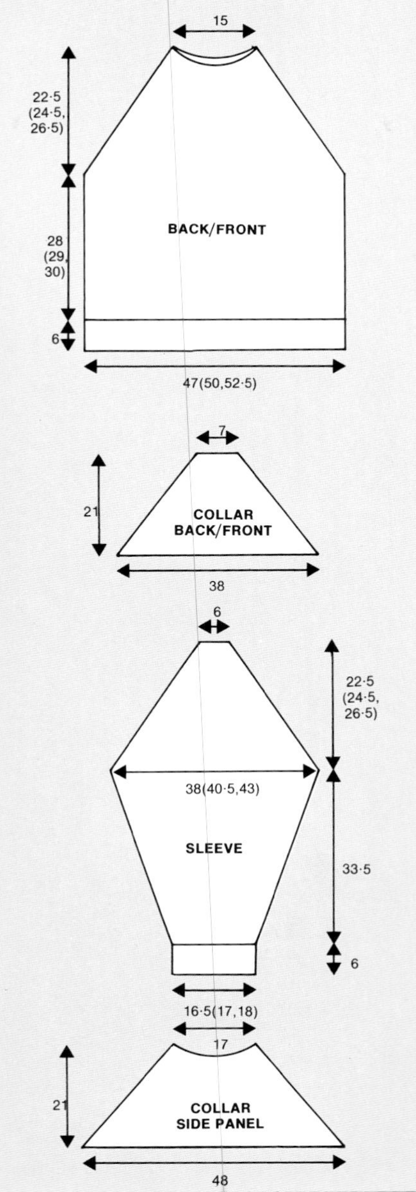

FINISHING

With knit side of work facing, block each piece by pinning out to correct measurements. Dampen with cold, clean water and leave to dry naturally. Join raglan and neckband seams of sweater. Join side and sleeve seams. Fold neckband in half to inside and slip stitch in position. Join panels of collar. Fold neckband in half to inside and slip stitch in position. Sew 2 beads to each corner of collar if required.

This sweater features the purl side of the fabric.

Pattern variations of the stitch technique featured in *Candy Floss*

PATTERN INSTRUCTIONS FOR
CANDY FLOSS

Team this neat double-breasted jacket with a skirt or trousers for a smart summer outfit.

MATERIALS

Yarn
Yarn A 300 (325)g fine-weight wool (natural)
Yarn B 275 (300)g medium-weight cotton/acrylic mixture yarn (multi-colour)

Notions
4 buttons 1.7cm in diameter
2 press-studs
Needles
1 circular needle size 2¾mm
1 pair size 2¾mm needles, if required

MEASUREMENTS

To fit chest 87 (91)cm (34, 36in)
Actual chest size 95 (102)cm (37½, 40¼in)
Length to shoulder 55cm (21¾in)
Sleeve seam 48.5cm (19in)

MAIN TENSION (MT)

34 sts and 96 rows measure 10cm over pattern (tension dial set at approximately 4)

SPECIAL NOTE

When shaping fronts, there must always be one st in UWP at front edge on every row. All the seams should be edge to edge seams, there are no extra stitches for seam allowances.

STITCH PATTERN 1

Work stitch pattern from chart. ** Knit 6 rows yarn B. * Push needles from HP to UWP. Release tucked loops from centre 4 needles of each 6 needle group and place below needles in UWP *. Knit 6 rows yarn A. Repeat from * to *. ** Repeat from ** to **.

STITCH PATTERN 2

Work stitch pattern from chart. ** Knit 6 rows yarn A. Repeat from * to *, above. Knit 6 rows yarn B. Repeat from * to *. Knit 6 rows yarn A. Repeat from * to *. Knit 6 rows yarn B. Repeat from * to *. ** Repeat from ** to **.

BACK

Push 78 (84) needles at left and 84 (90) needles at right of centre 0 to WP (162, 174 needles). With carriage at right and using yarn A, cast on by hand. * Set RC at 000. Continue in stitch pattern 1. Using MT, knit 120 rows *. Change to stitch pattern 2 and knit 168 rows. RC shows 288.
Shape armholes: Cast off 12 sts at the beginning of the next 2 rows (138, 150 sts). Knit 220 rows. RC shows 510. Using yarn A, knit 3 rows st st. Cast off loosely.

BLOCKS·AND·STRIPES

This fabric is produced using the partial knitting technique in the same way as the mock rib on pages 100-103, but by selecting wide blocks of needles the raised effect becomes less apparent. Although the surface of the knitting is flatter than the mock rib, it still retains a three-dimensional textural quality.

The fabric

When the partial knitting technique is used in this way, floats are formed on the purl side of the knitting, due to the yarn floating between selected sets of needles. This affects the physical quality of the knitting, making it warmer and bulkier than fabrics produced by some other stitch constructions. This should be borne in mind when designing garments using this technique.

Whereas floats in jacquard designs tend to look untidy, the floats created by this method can form attractive patterns, so the purl side of such fabrics may be used for the right side of a garment.

Experimenting with colours and yarns

Depending on how many rows are worked in each yarn, this pattern can be used to create a variety of geometric designs featuring squares and stripes of different colours. The double breasted jacket, *Candy Floss,* illustrated on the next page, shows a pleasing way of combining stripes and squares in one design. The stripes around the lower part of the jacket are repeated at the cuff ends of the sleeves.

The effects achieved with this technique may be considerably enhanced by the use of fancy yarns. Try mixing fluffy yarns with straight yarns, or knops and gimps with loops.

LEFT FRONT

Push 84 (90) needles at left and 36 (36) needles at right of centre 0 to WP, ** (120, 126 needles). With carriage at right and using yarn A, cast on by hand. Work as for back from * to *. Change to stitch pattern 2 and knit 5 rows.

Shape front edge: Decrease 1 st at right edge on the next and every following 6th row until 92 (98) sts remain. Knit 1 row. RC shows 289.

Shape armhole: Cast off 12 sts at the beginning of the next row (80, 86 sts). Continue to decrease at front edge only on every 6th row from previous decrease until 48 (54) sts remain. Knit 30 rows. RC shows 510. Using yarn A, knit 3 rows st st. Cast off loosely.

RIGHT FRONT

Push 42 (42) needles at left and 78 (84) needles at right of centre 0 to WP. Work as for left front from **, reversing shapings by reading left for right and right for left. At the same time, make a buttonhole over needles 4, 5 and 6 from left edge on rows 12 and 108.

SLEEVES

Push 42 (42) needles at left and 30 (36) needles at right of centre 0 to WP (72, 78 needles). With carriage at right and using yarn A, cast on by hand. Work as for back from * to * and at the same time, shape sides by increasing 1 st at each end of every 10th row (96, 102 sts). Change to stitch pattern 2 and continue to increase on every 10th row from previous increase until there are 158 sts. Knit 16 (46) rows. RC shows 446. Place marker at each end. Knit 34 rows. RC shows 480. Using yarn A, knit 3 rows st st. Cast off loosely.

CUFFS

Machines with ribber

Push 77 (83) needles to WP. With purl side facing, pick up 77 (83) sts evenly along lower edge of sleeve and place on to needles. With ribber in position, set machine and transfer sts for 1×1 rib. Set RC at 000. Using MT—1/MT—1 and yarn B, knit 6 rows. Cast off.

Machines without ribber

With knit side facing, join in yarn B and using 2$\frac{3}{4}$mm needles, pick up and knit 89 (95) sts evenly along lower edge of sleeve.

1st rib row: P1 * k1, p1; repeat from * to end.

2nd rib row: K1 * p1, k1; repeat from * to end.

Repeat these 2 rows for 2cm ending with a 1st rib row. Cast off in rib.

WELT

Join shoulder seams. Set in sleeves, sewing rows above marker to cast off sts on back and fronts. Join side and sleeve seams. With knit side facing, join in yarn B and using a 2$\frac{3}{4}$mm circular needle pick up and knit 496 (526) sts evenly along lower edge of body. Work 2cm in k1, p1 rib, increasing 1 st at each end of every row. Cast off in rib.

FRONT BAND

With knit side facing, join in yarn B and using a 2$\frac{3}{4}$mm circular needle, pick up and knit 224 sts evenly up right front, 53 sts evenly across back neck, and 224 sts evenly down left front (501 sts). Work 2cm in rib as given for cuff ending with a 1st rib row, increasing 1 st at each end of every row. Cast off in rib.

FINISHING

With purl side of work facing, block each piece by pinning out to correct measurements. Dampen with cold, clean water and leave to dry naturally. Join mitred corners of front band and welt. Finish buttonholes. Sew two buttons to left front to correspond with buttonholes. Lap right front over left and fasten buttons. Sew two remaining buttons to right front, level with first pair and in a position to come in line with centre of first stripe on left front edge. Sew one pair of press-studs behind each of these buttons.

STITCH PATTERN CHART

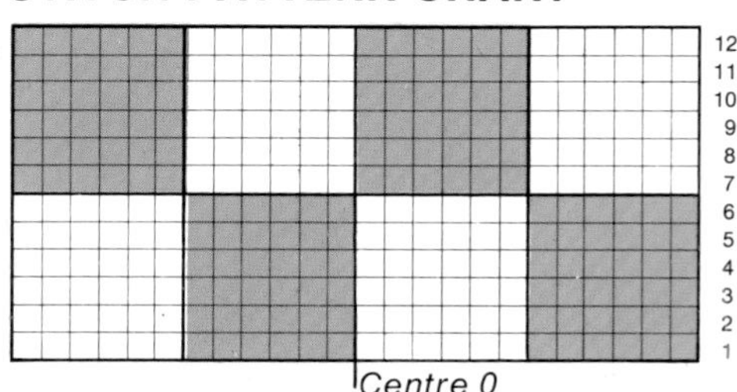

Push needle to HP (set carriage to hold)

SHAPE GUIDE

All measurements are given in centimetres. Figures in brackets refer to the larger size. Where only one figure is given, it applies to all sizes.

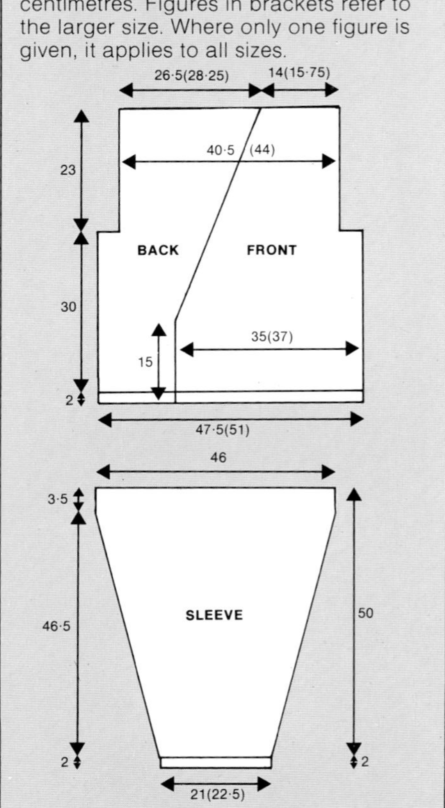

BOBBLES·AND·RIDGES

The partial knitting technique featured on *Anchors Away* and *Candy Floss* involves selecting and holding sets of needles regularly spaced across the needle bed, and carrying the yarn not being knitted across the purl side of the fabric. Here, sets of needles are selected at random across the needle bed, and the yarn is introduced and broken off separately for each bobble, so there are no floats on the back of the knitting.

The technique
To make bobbles push all the needles except the ones you wish to make a bobble on into the holding position. Set the carriage for partial knitting, so that the needles in the holding position will not knit. Knit one row with a contrasting yarn. Loop the contrast yarn around the adjacent needle in holding position on the same side as the carriage. Knit a few rows, each time looping the contrast yarn around the adjacent needle. When the bobble is the required size, push all the needles to working or upper working position. Knot the ends of contrast yarn together and continue knitting.

Experimenting with colours and yarns
Bobbles can be knitted in the same yarn as the main fabric, but from a different cone, this produces Aran type effects. Use different shades of the same colour for a subtle effect, or choose several contrasts for an eyecatching design. If you use fluffy yarn such as mohair for the bobbles, after removing the knitting from the machine the bobbles may be brushed with a teazle brush, as shown on sample 2. Whatever type of yarn you use it is important to tie the loose ends of yarn securely at the back of the fabric.

Experimenting with shape and size
The shape and size of the bobble is determined by the number of needles selected, the number of rows worked, the yarn used and the tension of the knitting. Experiment with different combinations to produce different shapes.

Patterning
Bobbles can be made at random, as in samples 2, 3 and 6, or in a regular sequence, as in samples 1, 4 and 5. Obviously the more you do the longer it will take to complete a garment. For added interest, stripe the background of the fabric as shown in samples 1, 2 and 4.

Pattern variations of the stitch technique featured in ***Confetti***

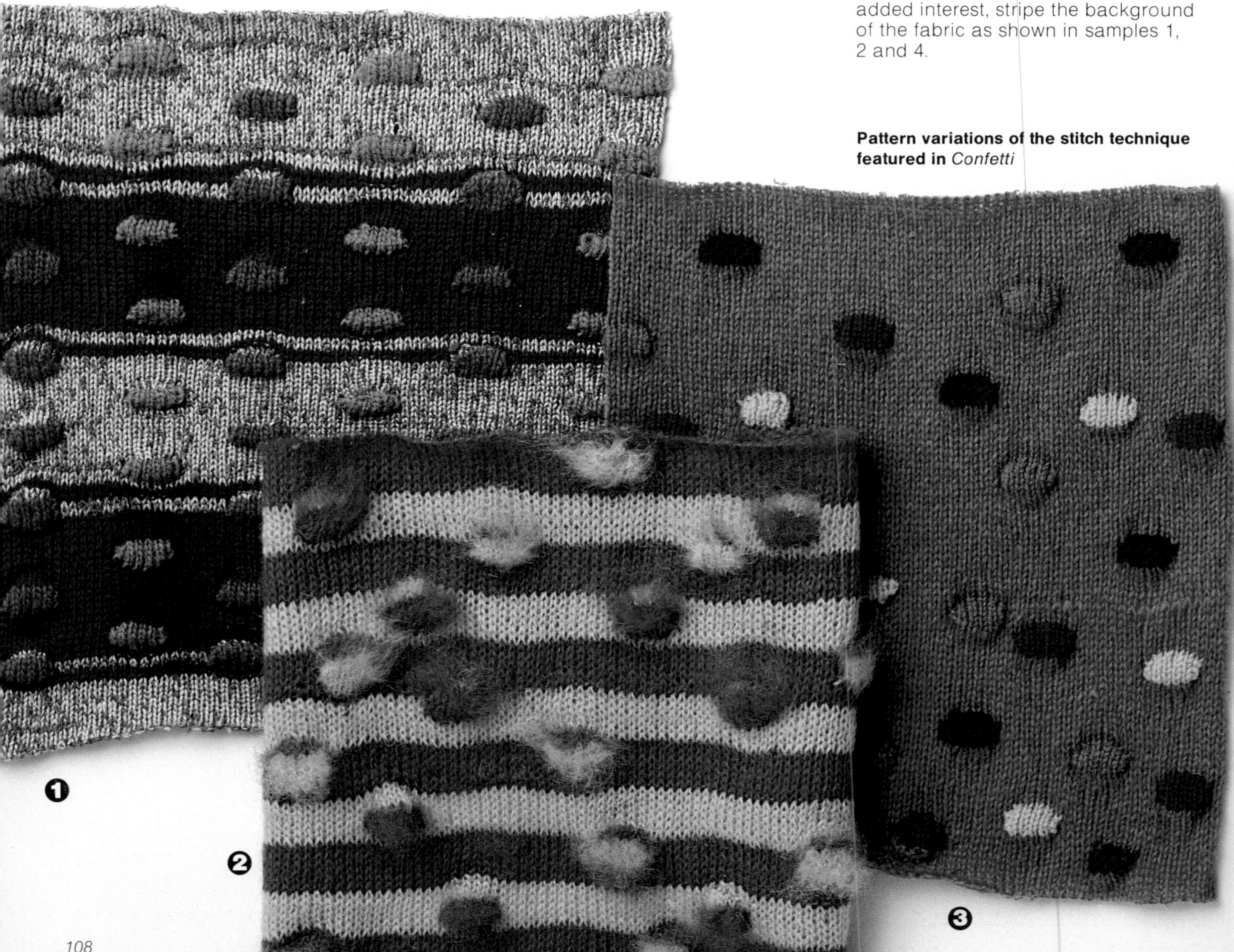

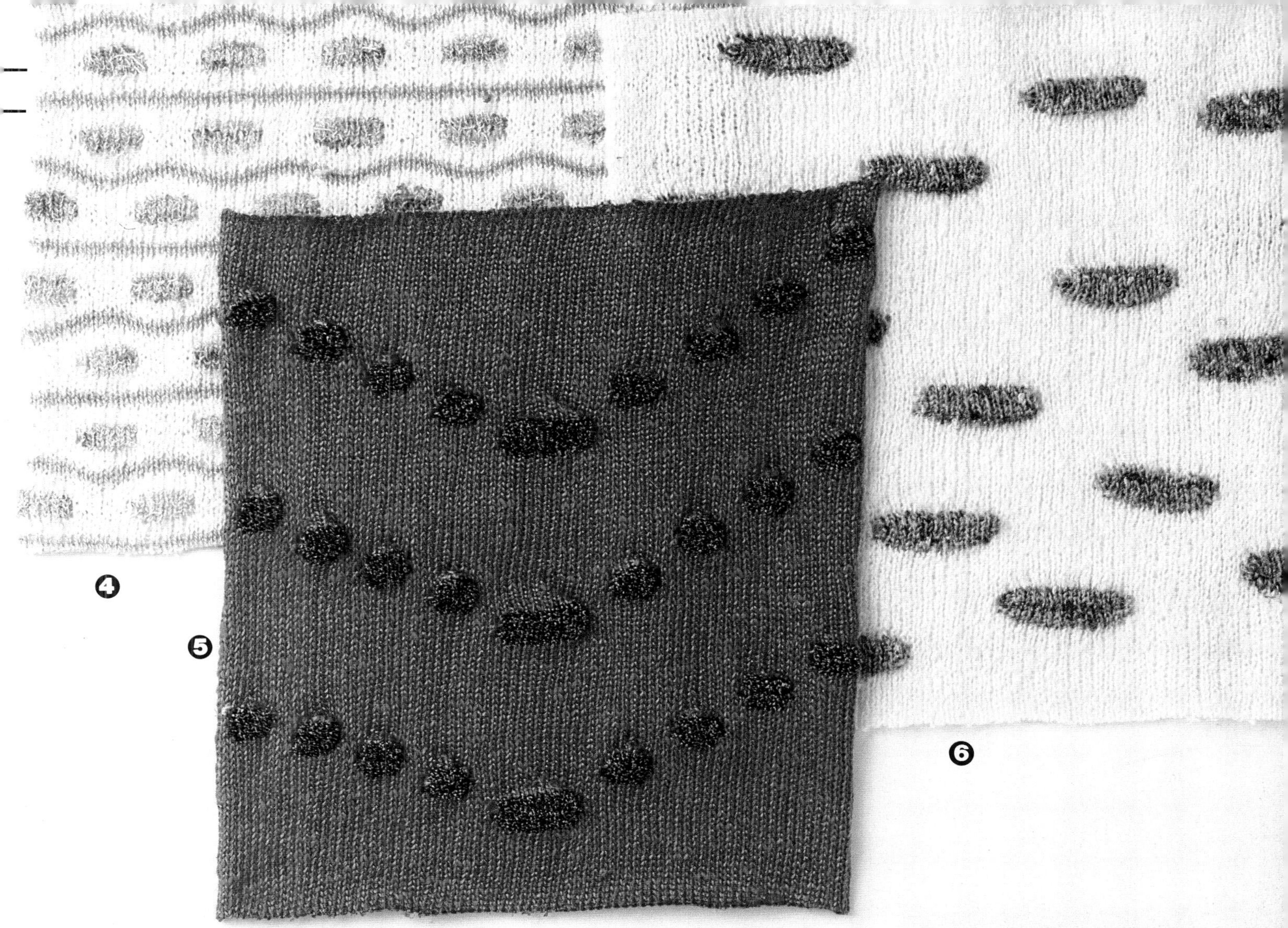

4

5

6

PATTERN INSTRUCTIONS FOR

CONFETTI

Make as many bobbles as you like on this comfortable, easy-to-wear sweater, scattering them at random across the front and back. The use of a fine gimp cotton for the main yarn produces a wonderful scrunchy texture which contrasts nicely with the shiny rayon yarn used for the stripes and bobbles. If you use rayon yarn, care must be taken to finish the bobbles well or the ends of the yarn will come undone.

MATERIALS

Yarn

Yarn A 350g fine-weight cotton gimp (ecru)
Yarn B 50g fine-weight rayon (pink) 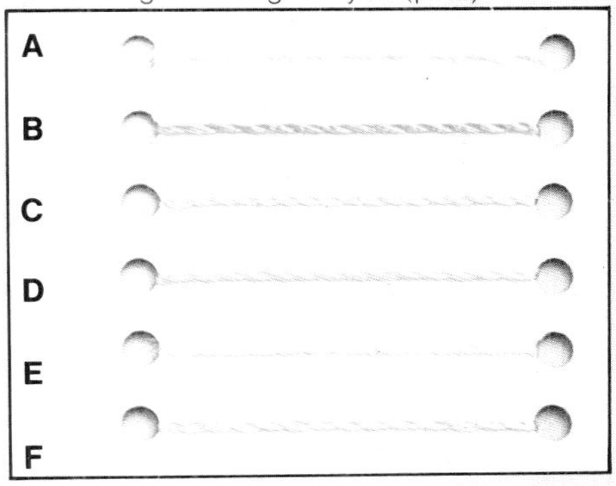
Yarn C 50g fine-weight rayon (beige)
Yarn D 50g fine-weight rayon (yellow)
Yarn E 50g fine-weight rayon (white)
Yarn F 50g fine-weight rayon (grey)

A
B
C
D
E
F

Needles

If you don't have a ribber, you need 1 pair size $2\frac{3}{4}$mm needles

MEASUREMENTS

To fit chest 86-91cm (34-36in)
Actual chest size 105cm ($41\frac{1}{4}$in)
Length at centre back 43.5cm ($17\frac{1}{4}$in)
Sleeve seam 38cm (15in)

MAIN TENSION (MT)

32 sts and 48 rows measure 10cm over stripe pattern (tension dial set at approximately 4)

STRIPE PATTERN

Knit 2 rows yarn C, 4 rows yarn A, 2 rows yarn B, 4 rows yarn A, 2 rows yarn F, 4 rows yarn A, 2 rows yarn D and 4 rows yarn A.

BOBBLE PATTERN

Disconnect RC and remove yarn A from feeder. Set carriage to hold stitches. Push all needles except the 6 to be worked into HP. Put a weight on these 6 sts. With B, C, D, E or F * knit 1 row, loop yarn around first needle in A at end of row; repeat from * 7 times more. Push these needles into HP.

For a pretty neckline oversew the edge with yarn to match the bobbles and stripes.

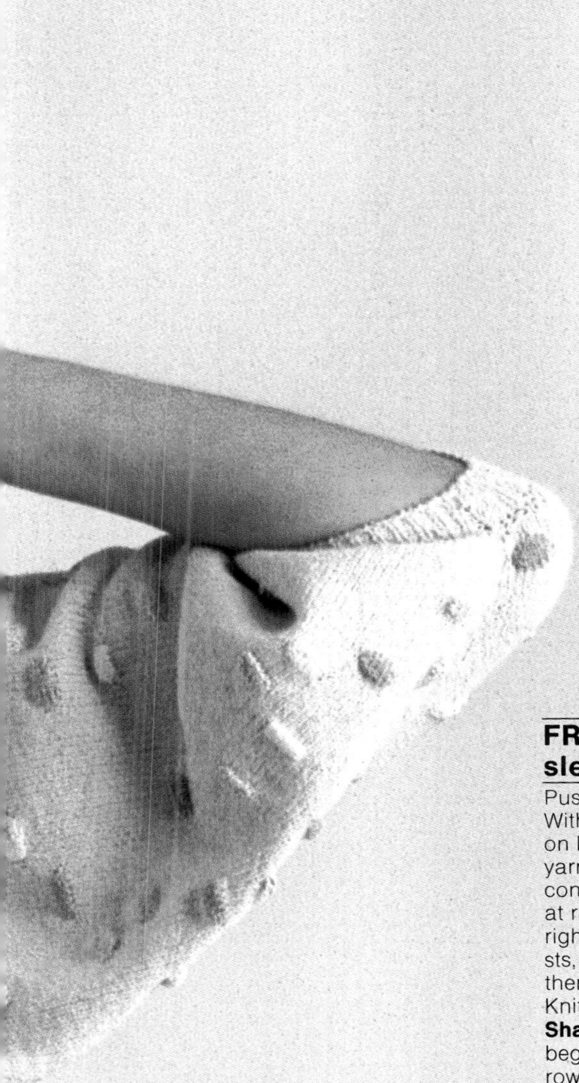

Knot ends. Repeat again (pushing 6 needles from HP to UWP), when a second or more bobbles are to be worked. When bobbles are completed, push all needles back in to WP, return yarn A to feeder and reconnect RC.

FRONT (beginning at left sleeve edge)

Push 50 needles at left of centre 0 to WP. With carriage at right and using yarn A, cast on by hand. Set RC at 000. Using MT and yarn A, except when working a bobble, continue in bobble pattern making bobbles at random, at the same time increase 1 st at right edge on every 4th row until there are 63 sts, on every 3rd row until there are 91 sts, then on every row until there are 122 sts. Knit 1 row. RC shows 168.
Shape body: Cast on 24 sts at the beginning of the next row (146 sts). Knit 42 rows. RC shows 211 *.
Shape neck: Cast off 4 sts at the beginning of the next row. Decrease 1 st at the left edge on every row until 127 sts remain, then on every following alternate row until 115 sts remain. Knit 43 rows. RC shows 294. Continue in stripe pattern, knit 44 rows. Increase 1 st at left edge on the next and every following alternate row until there are 128 sts, then on every row until there are 142 sts. Cast on 4 sts at the beginning of the next row (146 sts). ** Knit 42 rows. RC shows 420.
Shape sleeve: Cast off 24 sts at the beginning of the next row, knit 1 row. Decrease 1 st at the right edge on every row until 90 sts remain, on every following 3rd row until 62 sts remain, then on every following 4th row until 50 sts remain. Knit 2 rows. RC shows 588. Cast off.

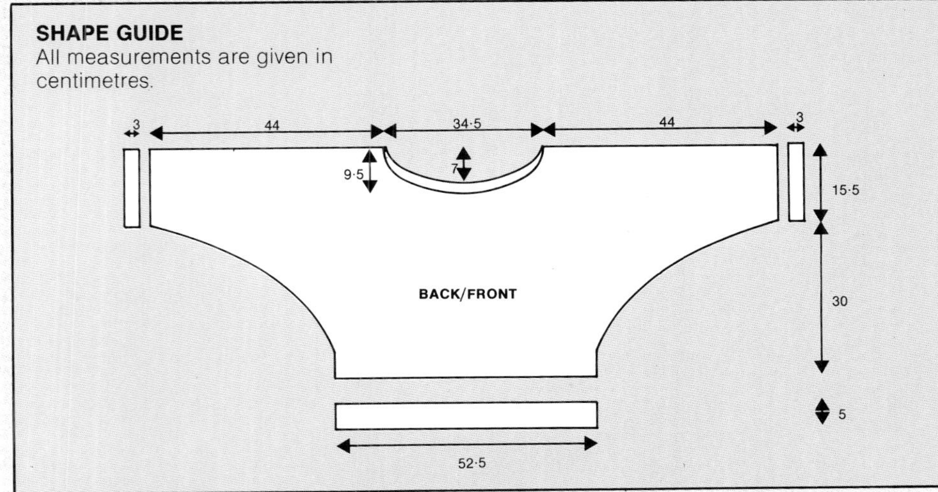

BACK (beginning at left sleeve edge)

Work as for front to *, reversing shaping by reading left for right and right for left.
Shape neck: Decrease 1 st at the right edge on the next and every following alternate row until 123 sts remain. Knit 38 rows. RC shows 294. Continue in stripe pattern, knit 39 rows. Increase 1 st at the right edge on the next and every following alternate row until there are 146 sts. Work as for front from ** to end reversing shaping by reading left for right and right for left.

NECK EDGING

Using yarn A, cast on 7 sts by hand. Using MT, knit until long enough to go around neck edge. Cast off.

WELTS

Machines with ribber
With ribber in position, set machine for 1 × 1 rib. Using yarn A, cast on 141 sts in 1 × 1 rib. * Knit 5 tubular/circular rows. Set carriage for 1 × 1 rib knitting. Set RC at 000. Use MT − 2/MT − 2 *. Knit 32 rows. Cast off.
Machines without ribber
Using 2¾mm needles and yarn A, cast on 121 sts.
1st rib row: K1, * p1, k1; repeat from * to end.
2nd rib row: P1, * k1, p1; repeat from * to end.
Repeat these 2 rows for 5cm ending with a 1st rib row. Cast off in rib.

CUFFS

Machines with ribber
With ribber in position, set machine for 1 × 1 rib. Using yarn A, cast on 81 sts in 1 × 1 rib. Work as for welts from * to *. Knit 17 rows. Cast off.
Machines without ribber
Using 2¾mm needles and yarn A, cast on 69 sts. Work 3cm in rib as given for welt ending with a 1st rib row. Cast off.

FINISHING

With purl side of work facing, block each piece by pinning out to correct measurements. Depending on yarn used, press carefully following instructions on ball or cone band, or dampen with cold, clean water and leave to dry naturally. Join upper sleeve and shoulder seams. Sew on cuffs and welts. Join side and sleeve seams. Join ends of neck edging and sew into position. Fold neck edging to right side and roll. With lengths of rayon yarn, alternating colours to match stripe pattern, oversew tightly at intervals to form "shell" effect. Press seams, if necessary.

LACE

Whereas the partial knitting technique as used in the previous three garments produces solid fabrics, here the same technique is used to create a very open, lace fabric.

The technique
To produce the open mesh fabric, follow the instructions given in the pattern for *Stardust*. After mastering this basic pattern you will find that you can vary the number of needles selected, or the number of rows worked to produce different patterns. The best results are achieved by keeping the spaces created by the sets of needles in the holding position small, too large a space creates an extremely open, and often unusable fabric. It is important that you hang weights on the knitting as instructed in *Stardust*.

Experimenting with colours and yarns
Because of the way blocks of needles are selected it is quite easy to introduce other colours and yarns at random, to create attractive fabrics. Other interesting optical effects can also be created by using space-dyed yarns, or by knitting with two contrasting colours.

PATTERN INSTRUCTIONS FOR STARDUST

The slight spring in the fabric of this glamorous evening top gives it a fluidity of movement that is enhanced by the sparkle of the glitter yarn. It is important that the weights are used as instructed, or the work will fall from the needles.

MATERIALS

Yarn
Yarn A 325g very fine rayon/lurex (black/silver)

A 

Notions
4 small buttons 1cm in diameter

MEASUREMENTS

To fit chest 87-92cm (34-36in)
Actual chest size 104cm (41in)
Length at centre back 56cm (22in)

MAIN TENSION (MT)

$4\frac{1}{2}$ patterns measure approximately 10cm wide and 30cm high (tension dial set at approximately 8)

SPECIAL NOTE

When working in HP do not take yarn round first inside needle in HP.

BACK AND FRONT (alike)

Push 148 needles to WP. Using MT and waste yarn, cast on and knit a few rows ending with carriage at left. Set RC at 000. Using MT – 4 and main yarn, knit 50 rows. Make a hem by placing loops of first row worked in main yarn on to corresponding needles. Unravel waste yarn when work is completed. Disconnect RC and continue in pattern as follows:
Counting from left edge, transfer the 5th st on to the 4th needle, the 6th st on to the 7th needle, the 11th st on to the 10th needle, the 12th st on to the 13th needle and so on across the row. Push empty needles to NWP. (Thus leaving 4 needles in WP and 2 needles in NWP alternately and ending with 4 needles in WP, 25 groups of 4 needles in WP.) Set carriage to hold sts. Leave first group of 4 needles at left in WP and push all remaining needles from WP to HP. Put weight on first group. Use MT.
1st pattern row: * Knit 8 rows. Push second group into UWP, weight and knit 8 rows. Push third group into UWP. Knit 1 row. Push first group into HP. Weight and knit 7 rows across remaining 8 sts. Push fourth group into UWP. Knit 1 row. Push second group unto HP. Weight and knit 7 rows across remaining 8 sts. Continue in this way until 25th group is pushed to UWP. Knit 1 row. Push 23rd group into HP. Weight and knit 8 rows. Push 24th group into HP. (4 needles remaining in WP at right.) It is important to move weights along the row as you work.
2nd pattern row: Work as for 1st pattern row from *, but work from right to left and read left for right.
These 2 rows form the pattern. Repeat them 6 times more, then the first row again. Push needles from HP and NWP to WP. Place loop from row below adjacent st on to empty needles (148 needles). Set RC at 000. Using MT – 2, knit 3 rows.
Shape shoulders: Cast off 30 sts at the beginning of the next 2 rows (88 sts). Knit 38 rows. RC shows 43. Cast off very loosely.

ARMHOLE BORDERS

Join shoulder seams and sides of neckband, reversing seam on neckband to allow for turning. Place a marker on each side of back and front, approximately 26cm from shoulders. Push 150 needles to WP. With purl side facing, pick up 150 sts evenly between markers and place on to needles. Set RC at 000. Using MT – 2 and main yarn, knit 20 rows. Cast off very loosely.

FINISHING

Join side seams, leaving st st hem open, but joining row ends of hem at each side on back and front. Roll neckband over to right side and fasten at each side of neck. Sew one button to each side at top of hem and one to each side at lower edge, make a button loop for each button and fasten.

SHAPE GUIDE
All measurements are given in centimetres.

BASIC·TECHNIQUES

THE KNITTING MACHINE

A typical knitting machine consists, basically, of a needle bed, into which are cut a number of channels or grooves. Each of these channels holds a latch needle. A cam box, or carriage is moved across the needle bed causing selected needles to slide forward. The yarn, the flow of which is controlled by a mast, tension spring and tension disc, is caught in the hook of the needle, and held in position by the latch which closes on to the yarn as the needle slides back. The yarn, held in the hook, is pulled through the previous stitch to form a new stitch.

Knitting machines can be divided into two main categories: those with one needle bed and those with two needle beds. The first type produces a basic single fabric in stocking stitch and is known as a single bed machine. The second produces a double knit or rib fabric and is known as a double bed machine. Most domestic machines are single bed, but can be converted to a double bed by the attachment of a ribber. The stitches and techniques described in this book may be done on the basic single bed machine.

Single bed machines
The main advantage of a single bed machine is that the knitting can be seen as it is produced, so it's easy to spot any mistakes and rectify them before it's too late. Also, being mechanically quite simple, the principal stitch variations and needle positions are easy to understand. Another factor in their favour is that they are much cheaper than double bed machines. The main drawback to single bed machines is that it is very difficult to use them to produce true rib. However single bed machines can easily produce mock rib, which may occasionally be used as a substitute for true rib, otherwise, a hand knitted rib may be used instead.

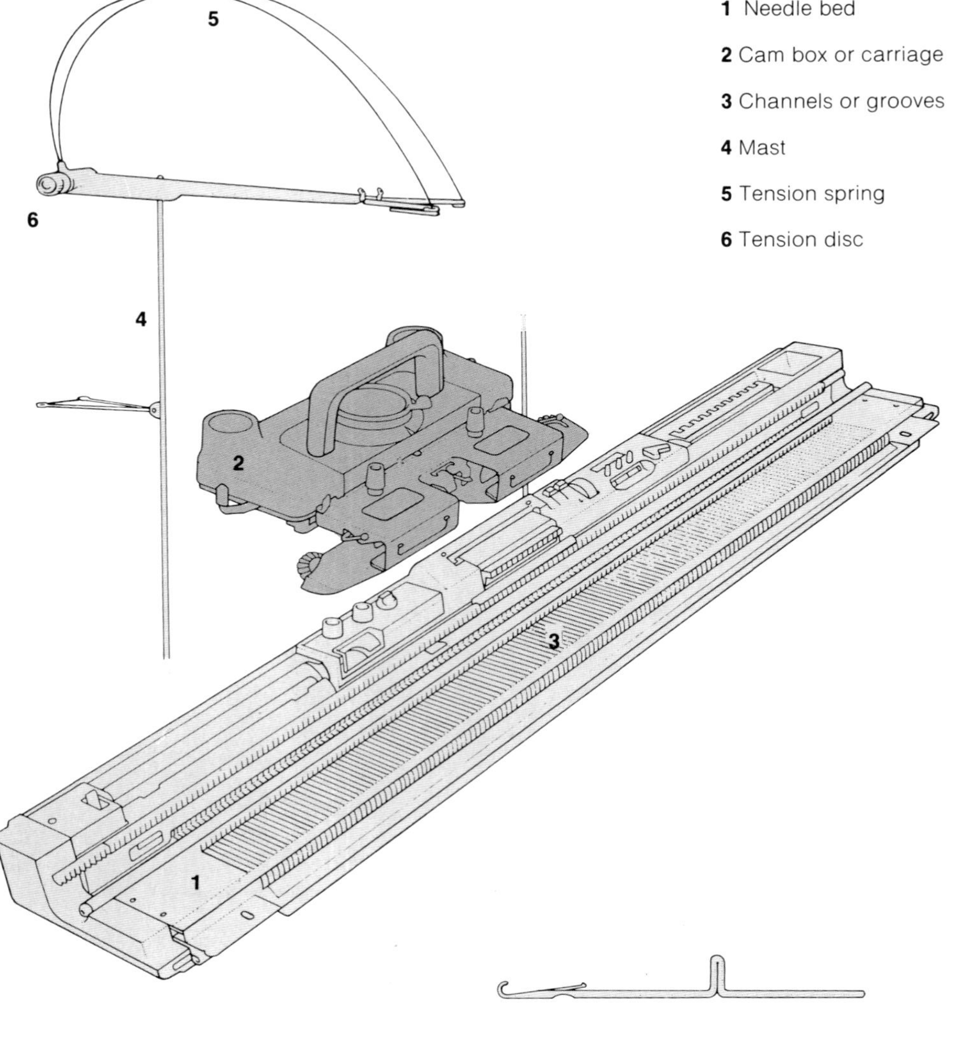

1 Needle bed

2 Cam box or carriage

3 Channels or grooves

4 Mast

5 Tension spring

6 Tension disc

Latch needle
Each channel contains a single latch needle.

Needle positions

On most machines, the needles may be moved into four basic positions:

Non-working position (NWP) – Needles pushed as far back in the slot as possible.
Working position (WP) – Needles pulled out approximately one-third of the depth of the needle bed.
Upper-working position (UWP) – Needles pulled out two-thirds of the depth of the needle bed.
Holding position (HP) – Needles pulled as far forward in the slot as possible.

NWP
WP
UWP
HP

Double bed machines

Having two needle beds instead of one gives you a choice: you can use just one of the beds, or both together, each one separately, or only partly separately. There are also an infinite number of stitch variations and combinations, and it is possible to produce true rib. However, some people find a double bed machine more difficult to master than a single bed machine, and the knitting produced is not visible until enough has been knitted to appear beneath the depth of the machine bed. It should also be noted that double bed machines are more expensive than single bed machines.

Stitch gauge

Stitch gauge refers to the number of needles to the inch across the needle bed. Depending on how far apart the needles are set, different thicknesses of yarn can be accommodated.
Basically, machines with three different stitch gauges are available: fine gauge, standard gauge and coarse gauge.

The fine gauge machine has a needle bed with about 250 needles and is suitable for knitting very fine yarns up to medium-weight yarns. The standard gauge machine, with 200 needles, is suitable for knitting fine yarns through to double knitting yarns. The coarse gauge machine, (often called a chunky machine) has about 100 needles and may be used for knitting double knitting yarns through to thick, chunky yarns. However, it is possible to extend these yarn boundaries slightly and use thicker yarns by either knitting on every other needle, or by using a special technique called "weaving", whereby rather than feeding yarn through the tension unit, it is laid across the needles and knitted in.

By far the most popular machine is the standard gauge machine, so all the patterns for the sweaters in this book have been given for this gauge. However, with the help of a shaping aid (see right) any of the sweater patterns may be adapted for use on different gauge machines.

Patterning

Patterning depends on needle selection – how, in each row, one can control which stitches will be plain and which will be fancy. To begin with, needle selection was done by hand, but, over the years, more efficient ways were devised. First a detachable lever or selector was introduced, then the punchcard system, and now, on the latest models, needle selection is electronically controlled.

Manual selection

On the simplest knitting machines, pattern needles are selected by bringing them forward, before knitting each row. Needle pushers may be used to push needles forward in certain sequences. For example, a 1 × 1 needle pusher gives a pattern stitch every other stitch, a 1 × 3 needle pusher gives a pattern stitch every fourth stitch. Although this method of selecting needles is slow, it has the advantage that there is no set repeat size, and the pattern can be non-repeating across the knitting.

Selector/lever

A selector or detachable lever provides a more efficient way of selecting pattern needles. With the selector the first pattern is hand selected, and the selector is then passed across the needle bed, automatically repeating the sequence across the row. With the lever system the first pattern is selected by pressing a set of buttons, a lever is then operated which brings needles forward in the same sequence across the knitting. With both these methods, the operation has to be repeated on every pattern row.

Punchcard

The punchcard system provides a much faster method of selecting pattern needles. The entire pattern is punched out on a plastic sheet before beginning knitting. The sequence of holes on the card controls which stitches will be patterned. The card is fed into the machine, and automatically moves down one row at a time.

The way the pattern is conveyed from the card to the needle varies from model to model, but the actual punchcards are all a standard size – 24 stitches wide by 60 rows deep. Pre-punched cards are available, or you can punch out your own designs. One punchcard may be used to produce a variety of different stitch patterns. For example, a punchcard suitable for tuck stitch may also be used for weaving or jacquard designs.

Electronic

Electronic machines have a built-in programming capacity, and have an even greater flexibility in patterning than manual or punchcard models. Instead of punching a card, the design is drawn onto a special graph, which is fed into the machine and "read" by electronic sensors. Very complicated patterns can be worked over a much larger pattern area.

Shaping aids

Shaping aids, or charting devices, are attachments which make it possible to draw out the required shape in diagram form, and then to commence knitting, without first working out the sequence of increases and decreases. (The different machine manufacturers call shaping aids by different names – knit radar, knit leader, knit tracer). Shaping aids make machine knitting faster, easier, and more creative.

How shaping aids work

Some machines work with a diagram which is the actual size of the garment, others work with half scale diagrams. But the principle is the same. With all makes, the shaping aid, which is fitted on to the machine (or sometimes built into it), holds a sheet on which is drawn the outline of the item to be knitted. The appropriate stitch scale, depending on the number of stitches to the inch or centimetre, is fed in; the row indicator is set in accordance with the number of rows to the inch or centimetre. The diagram moves down one space each time a row is knitted, and the knitter simply reads off the number of stitches to be increased or decreased. There is no need to count rows, or even to consult a row counter on the machine, because as the sheet moves down the knitter can see at a glance how far to knit and where to increase and decrease. Shaping aids are usually supplied with a set of basic shapes in a good range of sizes, but it is easy to alter or adapt these, or to draw your own shapes.

Advantages of using a shaping aid

These are many including speed, simplicity, and the fact that once you have found a shape you like, you can knit it again and again, varying yarn, stitch size, and stitch pattern. Bear in mind it must be subject to the laws of common sense and suitability – a garment designed to be knitted in a firm four-ply crêpe will be unsuitable in gossamer-fine baby yarn.

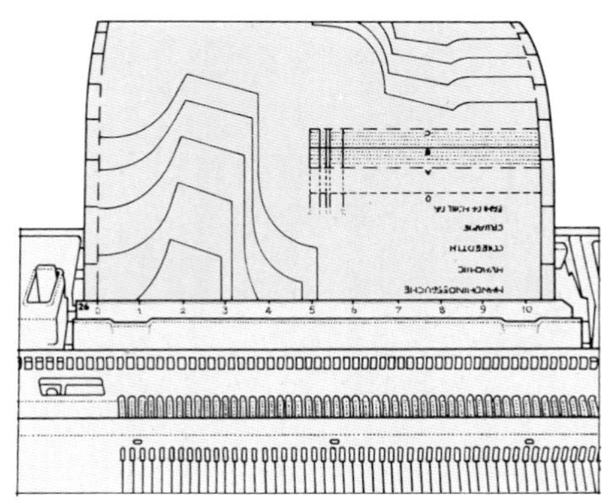

A typical shaping aid

Tools

Various items are supplied with each knitting machine; they vary slightly according to the manufacturer, but the basic, and most useful ones are described below.

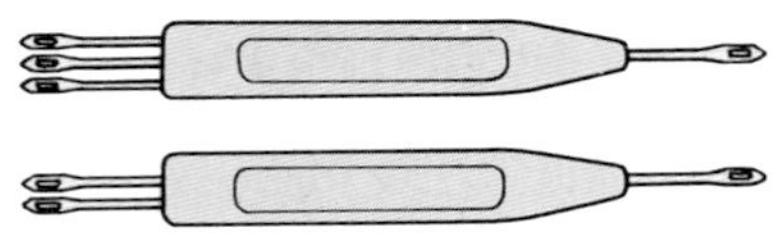

Transfer tool
This is used if you want to move a stitch from one needle to another, for increasing, decreasing, casting off or for making a hole in the fabric in lace patterns.

Latch tool
This looks just like one of the needles from the needle bed, set into a holder. It is used for casting off, picking up dropped stitches, and for producing ribbing manually on a single bed machine.

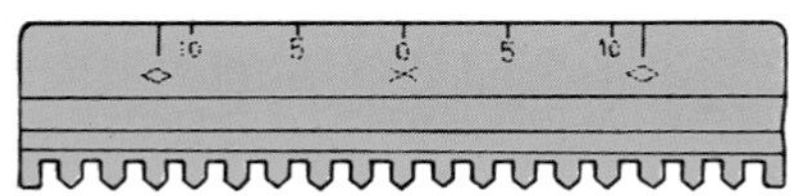

Needle pusher
This is a simple device which speeds up needle selection.

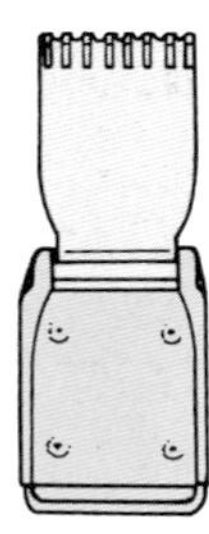

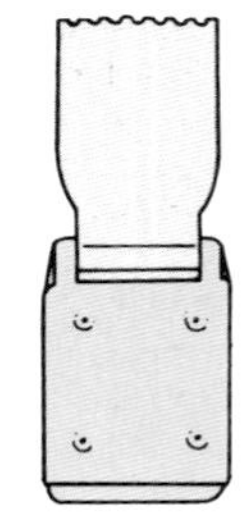

Weights
Some machine knitting techniques are made much easier if weights are hung on the knitting, so preventing the loops from slipping off the needles.

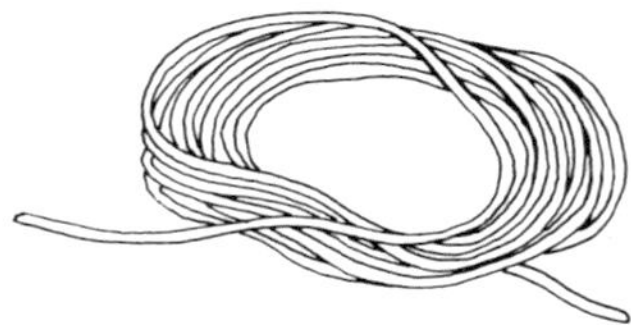

Nylon cord
This is useful for casting on when an open edge of loops is required.

PREPARING YARN

When knitting it is very important that the yarn is fed into the machine smoothly and evenly. Yarn sold on cone will do this, but balls or skeins must be re-wound before use (unless you are laying the yarn in by hand). The reason for this is that a knitting machine operates at a considerable speed, and unprepared yarn is likely to cause dropped stitches, machine jams or other hindrances. The machine manufacturers used to recommend waxing the yarn before using it, however the machines available today tend to be able to cope more easily with hairy yarn. However if you do have problems knitting with certain yarns it might be worth waxing them.

Winding

You must keep a constant tension as you wind the yarn. The best way to do this is by using a gadget known as a yarn winder. When rewinding a skein you will need to stretch it over a skein holder. It is a good idea to wind a good supply of yarn before starting to knit.

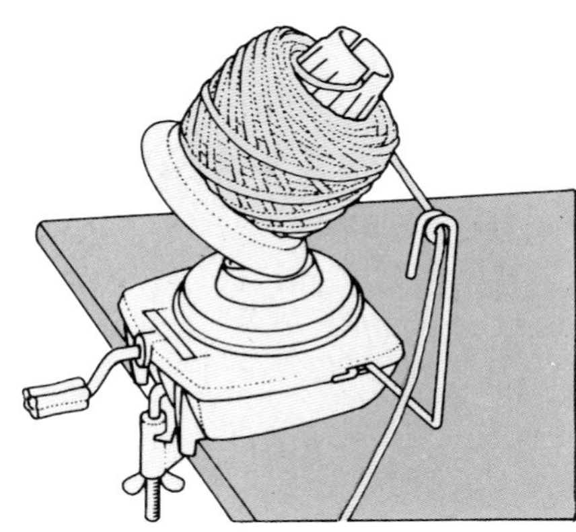

Waxing

Waxing yarn serves two purposes; it smooths the outer fibres, thus "stream-lining" the yarn, it also rubs off on to the knitting machine providing lubrication which keeps it running smoothly. Paraffin wax discs can be purchased but if you do not have any, candle wax is a good substitute.

Waxing should be done very lightly, synthetic yarns need less wax than natural ones. Hold the wax in the hand you are feeding the yarn through while winding, letting the yarn pass over it. If your yarn is already wound but not waxed just rub some wax on to the outside of the cone at regular intervals while knitting, do not apply too much pressure. You will probably find the wax rubs off the yarn while knitting and the finished garment looks unaffected, however, if some wax remains this will certainly come off in the first wash.

CASTING ON

Placing the first row of stitches on to the needles is known as "casting on". All further rows are worked into these initial loops. There are several different methods of casting on. Techniques differ slightly for different machines, and for the type or part of the garment you are making. The most frequently used techniques are described below.

For all four methods set the controls on your knitting machine as advised by your manual, into the neutral, or plain knitting position. Thread the yarn through the tension unit and bring it down through the feeder on the carriage. Make sure the tension setting is appropriate for the type of yarn you are using.

Simple cast on

This is a quick and easy cast on method for machines with weaving brushes. The edge it produces is not very stable, so it is most suitable for tension swatches, samples, and when turning up a hem.

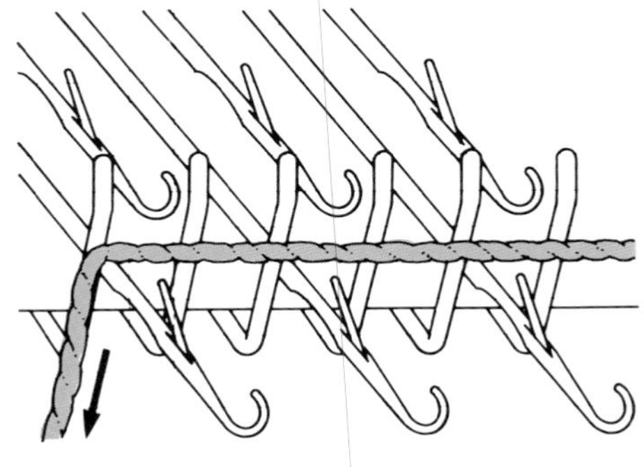

1 Bring the required number of needles forward into WP. Using the 1 × 1 needle pusher, push alternate needles into HP. Bring the weaving brushes on the carriage into operation. Pull the yarn from beneath the carriage so it lies across the needles in HP. Keep the yarn fairly taut.

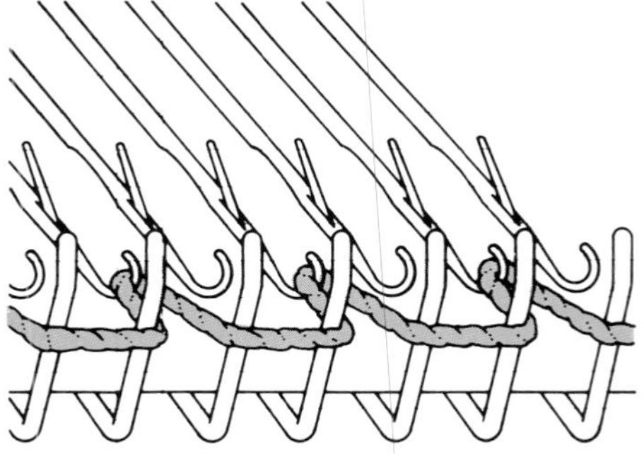

2 Move the carriage across the needle bed until it has passed all the needles.

3 Knit a few more rows, then attach weights to stop the knitting flying off the needles. Lift the weaving brushes so they are no longer in contact with the needles. Refer to your manual to see if any other controls should be changed before continuing.

Nylon cord cast on

This method produces an open edge of loops, so it is suitable for tension swatches, samples, and when turning up a hem.

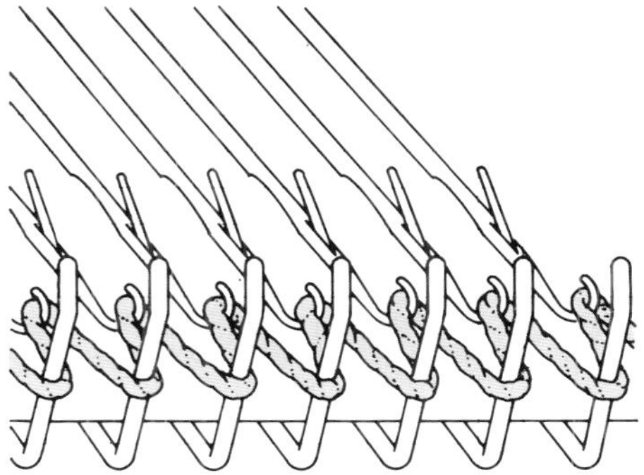

1 Bring the required number of needles forward into WP. Knit one row, by holding on to the end of the yarn and moving the carriage across the needles. This will look like a row of loops rather than a row of stitches.

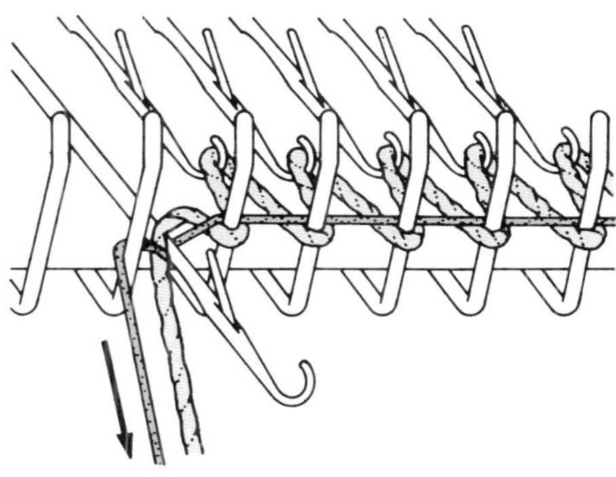

2 Lay the nylon cord across the loops, between the sinker hooks and the needles. Hold both ends of the cord in one hand, below the needle bed, pulling down firmly. Push the centre and end needles into HP, over the nylon cord.

3 Keeping the cord taut and with the carriage set to knit back the needles in HP, knit about six rows, then pull the nylon cord out of the knitting.

Waste yarn cast on

Knitting patterns frequently contain the instruction "cast on with waste yarn". This is so that an open edge of loops may be left that can later be knitted on to, or turned up to form a hem.

1 Set the tension dial at a slightly looser setting than would normally be used for the yarn you are casting on with.

2 Thread waste yarn, which should be of the same type and thickness as the main yarn, but of a different colour, through the tension unit and through the feeder on the carriage.

3 Bring the required number of needles forward into WP. Cast on using the simple cast on or the nylon cord cast on.

4 Knit approximately six rows, and then remove the waste yarn from the feeder.

5 Change the tension dial to the required setting. Thread the machine with the main yarn and continue knitting.

Hand wound cast on

This cast on gives a firm, solid edge. With practise you will achieve a neat edge quite quickly. Make sure you wind the yarn evenly, and fairly loosely, or else the carriage will jam when you try to knit a row.

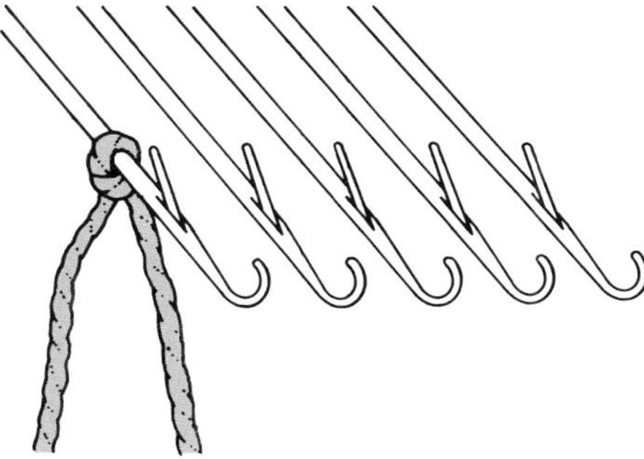

1 Position the carriage on the right of the needle bed. Bring the required number of needles forward into HP. Tie a slip knot in the end of the yarn and place the loop on the left-hand needle in HP.

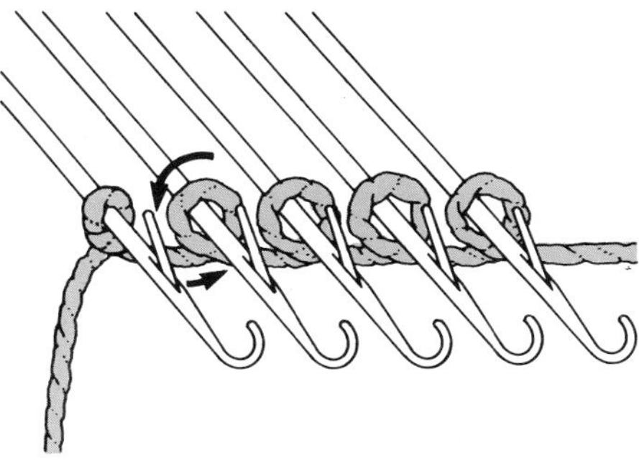

2 Pull the yarn through the tension unit so the yarn is not stretched tight. Loop the yarn around the next needle on the right in an anti-clockwise direction. Repeat, looping the yarn around all the needles in HP.

3 Pull the yarn back through the tension unit so that any slack is "taken up". Use a tension setting slightly looser than normal for the type of yarn you are using. Pass the carriage from right to left across the needles. Attach weights to the first row and continue to knit at the normal tension.

Dropped stitches

If a stitch has dropped through several rows, it can be picked up and re-knitted with the latch tool.

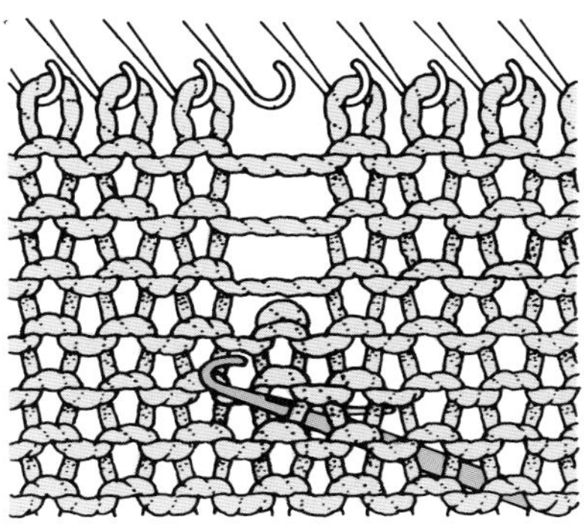

1 Insert the latch tool from behind the knitting into a stitch one or two rows below the dropped stitch. Unravel the knitting down to the latch tool.

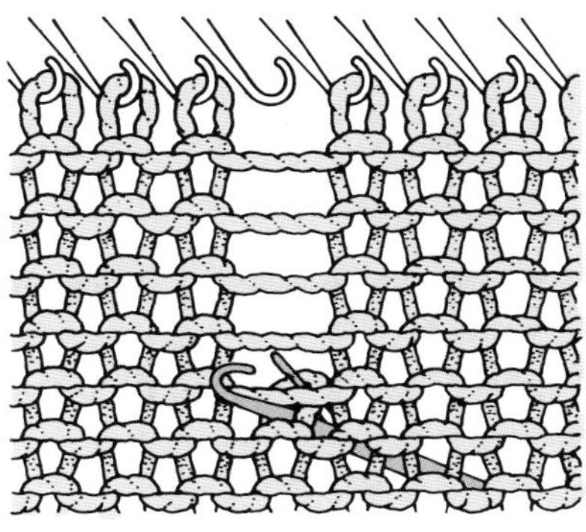

2 Push the latch tool towards you so that the stitch comes behind the latch. Catch the next cross thread in the hook and pull the latch tool back so the latch closes and the cross thread is trapped in the hook. Continue pulling backwards so the stitch that was behind the latch slides down over the closed latch thus forming a new stitch in the hook.

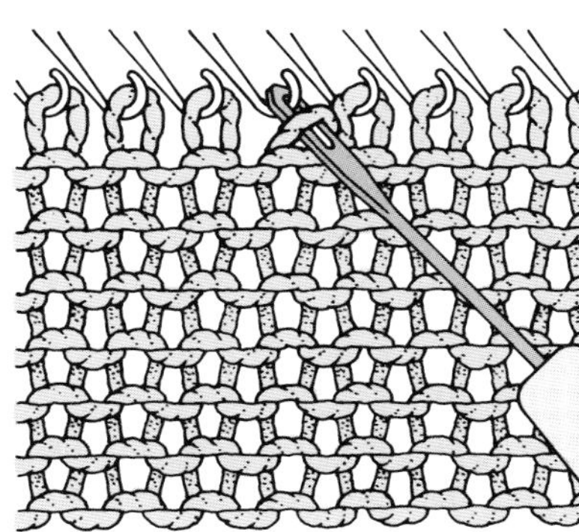

3 Repeat this until you reach the top. Using a single transfer tool place the stitch on to the empty needle.

CASTING OFF

When you end a piece of knitting, such as a sleeve, or part of a piece of knitting, such as up to the neck, you must secure all the stitches by "casting off". As with casting on, there are many different methods. Given below are four of the most useful. Inexperienced knitters are advised to practise the techniques on samples before using them on a garment.

Open edge cast off

This cast off method is very quick and easy to do, but since it leaves an open edge of loops it is only suitable for tension swatches, samples, and finishing off a waste yarn cast off.

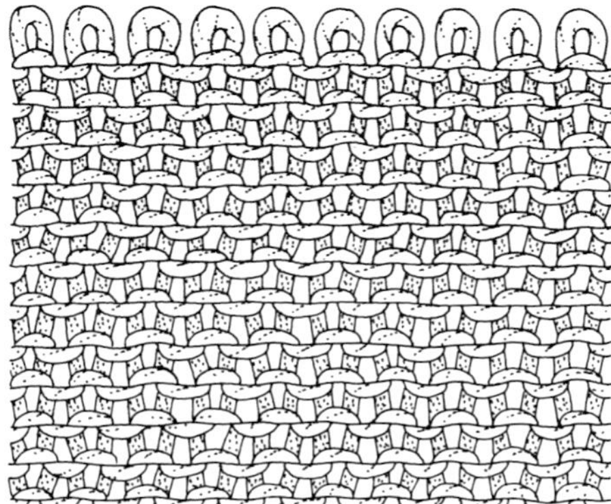

When you have finished knitting, cut the yarn at any point between the carriage and the knitting. Pull the yarn out of the yarn feeder. Push the empty carriage across the work once. The knitting will fall from the needles.

Waste yarn cast off

This method is used when you need to pick up stitches at a later stage in a pattern, for example when attaching a welt.

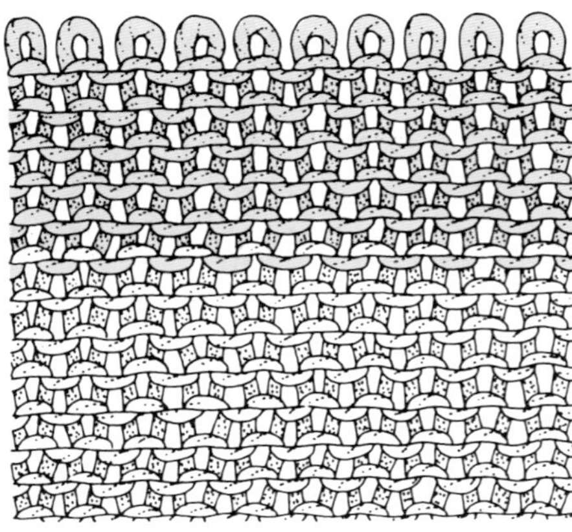

When you have finished knitting rethread the machine with waste yarn. This should be of the same type and thickness as the main yarn, but in a different colour. Knit about six rows with the waste yarn, then cast off using the simple cast off method described above.

Latch tool cast off

This produces a firm, secure, neat edge. For this method of casting off the last row of knitting should be done with the tension setting at least three sizes higher than the main knitting, so it can generally only be used with yarns knitted at tension setting seven, or less. Start the casting off at the opposite end of the knitting from the carriage.

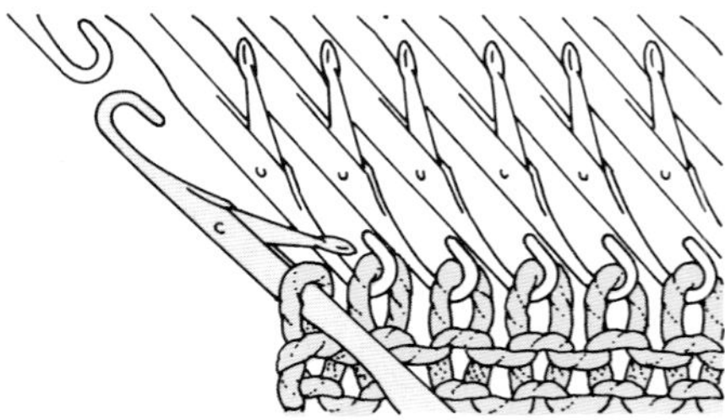

1 Insert the latch tool into the first stitch and remove it from the needle. Push the empty needle back to NWP. Push the latch tool away from you so the stitch is placed behind the latch of the latch tool. Put your forefinger on top of the latch so the stitch is held under the latch.

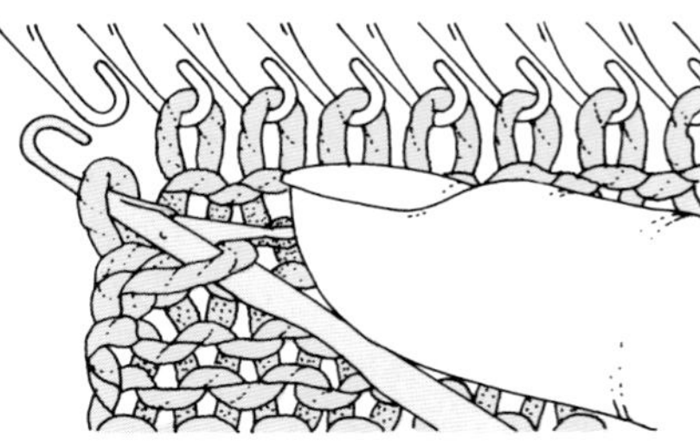

2 Insert the latch tool into the second stitch and remove it from the needle. Push the second needle to NWP.

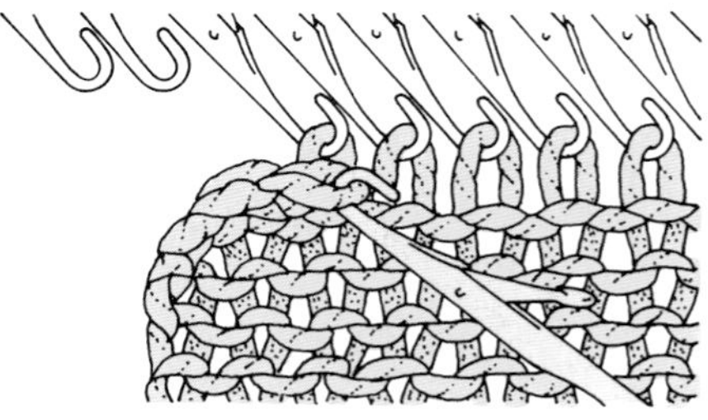

3 Pull the second stitch through the first stitch.

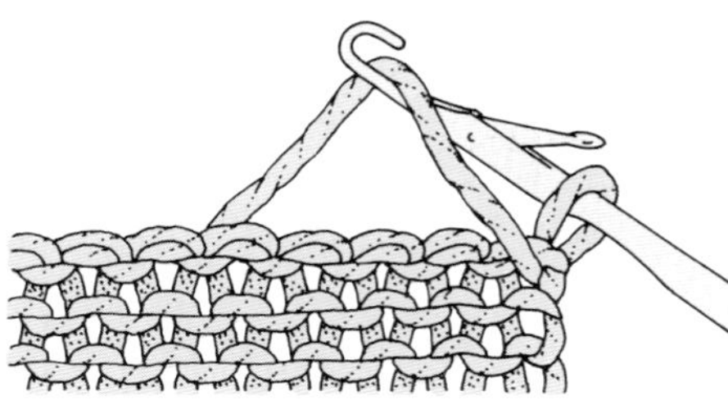

4 Repeat the process along the row. Cast off the last stitch by pulling the yarn end through the stitch.

Transfer tool cast off

This also produces a neat, firm edge. Start the casting off at the same side of the work as the carriage.

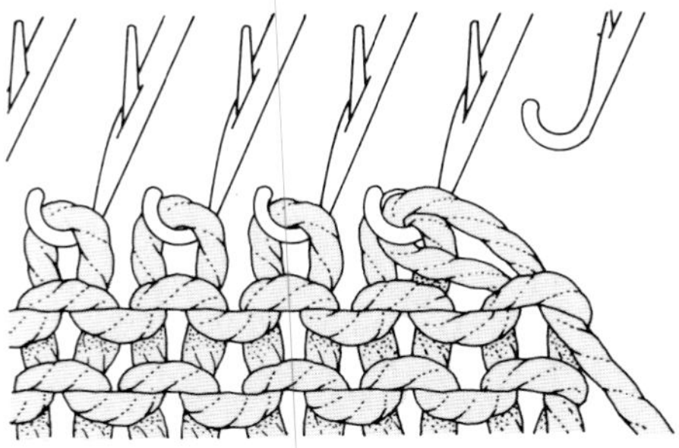

1 Using the single transfer tool, move the end stitch on to the adjacent, occupied needle. Push the empty needle back to NWP.

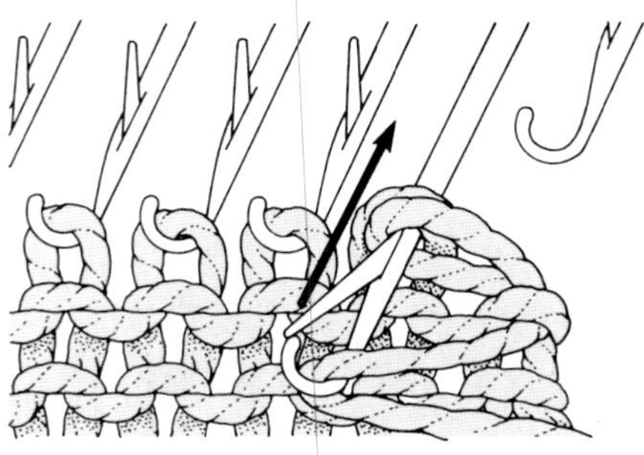

2 Push the needle with two stitches on forward to HP. This pushes both stitches behind the latch. Open the latch. Pull the yarn from the carriage and lay it loosely across the needle hook.

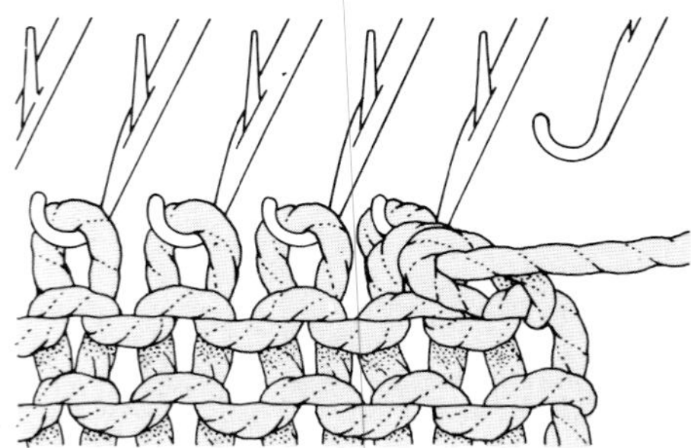

3 Push the needle with two stitches back to WP. This pulls the yarn through the two stitches, creating one stitch.

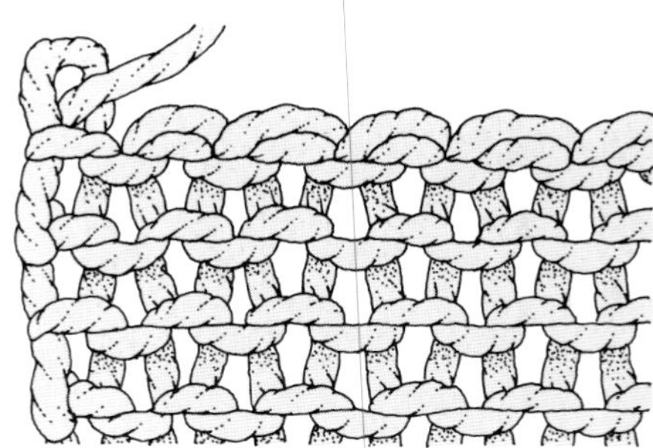

4 Repeat the process all along the row. Cast off the last stitch by pulling the yarn end through the stitch.

HEMS AND RIBS

A simple cast on or cast off edge is not adequate for many edges on machine knitted work – especially if you are making clothes. This is because it stretches and distorts no matter how well you prepare and steam it. Knit and purl ribbing – a combination of knit and purl stitches in the same row – is usually used to finish off edges on hand knitted garments, however standard knit and purl ribbing cannot easily be produced on a single bed knitting machine without a ribbing attachment. Several alternative finished edges which may be used instead are given below and overleaf.

Basic Hem

It is quick and easy to make this hem, the finished result is neat and secure.

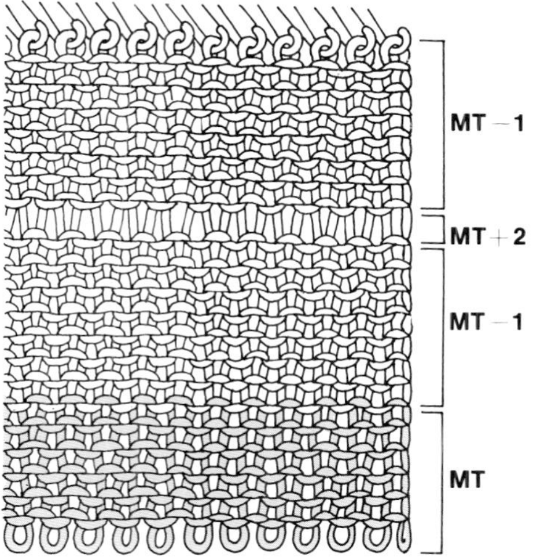

1 Using waste yarn and main tension (MT) cast on the number of stitches required. Knit about 6 rows, then remove the waste yarn from the yarn feeder. Set the tension dial one full size tighter than the main tension (MT – 1), and using the main yarn knit the number of rows required for the depth of the hem. Change the tension to three full sizes looser (MT + 2) and knit one row. Return the tension dial to MT – 1 and knit the number of rows required for the depth of the hem.

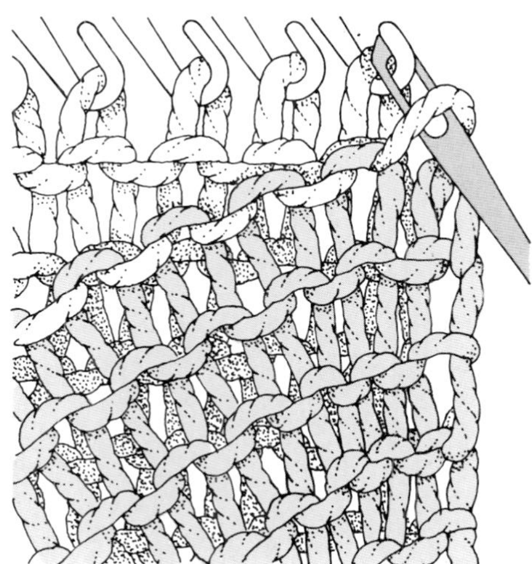

2 Open the latches of the needles in use. Using a single transfer tool pick up the first main yarn stitch (after the waste yarn) and put it on to the first needle.

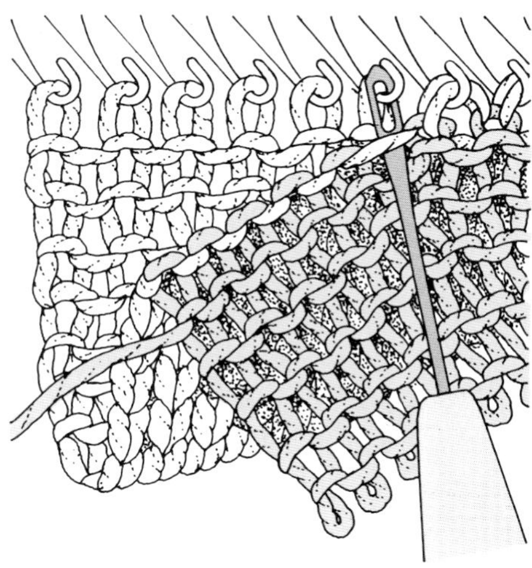

3 Continue across the row being careful to keep each stitch with its corresponding needle.

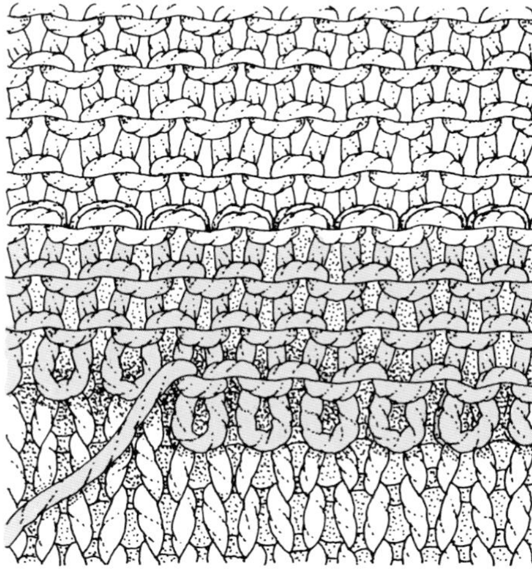

4 When this is completed – each needle should hold two stitches – bring the needles into UWP to make sure that all the loops are caught in the next row. Continue knitting at MT. Unravel the waste yarn after removing the completed knitting from the machine.

Latch tool rib

A true rib can be made on a knitting machine by creating purl stitches with the latch tool. You may find it rather time consuming to produce this rib on a knitting machine, however the column of purl stitches may be made every other stitch, every third stitch, or every fourth stitch. Described below is a 1 × 1 rib.

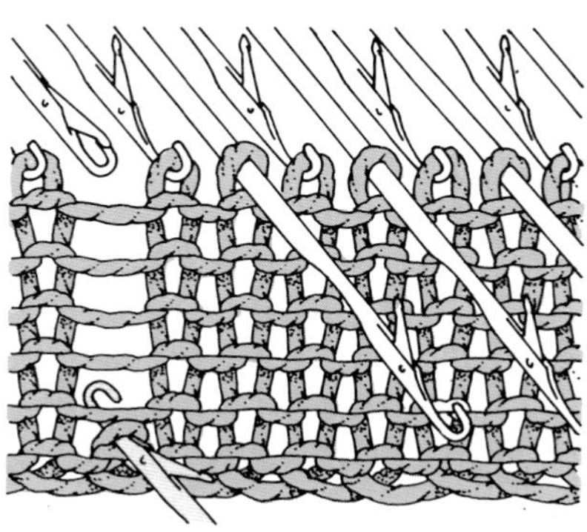

1 Cast on the required number of stitches by hand. Using MT – 2 knit the number of rows required for the depth of the rib. Push every alternate needle into HP. The stitches on these needles are to be reformed into purl stitches. Push the first needle in HP to NWP, then push the now empty needle to WP. Insert the latch tool into the bottom stitch in the column, and drop the stitches above it. * Holding the knitting firmly, push the latch tool away from you so the stitch on the latch tool is behind the latch. Catch the next cross thread with the hook of the latch tool.

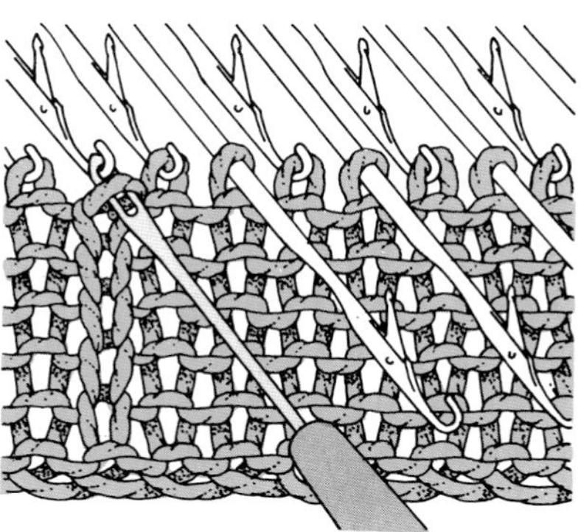

2 Pull the latch tool towards you so the cross thread is pulled through the stitch on the latch tool, thus forming a new stitch. Repeat from * up the column of dropped stitches. Use a transfer tool to place the last new stitch back on the empty needle.

3 Repeat this procedure over the remaining stitches on the needles in HP.

Continental rib

It is very time consuming to produce a true rib with a latch tool on a single bed machine, but a mock rib known as continental rib may be made quite quickly. Continental rib lacks the elasticity of true rib. It may be produced in various stitch formations such as 1 × 1, 2 × 1, and 3 × 1. To make a neat edge, turn up continental rib to form a hem.

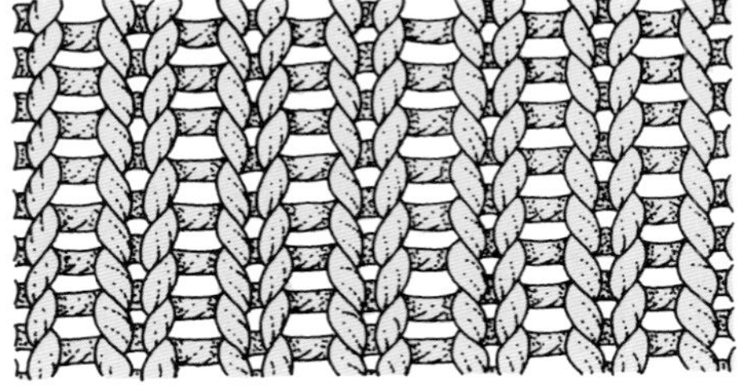

1 × 1 continental rib

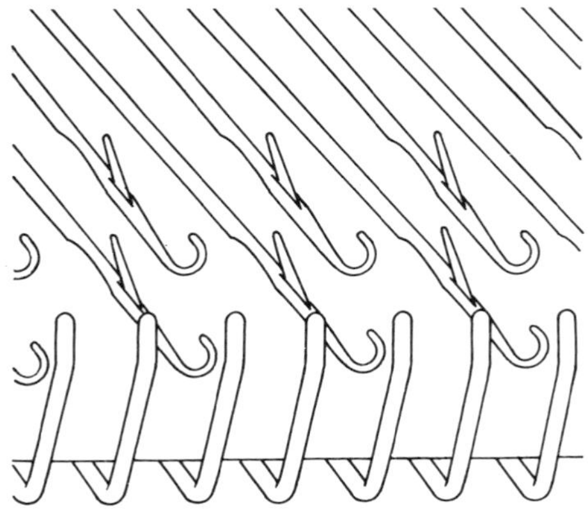

1 This is always produced over an odd number of needles. Bring the required quantity of needles into WP. Using a 1 × 1 needle pusher, push every other needle back to NWP.

2 Cast on using waste yarn and main tension (MT). Using the nylon cord or a cast on comb will help prevent the knitting falling from the needles. Knit about 10 rows, then remove the waste yarn from the yarn feeder. Set the tension dial three full sizes tighter than the main tension (MT − 3), and using the main yarn knit the number of rows required for the depth of the hem. Change the tension to four full sizes looser (MT + 1) and knit one row. Return the tension dial to MT − 3 and knit the number of rows required for the depth of the hem.

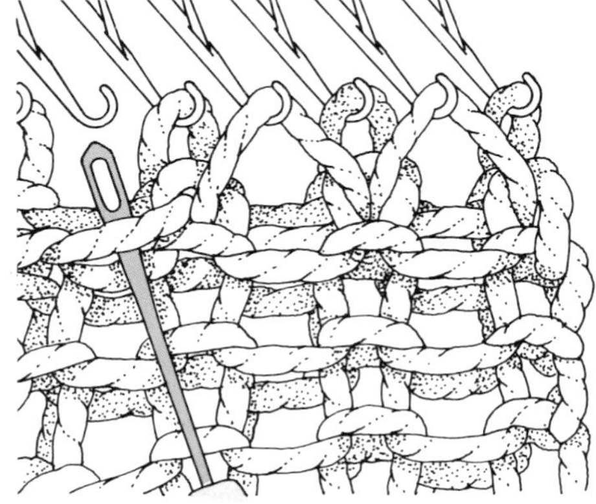

3 Push the empty needles to WP. Remove any combs or weights from the work. Using the single transfer tool, pick up the first stitch of the first row worked in main yarn and place it on the first empty needle. Continue across the row, hooking one main yarn loop on to each empty needle until you come to the last loop; attach this one to the last working needle (although it already has one stitch on it).

4 Bring all the needles to UWP to make sure that all the loops are caught in the next row. Continue knitting at MT. Unravel the waste yarn after removing the completed knitting from the machine.

2 × 1 continental rib

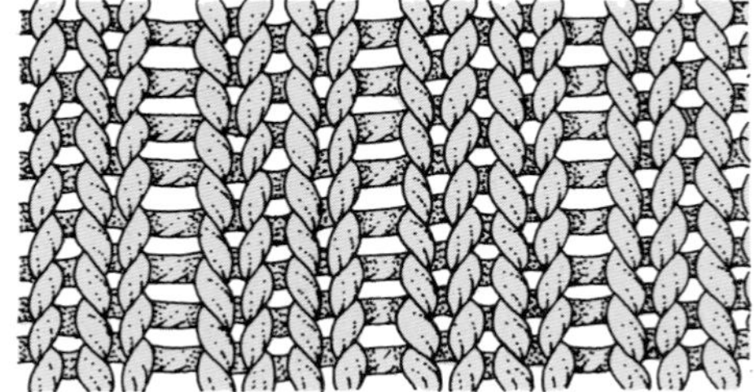

This is always produced over a multiple of three needles plus two. It is worked in just the same way as a 1 × 1 rib, except the needle arrangement is different; push two forward into WP and leave one in NWP. Knit the hem at MT − 2, instead of MT − 3. Work the loose row at MT + 1.

3 × 1 continental rib

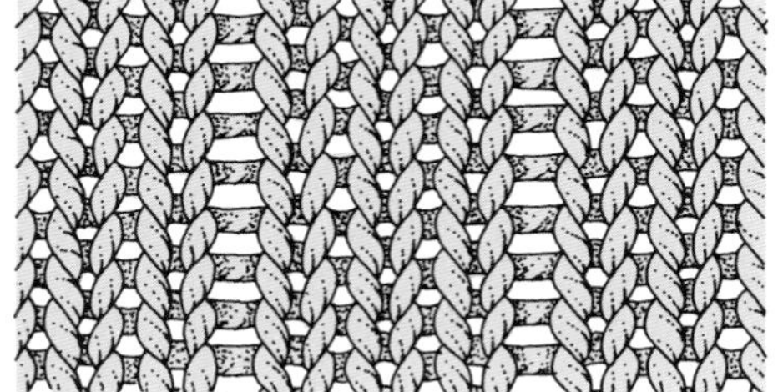

For this you need a multiple of four needles, plus three. It is worked in just the same way as a 1 × 1 rib, except that the needle arrangement is different; push three forward into WP and leave one in NWP. Knit the hem at MT − 1, instead of MT − 3, and work the loose row at MT + 1.

Hand knitted rib

If you want the effect of a true rib, you can use a hand knitted rib. Depending on the pattern, you can either hand knit a rib and then transfer it to the machine needles, or you can pick up stitches on a piece of knitting, or you can knit a separate rib and sew it to the garment at the finishing stage.

Casting on

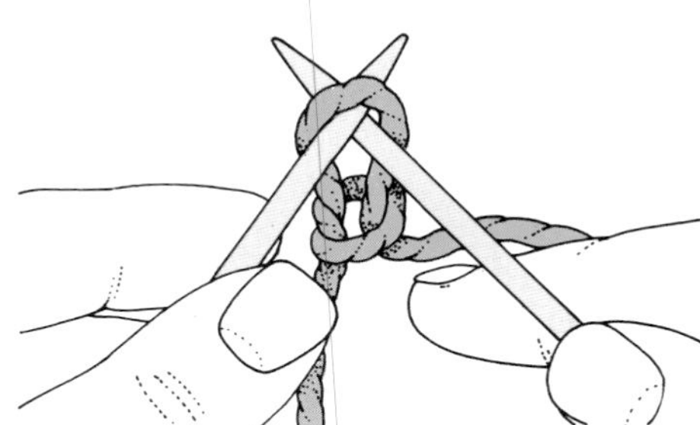

1 Make a slip loop and place it on your left-hand needle. Insert your right-hand needle through the loop from front to back.

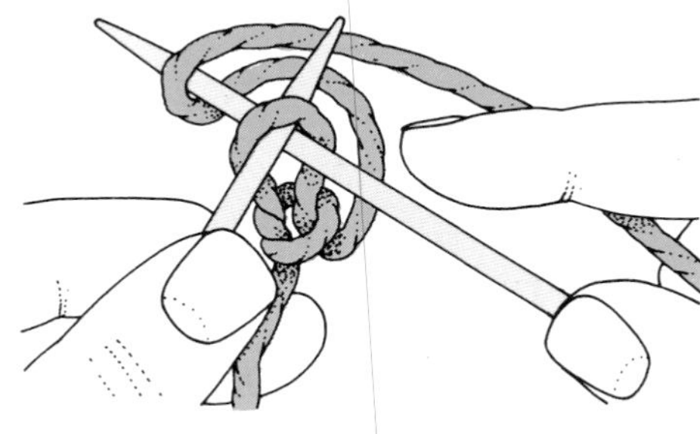

2 Bring the yarn under and over your right-hand needle.

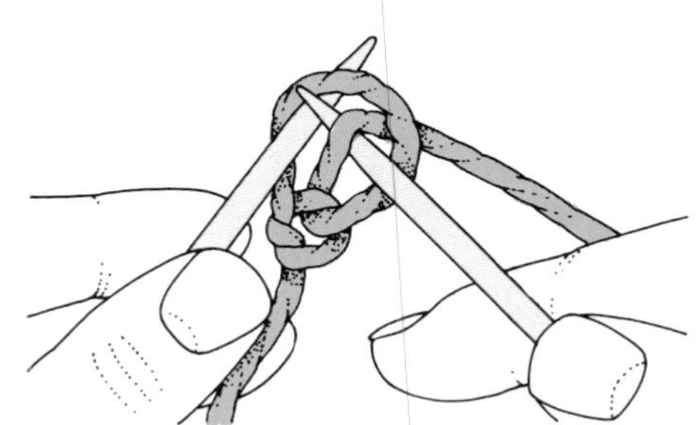

3 Draw up the yarn through the slip loop to make a stitch.

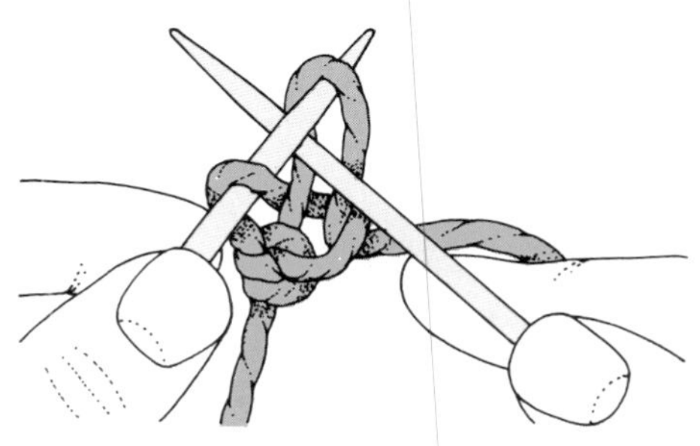

4 Place the stitch on the left-hand needle. Continue to make more stitches inserting the right-hand needle between the last two stitches worked.

Knit stitch

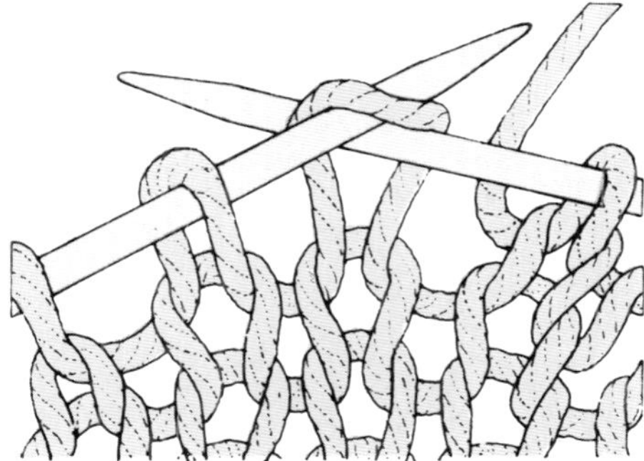

1 With the yarn at the back, insert your right-hand needle from front to back into the stitch on your left-hand needle.

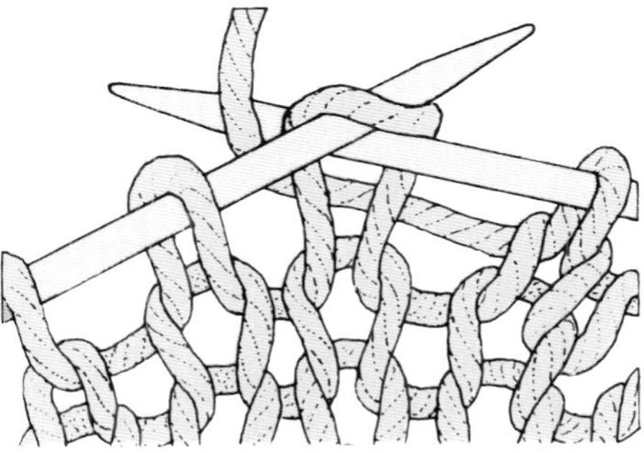

2 Bring your working yarn under and over the point of your right-hand needle.

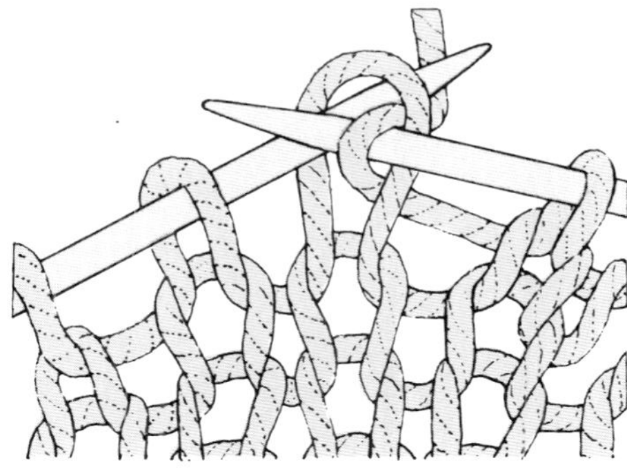

3 Draw a loop through and slide the first stitch off your left-hand needle while the new stitch is retained on your right-hand needle.

Purl stitch

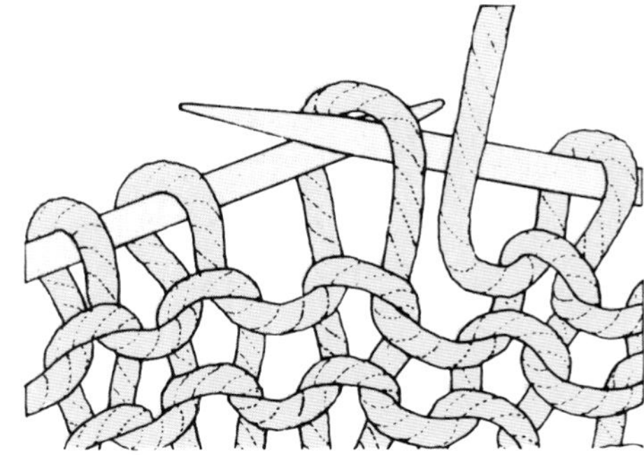

1 With the yarn at the front, insert your right-hand needle from back to front into the stitch on your left-hand needle.

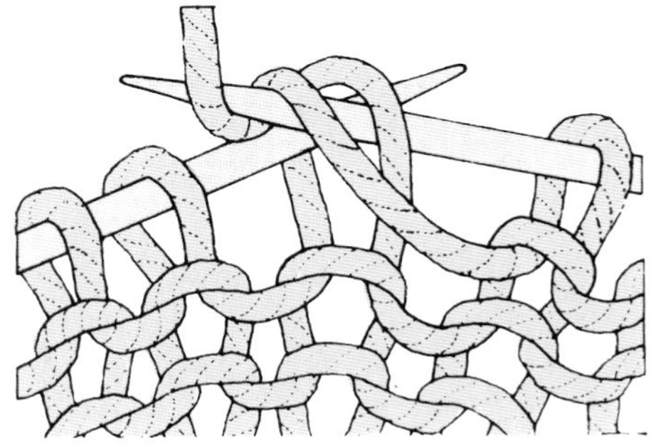

2 Bring your working yarn over and around the point of your right-hand needle.

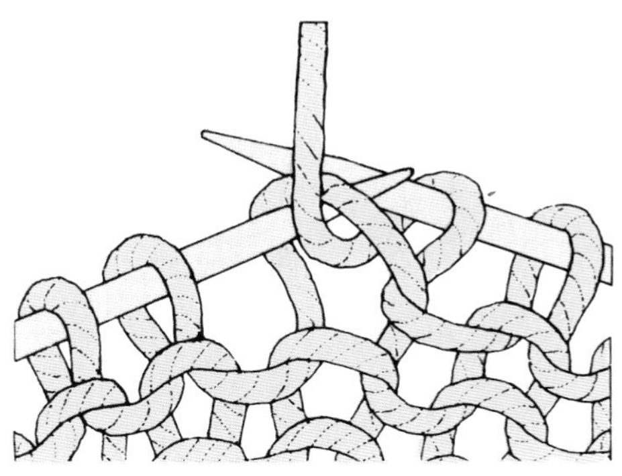

3 Draw a loop through and slide the stitch off your left-hand needle while the new stitch is retained on your right-hand needle.

Casting off

Casting off should be done quite loosely. When casting off in rib you must follow the pattern and cast off in both knit and purl. Whether casting off in knit or purl the basic technique remains the same, but instead of knitting all the stitches, knit and purl alternately for single rib, knit two, purl two for double rib.

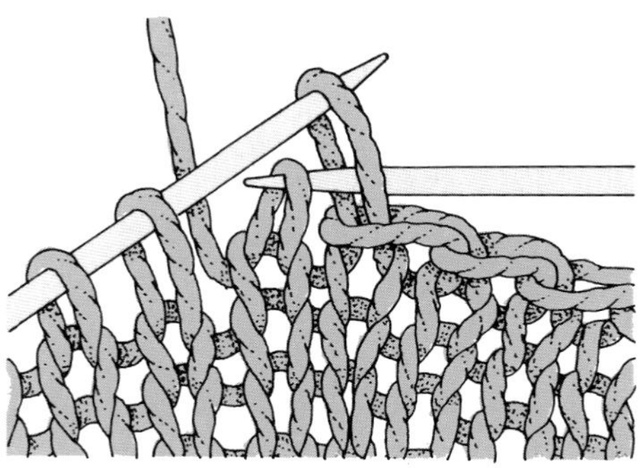

1 Knit the first two stitches and insert the tip of your left-hand needle through the first stitch.

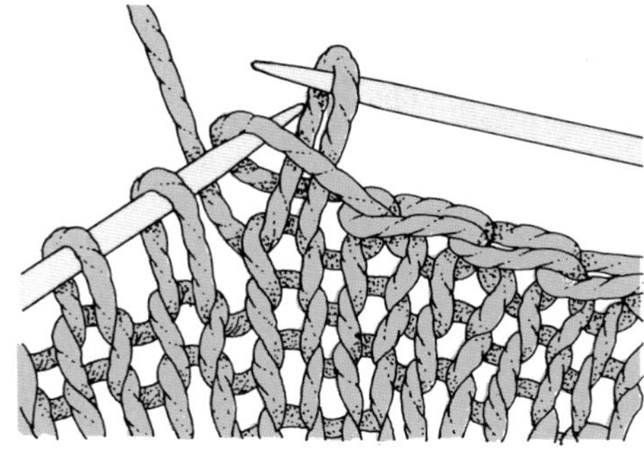

2 Lift the first stitch over the second stitch and discard it. Work the next stitch and continue to lift the first stitch over the second stitch to the end of the row. Be careful not to knit too tightly.

3 For the last stitch, cut your yarn, slip the end through the stitch and pull the yarn tight to fasten off securely.

Single rib

When changing from a knit stitch to a purl stitch bring the yarn to the front. When changing from a purl stitch to a knit stitch bring the yarn to the back. Cast on an odd number of stitches.

Row 1 *Knit 1, purl 1; repeat from * to last stitch, knit 1.
Row 2 *Purl 1, knit 1; repeat from * to the last stitch, purl 1.
Repeat rows 1 and 2 until the rib is the required length.

Double rib

When changing from a knit stitch to a purl stitch bring the yarn to the front. When changing from a purl stitch to a knit stitch bring the yarn to the back. Cast on a multiple of 4 stitches, plus 2.

Row 1 *Knit 2, purl 2; repeat from * to the last 2 sts, knit 2.
Row 1 *Knit 2, purl 2; repeat from * to the last 2 sts, purl 2.
Repeat rows 1 and 2 until the rib is the required length.

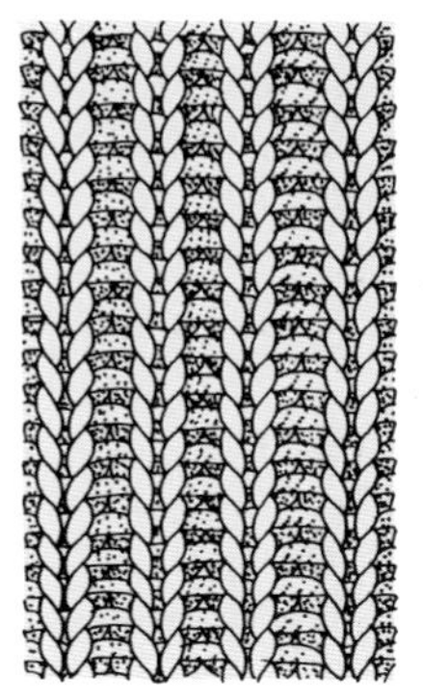

Single rib

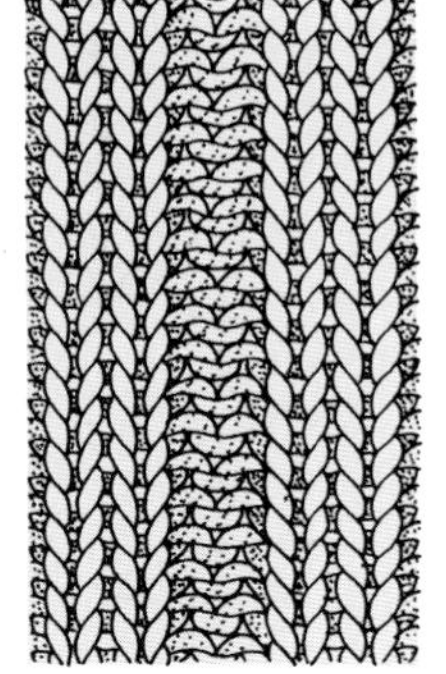

Double rib

INCREASING AND DECREASING

Shaping of machine knitting is done in much the same way as in hand knitting, by increasing and decreasing stitches. Increases and decreases can be made on the edge of the knitting, or one or more stitches in from the edge.

Simple increase

This method of increasing is quick to do but only one stitch at a time may be increased. It may be done on either side of the knitting, but a neater edge is produced if it is worked on the opposite side of the knitting from the carriage.

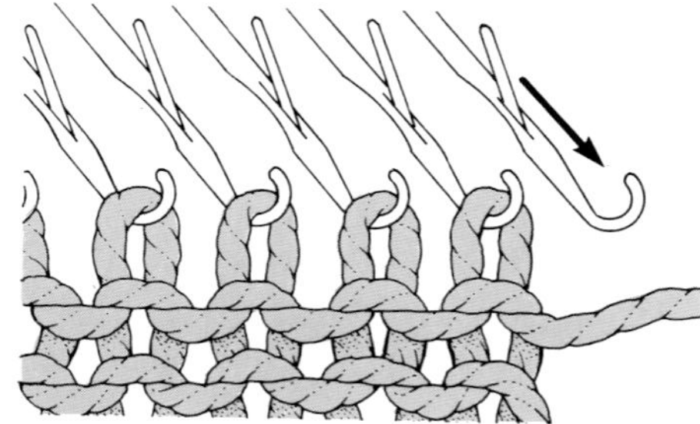

Push the needle at the edge of the knitting forward into WP. Operate the carriage and knit one row. The empty needle will pick up the yarn. Continue knitting.

Multiple increase

Using this method you can increase as many stitches as you require on one side of the work in any one row.

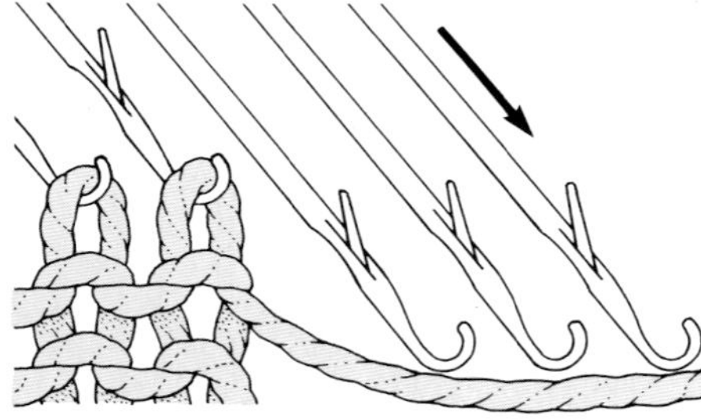

1 With the carriage on the same side of the knitting as the increase, pull as many needles as you need extra stitches from NWP to UWP.

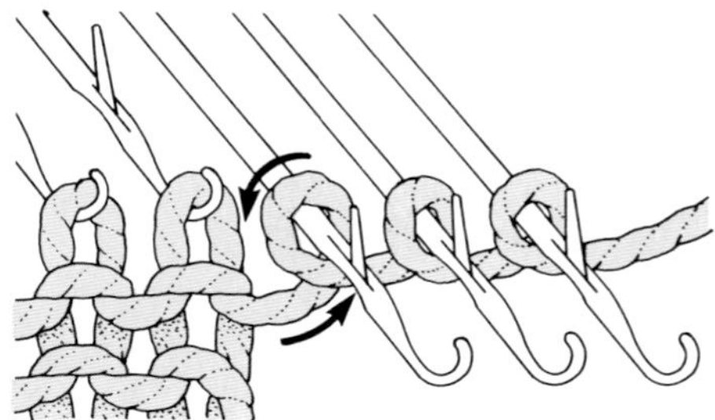

2 Pull a little yarn through the carriage, and wind it around the needles, in the same way as a hand wound cast on. Wind as evenly as possible. Before knitting the next row, pull slack yarn back through the tension unit.

Fully fashioned increase

This method produces a neater, straighter edge than the simple increase method, so it is easier to sew the pieces of knitting together. You can use a single, double or treble transfer tool to move one, two or three stitches. The method using a treble transfer tool is described below.

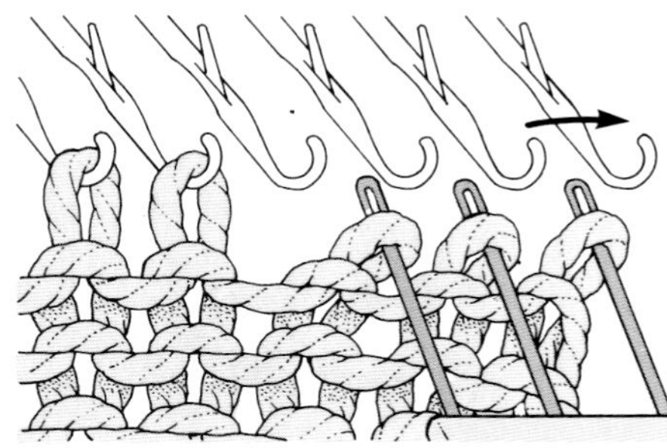

1 Push the needle at the edge of the knitting forward into WP. Using the treble transfer tool, move the three end stitches out one needle, so that the fourth needle from the end is empty.

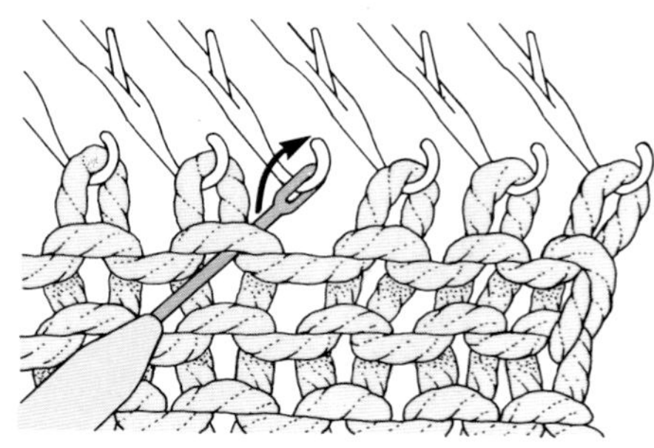

2 Insert a single transfer tool into the loop below the fourth stitch. Place the loop on to the empty needle. Continue knitting.

Simple decrease

It is very quick to decrease stitches with this method, however only one stitch at a time can be decreased.

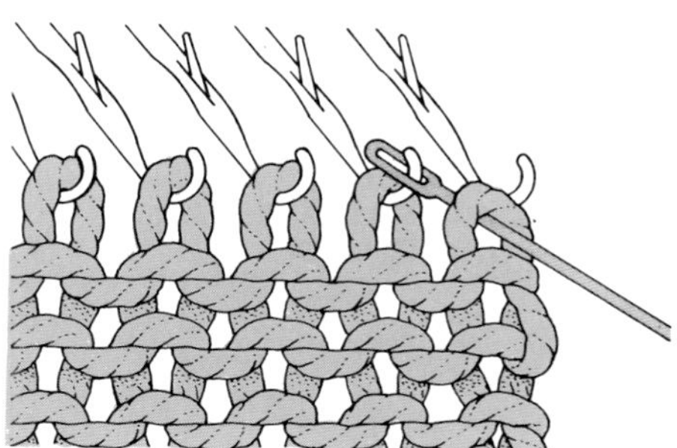

Using a single transfer tool, pick up the stitch on the needle at the end of the knitting. Transfer the stitch to the next needle along and push the empty needle to NWP. Continue knitting.

Fully fashioned decrease

This decrease produces a neat straight edge. Generally only one stitch at a time is decreased. As with the fully fashioned increase, you can use a single, double or treble transfer tool to move one, two or three stitches.

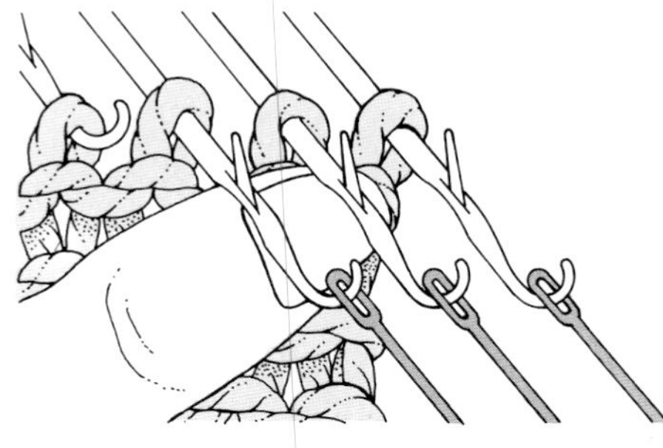

1 Place the transfer tool over the hooks of the last three needles on the side of the decrease. Pull these needles out to HP.

2 Close the needle latches, and push the needles back to NWP, and then forward to WP, the stitches should now be held on the transfer tool.

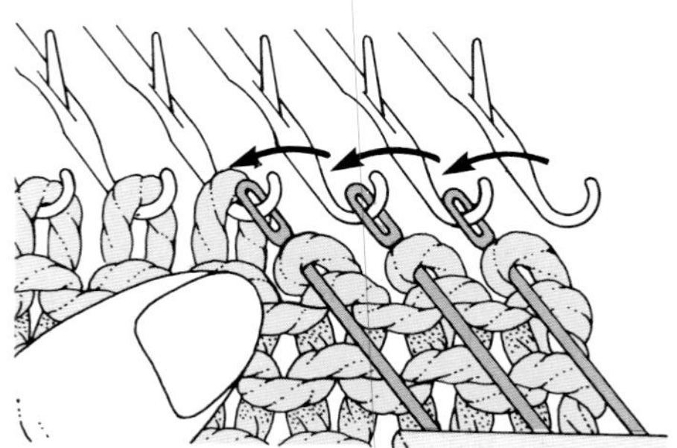

3 Lift the transfer tool off the needle hooks and move it one stitch along.

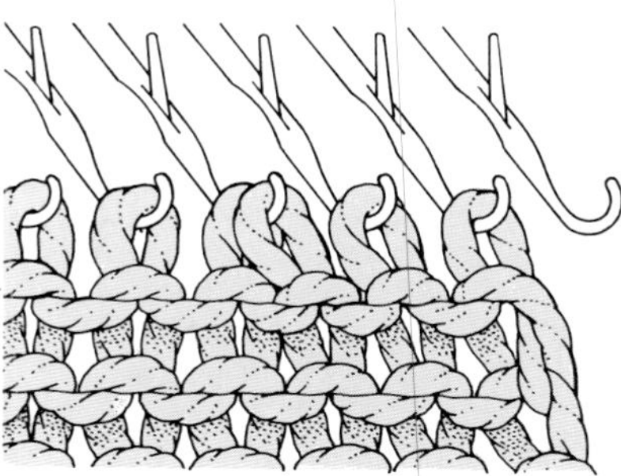

4 Push the loops on the transfer tool on to the needles. Push the empty end needle back to NWP.

Multiple decrease

With this method several stitches may be decreased on one side of the work in any one row. It uses the same technique as the transfer tool cast off.

1 With the carriage on the same side of the work as the decrease, use the single transfer tool to move the end stitch on to the adjacent, occupied needle. Push the empty needle back to NWP.

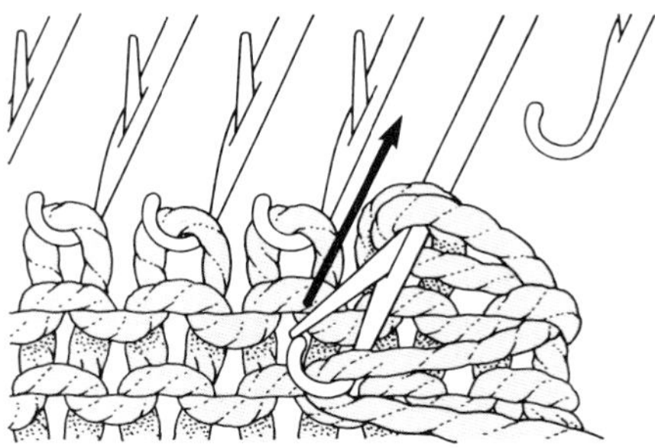

2 Push the needle with two stitches on forward to HP. This pushes both stitches behind the latch. Open the latch. Pull the yarn from the carriage and lay it loosely across the needle hook. If the carriage is at the right, lay the yarn from right to left, and if the carriage is at the left lay the yarn from left to right.

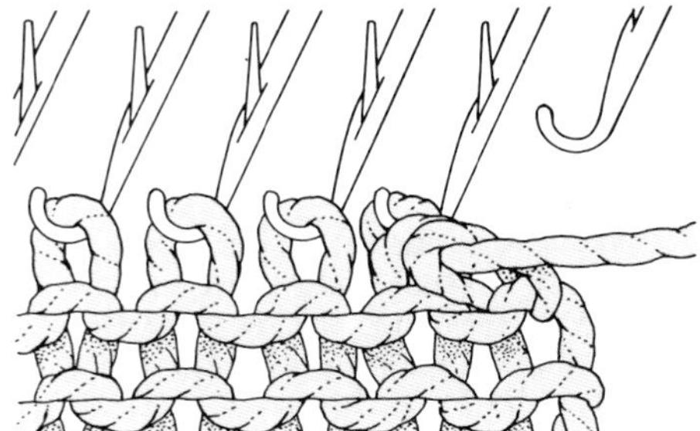

3 Push the needle with two stitches back to WP so it is in line with the other needles. This pulls the yarn through the two stitches, creating one stitch.

Repeat this process until you have decreased the required number of stitches.

THE TENSION SWATCH

Before knitting any garment it is vital to make a tension swatch to check that your knitting is worked at the same tension as that given in the pattern.

At the beginning of every pattern the tension measurement required to make the garment the correct size is given, for example: 30 stitches and 40 rows to 10 centimetres. You have to make up tension swatches at different tension settings until you make one exactly the same as stated in the pattern.

It is useful to take note of tension swatch results for future reference, but you must remember that you have to consider not just the type and thickness of the yarn, but also the brand and colour.

There are many different ways of making tension swatches, and each knitter usually develops her own technique. One way is described below.

1 Thread the machine with waste yarn of the same type and thickness as the yarn to be used in the pattern, but in a contrasting colour. Set the tension to one stop lower than suggested in the pattern. Cast on a number of stitches so that the finished width of the knitting will be approximately 15cm (6in). Using the needles in the centre of the needle bed, count the same number of needles as given in the tension measurement, and push one needle each side to NWP.

2 Knit a few rows in waste yarn. Change to the same yarn as you will be using for the garment. Knit the number of rows stated in the tension measurement.

3 Change to waste yarn and change the tension setting to that suggested in the pattern. Knit a few rows in waste yarn and then change to the yarn used in the pattern. Knit the number of rows given in the tension measurement.

4 Change to waste yarn and change the tension setting to one stop higher than suggested in the tension measurement. Knit a few rows in waste yarn and then change to the yarn used in the pattern. Knit the number of rows given in the tension measurement.

5 Change to waste yarn and knit a few rows. Remove the knitting from the machine and make a note of the tension settings that were used.

6 Since machine knitting distorts the stitches considerably you have to give the tension swatch time to settle after removing it from the machine. Ideally, allow it to settle overnight. However, if time is short you may measure the swatch after about an hour.

7 Place the swatch on a smooth, flat surface and measure the three different tension areas. Hopefully, one of them will correlate with the tension measurements given in the pattern. If not, using the swatch as a guide, knit up another at different settings, based on the results you have already obtained.

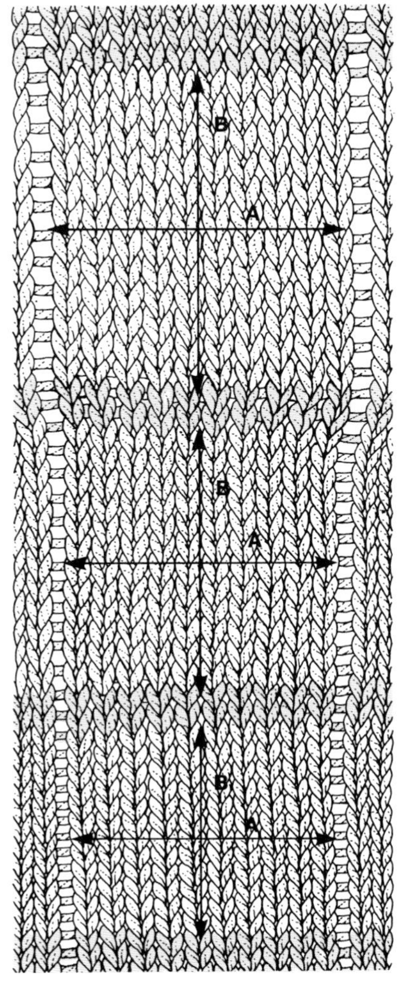

A number of stitches

B number of rows

FINISHING

The way you finish off your garment makes a great deal of difference to the final result. Finishing involves three different stages: blocking, setting, and sewing together.

Blocking

Basically this is just pinning each garment piece out on a flat surface, to the correct measurements. This pulls all the stitches into place and makes it easier to sew the pieces together.
If you omit this stage, your garment will not have a professional finish.

The blocking surface can be a blanket, folded in half, or foam, covered with lightweight cotton fabric such as sheeting or gingham. Using gingham makes the process slightly easier, since it provides straight lines and right angles to work with.

Lay the piece of knitting wrong side up on the blocking surface and gently coax it into the right shape and size. Pin the knitting to the surface, spacing the pins two or three centimetres apart.

Setting

After blocking, each piece has to be set so that it will remain the right shape. The way you set depends on the yarn and stitch construction used. Generally, natural yarns should be pressed or steamed, blended yarns should be pressed only, and synthetic yarns need to be treated with great care. If a textured stitch construction, such as tuck stitch, has been used, do not press the pieces, even if natural yarns have been used. Instead, dampen them using one of the methods given on the right.

Pressing natural yarn
Lay a wet, cotton cloth over the knitting and hold a hot iron over the cloth, evaporating the water. Do not actually make any ironing movements, just hold the iron over each section in turn until the cloth is completely dry. Remove the cloth and check you have pressed the piece correctly. Leave the knitting to dry before removing the pins, and store it flat until you are ready to sew.

Pressing synthetic yarn
The only safe way to press synthetic yarn is according to the manufacturer's instructions. You have to proceed with extreme caution with all synthetic yarn, checking the results as you go along.

Pressing synthetic/natural mixes
This depends on the proportions of synthetic and natural yarn. If the manufacturer's instructions are available, you should refer to them. If they are not, it is safest to place a dry cloth over the work and then press lightly with a warm iron. To avoid iron marks, make your actions as smooth as possible, without actually sliding the iron across the work. Remove the pins on completion and store the pieces flat until you are ready to sew them together.

Dampening textured stitch constructions
- Dampen the cotton cloth that lays on top of the folded blanket or foam, then block the pieces on top of this. Do not remove the pins until the cloth and the knitting are dry.
- Using a plant spray, spray the blocked garment pieces when they are pinned out. Do not remove the pins until the knitting is dry.

Sewing together

Sewing together is a most important part of making knitted garments. None of the techniques are particularly difficult, and time and care spent on them will achieve professional-looking results. Described below are the various stitches you will need, and their uses.

Mattress stitch
This is the most versatile stitch. It provides a strong, invisible seam, the only real disadvantage being that it is bulky on the underside. However, it is well-suited to raglan-sleeve seams, side seams on all your garments, and seams that join two pieces of patterned knitting. This is because it is sewn with the right side facing, so you can match the pattern as you go. You will need a tapestry needle and some yarn.

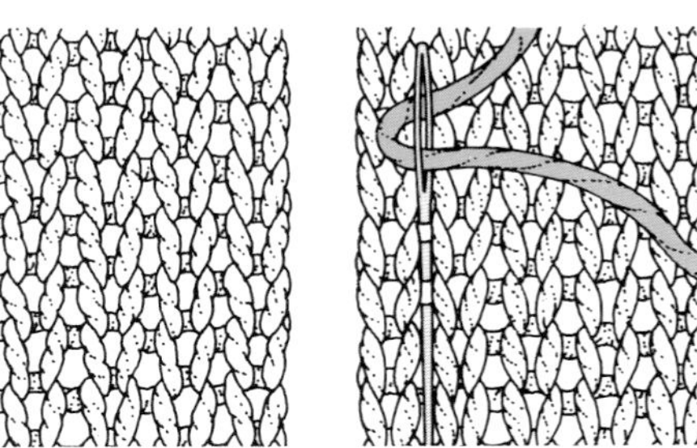

1 Place the two seam edges side by side, right side up. Thread the needle and stitch through two stitchbars, one stitch in from the edge on one side.

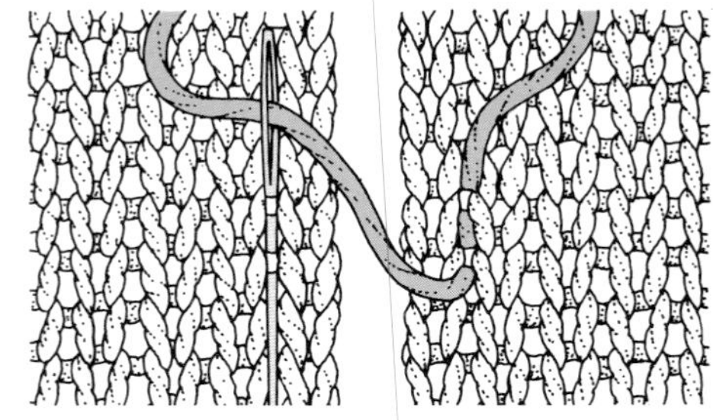

2 Pick up the two stitchbars one stitch in on the other side.

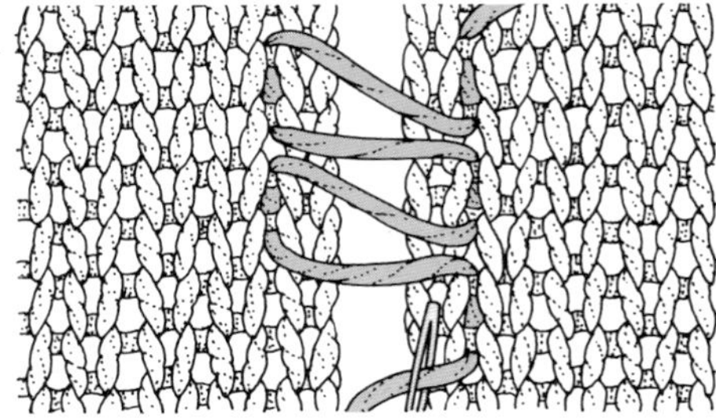

3 Without pulling the stitches taut, pick up the next two stitchbars on the first side. Then pick up the next two stitchbars on the other side, and so on.

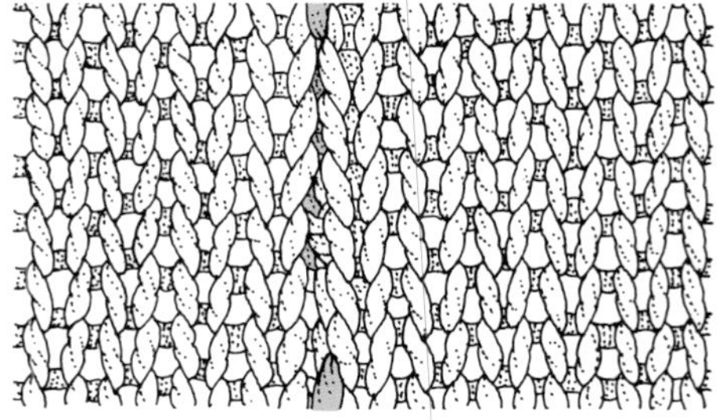

4 When the thread is zigzagged across the two seam edges about five times pull it taut – the seam will be pulled together. Continue picking up the next two stitchbars on each side in turn, pulling the thread taut after about every five stitches until the seam is complete.

Grafting

This is another hand-sewn seam that, if well done, is both invisible and firm. It is often used for shoulder seams or at any time when a flat seam is required. You will need a tapestry needle which you thread with the yarn remaining from the last stitch. Be sure to leave enough yarn on the work to cover the intended seam length, times three. If either of the edges you are joining are cast-on edges it is a good idea to cast on with the waste yarn method (using the same yarn for the waste yarn as for the garment). This ensures that you have enough yarn left to graft the seam.

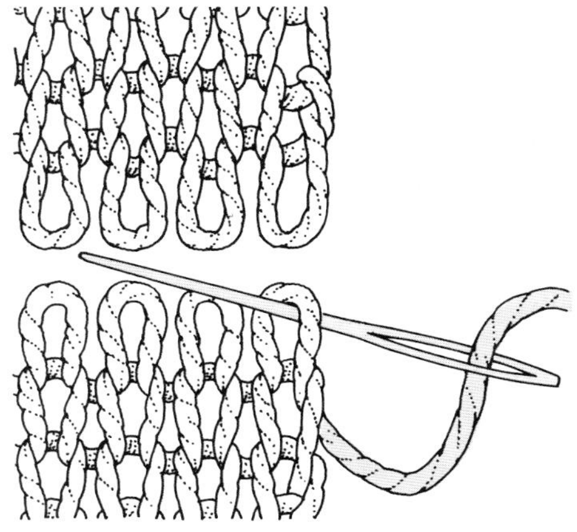

1 Lay the two seam edges side by side, right side up. Bring the needle back through the loop of the first stitch.

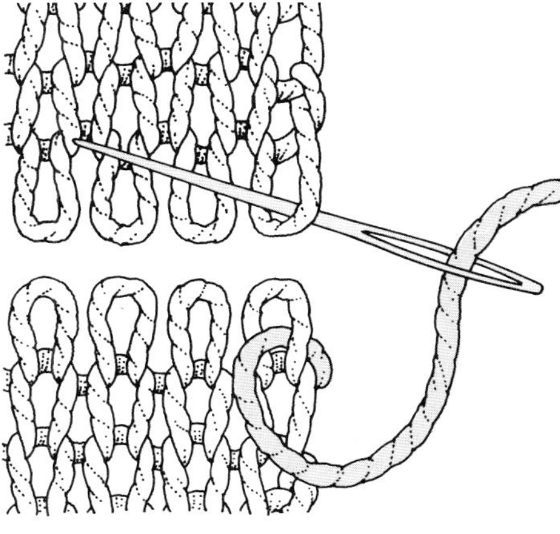

2 Take the needle up through the first loop on the other side.

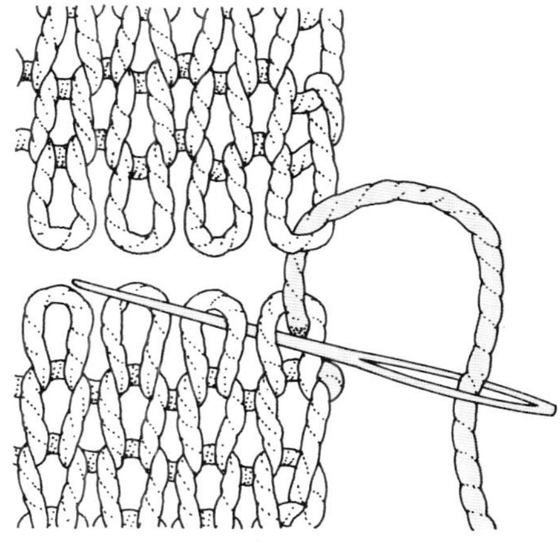

3 Stitch the needle back down through the first loop on the first side, and through the second loop on the same side.

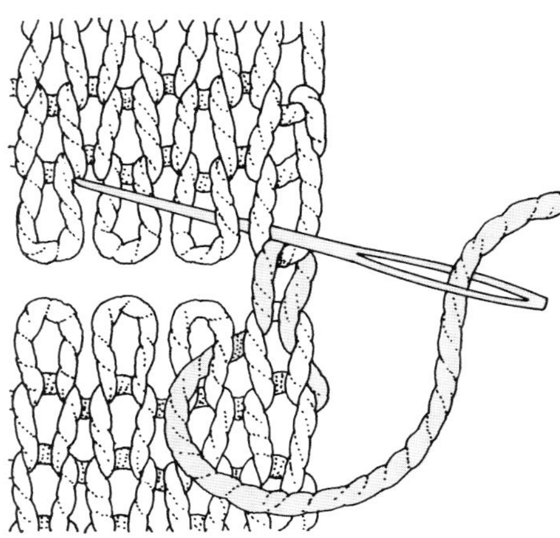

4 Take the needle through the first and second loops on the other side.

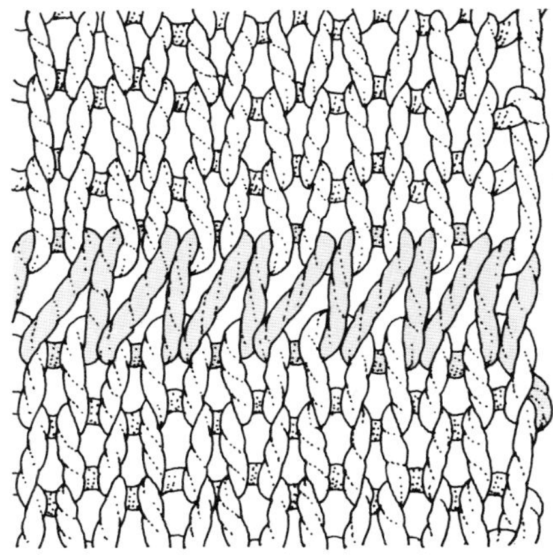

5 Repeat across the row, keeping the tension as close as you can to the tension of the two pieces you are joining. The more time you spend getting the tension right the more "invisible" the seam will be.

Backstitch

Backstitch provides a quick, satisfactory seam for many purposes, as well as being a technique that most people already know. However, it is difficult to get as neat a finish as with either mattress stitch or by grafting. When you sew through both pieces of knitting check that the corresponding stitches are in line with each other. You will need a tapestry needle and yarn to match the knitting.

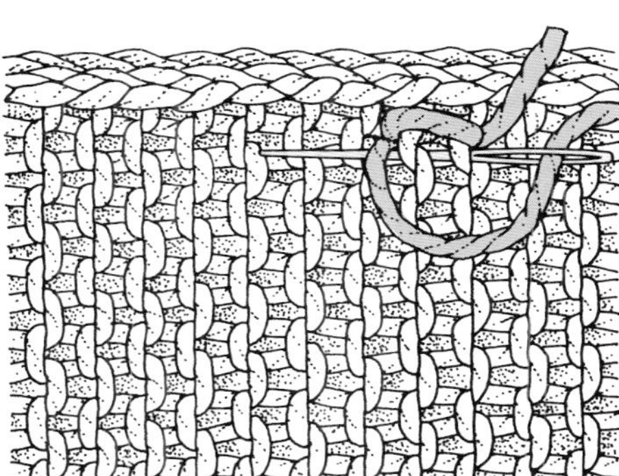

1 Lay the two pieces you are joining with right sides together. With the needle threaded, sew three small stitches one on top of the other at the beginning of the seam.

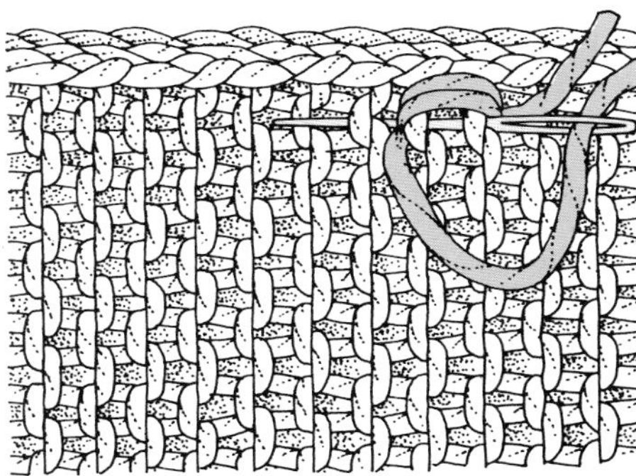

2 Insert the needle into the back of the first stitch and take it out one stitch along.

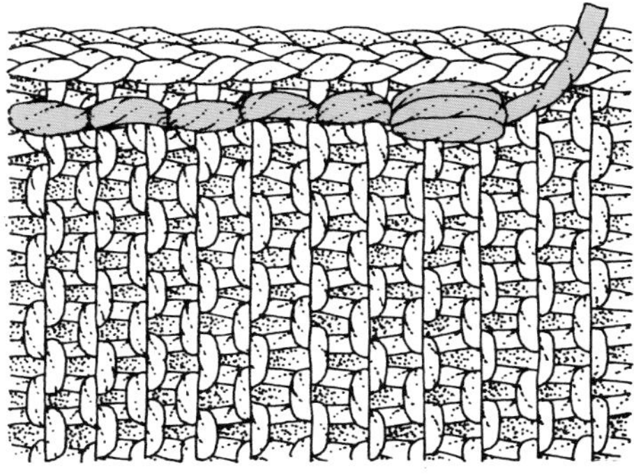

3 Repeat this process all along the seam, keeping the tension constant and the stitches as tight as you can without puckering or distorting the knitting.

USEFUL·ADDRESSES

YARN SUPPLIERS

The suppliers marked with an asterisk sell their yarn only through retailers. Write to them for the address of your nearest stockist.

S+J Andrews (WY) Ltd
Brockwell Wools
Stansfield Mill
Triangle
Halifax
West Yorkshire HX6 3LZ
Extensive range of coned yarns, including Botany wool, oiled or scoured lambswool, plain, slub and mercerised cotton.

***Argyll Wools Ltd**
PO Box 15
Priestley Mills
West Yorkshire LS28 9LT
Wide range of hand and machine knitting yarns, including 2-, 3-, 4-ply, double knitting, mohair, cotton, Aran, chunky and fancy yarns.

***F W Bramwell & Co Ltd**
Holmes Mill
Greenacre Street
Clitheroe BB7 1EA
A wide range of yarns on cone from 1-ply to chunky in wool, cotton, acrylic and blends.

***James Brett**
32-34 Clyde Street
Bingley
West Yorkshire BD16 2NT
Good range of quality yarns available on cone.

British Mohair Spinners Ltd
Grove Mills
Ingrow
Keighley BD21 5EG
A very good colour range of coned mohair, also British wool in natural shades, and Icelandic and chunky yarns.

Hilary Chetwynd
Kipping Cottage
Cheriton
Alresford
Hampshire SO24 0PW
Interesting variety of silks, mainly in natural shades. Most available on cone. Mail order service or collect by appointment No wholesale.

***Coats Domestic Marketing Division**
39 Durham Street
Glasgow G41 1BS
Wide range of knitting and crochet cotton suitable for use on a knitting machine.

Colourtwist
10 Mayfield Avenue
Industrial Park
Weyhill
Andover
Hampshire SP11 8HU
Specialists in fancy coned yarns. Also can supply some of the fancy yarns used in the patterns. Please write for details.

Cumbrian Crafts
58 Main Street
Keswick
Cumbria CA12 5JS
Suppliers of undyed British wool from named varieties of sheep, available on cone. Also stock unspun Icelandic lopi.

***Emu Wools Ltd**
Leeds Road
Greengates
Bradford
West Yorkshire BD10 9TE
Comprehensive selection of fancy and straight yarns in a wide range of colours. Not available on cone.

Falcon-by-Post
Falcon Mills
Bartle Lane
Bradford
West Yorkshire BD7 4QJ
Mail-order retailer, selling own range of coned yarns as well as hand-knitting yarns by other leading manufacturers.

***T Forsell & Son Ltd**
Blaby Road
South Wigston
Leicester LE8 2SG
Selection of straight yarns in a wide range of colours, some available on cone, including a good range of pure wool yarns.

Jamieson & Smith
90 North Road
Lerwick
Shetland
Best quality Shetland wool in a very wide colour range. Mail order service, no wholesale.

***Knitmaster**
39-45 Cowleaze Road
Kingston-upon-Thames
Surrey KT2 6DT
Range of straight yarns available on cone.

***Lister Handknitting Ltd**
Whiteoak Mills
Westgate
Wakefield WF2 9SF
Comprehensive selection of fancy and straight yarns in a wide range of colours. Not available on cone.

***Loweth Wools Ltd**
PO Box 140
Murrayfield Road
Leicester LE3 1UL
A range of straight and fancy yarns for hand and machine knitting, some available on cone.

Neveda Yarns
Smallwares Ltd
17 Galena Road
London W6 0LU
Small but interesting selection of fancy hand-knitting yarns. Also supply unusual, high-fashion Japanese yarns.

***Patsy Yarns**
(Div John Crowther Group PLC)
PO Box A24
Union Mills
Milnsbridge
Huddersfield HD3 4NA
Good range of quality fashion yarns for machine and hand knitters, including fancy and straight yarns.

Ries Wools of Holborn
242-243 High Holborn
London WC1V 7DZ
Large multi-brand wool shop in central London with many high fashion European yarns. Mail order service available.

***Rowan Yarns Ltd**
Green Lane Mill
Washpit
Holmfirth
Huddersfield HD7 1RW
Wide selection of straight yarns, all natural fibres, also good colour range of cotton chenille. Most yarns available on cone.

St John's Knitting Wool Co Ltd
PO Box 55
Parkside Mills
Bradford BD5 8DZ
Mail-order company selling patterns and books as well as a wide range of yarns. Some yarn available on cone.

***Scapa Yarns Ltd**
Mossfield Mill
Chesham Fold Road
Bury
Lancashire BL9 6XJ
A range of straight and fancy yarns for hand and machine knitting, some available on cone. Specialize in pure, new wool yarns.

Silverknit
Park Road
Calverton
Nottingham NG14 6LL
Good selection of fancy and straight yarns, including wool, silk, cotton, viscose and mixtures. All supplied on cone.

***Sirdar PLC**
Flanshaw Lane
Alverthorpe
Wakefield
West Yorkshire WF2 9ND
Comprehensive selection of fancy and straight yarns in a wide range of colours. Not available on cone.

Texere Yarns
College Mill
Barkerend Road
Bradford BD3 9AQ
Specialists in unusual and expensive yarns, including silk, angora, mohair, mercerised cotton, lurex and fancy yarns. Available on cone.

***H G Twilley Ltd**
Roman Mill
Little Casterton Road
Stamford
Lincs PE9 1BG
Specialists in cotton yarns. Also distribute fancy yarns from Continental spinners.

Woolgatherers
10 Devonshire Road
London W4
Specialize in natural fibres, unusual and fancy yarns, including Angora and silk.

MACHINE MANUFACTURERS

Jones+Brother
Shepley Street
Audenshaw
Manchester M34 5JD

Knitmaster
39-45 Cowleaze Road
Kingston-upon-Thames
Surrey KT2 6DT

Passap
Bogod Machine Company Ltd
50-52 Great Sutton Street
London EC1V 0DJ

Singer Distribution Limited
Grafton Way
West Ham Industrial Estate
Basingstoke RG22 6HZ

Toyota Aisin UK Ltd
34 High Street
Bromley
Kent BR1 1EA

International Wool Secretariat
Wool House
Carlton Gardens
London SW1 5AE

INDEX

ACKNOWLEDGEMENTS

I would like to thank the Dorling Kindersley team for the patience and consideration shown to me during the production of this book, particularly Melanie Miller, whose invaluable help, support and advice was always so readily available. I would also like to thank Jon Crane and Lillian Dodds for their availability and tolerance while I was writing the manuscript. I am especially grateful to Clare Rowland and her company *Colourtwist* without whose encouragement and enthusiasm I might never have written the book. Clare also translated my garment designs into pattern form, thus enabling me to concentrate on the design and text. I cannot thank Clare enough for her unstinting help and patience throughout.

John Allen

Dorling Kindersley would like to thank Anne Smith and Sue Roberts for their careful checking of the patterns; Knitmaster for the loan of a 360K knitting machine; Debra Grayson and Sally Powell for editorial and design assistance; Argyll Wools, British Mohair Spinners, Emu Wools Ltd, Falcon-by-Post, Jamieson and Smith Ltd, Lister Handknitting Ltd, Patsy Yarns, Ries Wools of Holborn, Silverknit, Sirdar and Texere Yarns for providing yarns for photography; and the following companies for the loan of clothes and jewellery:

p. 27 trousers by Pepe, belt by Chelsea Girl, hat from The Hat Shop, jewellery from Detail; p. 31 skirt and hat by Donna Weight, jewellery by Adrien Mann; p. 34 trousers by Reldan, hat from The Hat Shop, gloves from John Lewis, jewellery from Detail; p. 36 trousers by Reldan, gloves from Liberty, jewellery from Detail; p. 41 skirt by Ten Big Boys, trousers by Penny Warner, jewellery from Detail; p. 45 trousers by Chelsea Man; p. 47 skirt by No?Yes!, hat from The Hat Shop, gloves from Liberty, jewellery from Detail; p. 51 jeans by Pepe, watch from Detail; p. 53 skirt by PX, jewellery from Detail; p. 57 skirt by No?Yes!, jewellery by Adrien Mann; p. 60 blouse by Reldan, skirt by Ditto, trousers by Robin Archer, skirt by Chelsea Girl, hats from The Hat Shop, gloves from Fenwick, belt by Christopher Trill, jewellery from Detail; p. 64 trousers by Su Barnes, belt by Christopher Trill, jewellery from Detail; p. 68 skirt by Ditto, gloves from Liberty, jewellery from Detail; p. 72 skirt by Roy Peach, blouse by Reldan, hat from The Hat Shop, gloves from Liberty, jewellery from Detail; p. 77 shirt from Pepe, jodphurs by Gail Bestwick, hat from The Hat Shop, sunglasses by Stephen Rothholz, belt by Chelsea Girl, jewellery by Adrien Mann; p. 78 top and skirt by Donna Weight, hat from The Hat Shop, jewellery from Detail, belt by Swanky Modes; p. 82 skirt by Heather Grattan, jewellery from Detail; p. 87 trousers by Pepe, hat from The Hat Shop, gloves from Liberty, jewellery and sunglasses from Detail; p. 90 skirt by Freeman's, jewellery from Adrien Mann; p. 95 skirt by Swanky Modes, hat from The Hat Shop, jewellery from Detail, belt by Christopher Trill; p. 99 skirt by Chelsea Girl, hat from The Hat Shop, jewellery from Detail; p. 103 skirt by Donna Weight, skirt by Gloria Vanderbilt, hats from The Hat Shop, gloves from Fenwick, earrings by Adrien Mann, jewellery from Detail; p. 107 skirt by Stephanie Cooper, blouse by Reldan, gloves from Fenwick, jewellery by Adrien Mann; p. 110 trousers by Roy Peach, gloves from John Lewis, jewellery from Detail; p. 113 dress by Minoan, jewellery from Detail, gloves from John Lewis, sunglasses by Stephen Rothholz.

Photography
Colin Thomas
Typesetting
Chambers Wallace
Reproduction
Reprocolor International
Illustrators
John Hutchinson
Vanessa Luff
Coral Mula
Lynne Robinson
Brian Sayers
Styling
Susie Slack